GeoAI and its Role in Planetary Health

ABHIJEET SARKAR

Published by ABHIJEET SARKAR, 2025.

GEOAI AND ITS ROLE IN PLANETARY HEALTH

First edition. January 17, 2025.

Copyright © 2025 ABHIJEET SARKAR.

ISBN: 979-8896992622

Written by ABHIJEET SARKAR.

Table of Contents

To my mother, whose unwavering love and support have been my foundation, and to my wife, whose encouragement and belief in me have fueled my journey. Your strength, motivation, and endless patience have made this work possible. This book is a reflection of your belief in me and the boundless possibilities you inspire every day. Thank you for walking with me every step of the way.

Introduction

Dear Reader,

Welcome to *GeoAI and its Role in Planetary Health,* a book that takes you to the forefront of one of the most exciting and transformative intersections of our time: where cutting-edge technology meets the urgent need to preserve our planet.The health of our planet is the health of humanity. Every forest cleared, every species lost, every degree of warming is a reminder of the interconnectedness of life. As we stand at a critical juncture, grappling with environmental challenges that threaten the very foundations of our existence, technology like GeoAI emerges as both a tool and a beacon of hope.

Planetary health is not just an academic term or a distant ideal—it's the pulse of our shared existence, a reflection of the delicate balance between humanity and the environment. Today, this balance is under unprecedented strain. Rising global temperatures, deforestation, water scarcity, and biodiversity loss are urgent alarms, reminding us of the consequences of inaction. But amidst these challenges lies an opportunity—a chance to reimagine our relationship with the planet using the transformative potential of GeoAI.

Picture a world where AI-driven models accurately map pollution in real-time, helping cities take swift action to protect vulnerable communities. Imagine conservation efforts amplified by satellite-powered algorithms that monitor wildlife habitats and track illegal poaching with pinpoint accuracy. Visualize the global fight against climate change strengthened by GeoAI systems that optimize renewable energy deployment or predict extreme weather events weeks in advance. These are not visions of a distant future—they are breakthroughs happening today, and their implications are profound.

Imagine a future where AI-driven technologies provide real-time insights into deforestation trends, predict extreme weather events with unmatched accuracy, or optimize urban planning to mitigate the effects of climate change. Envision communities empowered by data to make informed decisions about their environment, from managing water resources to restoring degraded lands. These aren't just abstract possibilities—they are the tangible realities GeoAI is already beginning to deliver.

But this book isn't just about technology—it's about storytelling. It's about the countless ways humanity and nature intersect, the challenges we face together, and the solutions we can craft with creativity and compassion. It's about how GeoAI, when wielded wisely, can become a force for equity, sustainability, and resilience in a rapidly changing world.

Throughout this book, we'll dive into stories of innovation and impact:

- Real-world examples of how GeoAI is transforming fields like agriculture, disaster management, and urban planning.

- Insights into the challenges of adopting GeoAI on a global scale and the innovative solutions being proposed.

Yet, alongside these triumphs, we must confront the ethical and practical challenges of deploying such a powerful tool. Who has access to this technology? How do we prevent bias in AI models? How can we ensure GeoAI empowers marginalized communities instead of perpetuating existing inequalities? These are the critical questions we must explore together.

Whether you're a technologist eager to understand the potential of AI, a policymaker shaping the future of sustainable development, or simply someone who cares deeply about the Earth, this book is for you. It's a call to action for dreamers and doers, a roadmap for using GeoAI to turn data into decisions and knowledge into impact.

So, I invite you to join me on this journey. Let's uncover the possibilities of GeoAI, learn from its challenges, and envision a future where human ingenuity and technological innovation harmonize with the rhythms of the natural world.

Welcome to *GeoAI and its Role in Planetary Health*—a book about hope, collaboration, and the power of technology to create a better tomorrow.

Warm regards,

— **Abhijeet Sarkar**

Chapter 1: Introduction to GeoAI and its Role in Planetary Health

1.1 Introduction

In the face of unprecedented environmental challenges, such as climate change, biodiversity loss, and pollution, the need for advanced tools to monitor and manage Earth's ecosystems has never been greater. GeoAI, an emerging field at the intersection of geospatial science and artificial intelligence, offers an innovative approach to solving some of these critical global problems. This chapter serves as an introduction to GeoAI, its fundamental concepts, its role in Earth observation (EO), and its potential to protect planetary health.

GeoAI combines the power of geospatial data with artificial intelligence (AI) technologies, such as machine learning (ML), deep learning, and data mining, to analyze and interpret complex environmental phenomena. With its ability to process vast amounts of data, identify patterns, and make predictions, GeoAI is transforming the way we monitor, manage, and conserve Earth's ecosystems. By leveraging data from various Earth observation platforms—ranging from satellites and drones to terrestrial sensors—GeoAI enables a more accurate, timely, and comprehensive understanding of planetary health.

This chapter will provide an overview of GeoAI's key concepts, discuss the importance of Earth observation technologies in monitoring environmental changes, and examine how GeoAI is contributing to the protection of planetary health. In doing so, it will lay the groundwork for the more detailed case studies and applications explored in the subsequent chapters of this book.

1.2 What is GeoAI?

GeoAI refers to the integration of geospatial data with artificial intelligence techniques to analyze, model, and predict Earth's environmental processes. This multidisciplinary field combines the capabilities of Geographic Information Systems (GIS), remote sensing, and AI to address some of the most pressing environmental issues facing humanity today.

Defining GeoAI

GeoAI is, at its core, the marriage of spatial data with advanced algorithms, enabling more sophisticated analysis and predictions. It involves the use of AI technologies—such as supervised and unsupervised machine learning, deep learning, and neural networks—on geospatial data sources like satellite imagery, geographic databases, and sensor networks.

Unlike traditional geospatial analysis, which is largely based on static models and human interpretation, GeoAI can automatically process, analyze, and even predict environmental trends based on the patterns detected in large datasets. This enhances the capability to make real-time decisions about environmental monitoring, urban planning, disaster management, and conservation.

Core Components of GeoAI

1. **Geospatial Data Sources**: The foundation of GeoAI lies in geospatial data, which includes satellite images, radar data, GPS information, and environmental sensor data. This data is collected from various platforms, such as remote sensing satellites, unmanned aerial vehicles (UAVs), drones, and IoT sensors.
2. **AI Techniques**: At the heart of GeoAI are advanced AI methods that enable the extraction of actionable insights from geospatial data. Machine learning (ML) is used to identify patterns, while deep learning techniques, such as convolutional neural networks (CNNs), are used for complex image recognition tasks. Natural

language processing (NLP) may also be used to analyze textual data from social media or scientific literature related to environmental changes.

3. **Tools and Frameworks**: GeoAI relies on a range of tools and frameworks to process and analyze data. Geographic Information Systems (GIS) are commonly used to map and visualize geospatial data. Remote sensing platforms allow for the collection of satellite data, while cloud computing enables large-scale data storage and real-time processing. AI-driven software and platforms further enhance the efficiency and accuracy of GeoAI applications.

1.3 Significance of GeoAI

The growing scale of environmental problems, combined with the vast amount of data generated by Earth observation technologies, presents a challenge for traditional methods of environmental monitoring and analysis. GeoAI addresses this challenge by enabling more efficient, accurate, and scalable solutions.

Transforming Earth Observation

Earth observation (EO) refers to the collection and analysis of data about the Earth from remote sensing satellites, airborne sensors, and ground-based systems. Traditionally, EO has been limited by the manual processing of large volumes of data and the inability to extract deep insights quickly. However, GeoAI has revolutionized the field by automating data processing, allowing for faster and more accurate analysis.

For example, satellite imagery has long been used to monitor deforestation, but the sheer volume of data produced by modern satellite missions made it difficult to track and assess environmental changes in real time. GeoAI algorithms can now process satellite imagery at unprecedented speeds, identify areas of deforestation, and even predict future changes based on historical data trends. By automating these processes, GeoAI not only saves time but also improves the accuracy of environmental monitoring efforts.

Applications in Planetary Health

Planetary health refers to the health of Earth's ecosystems and their capacity to support human life. The global environment is increasingly under threat due to issues like climate change, biodiversity loss, and the degradation of natural resources. GeoAI plays a pivotal role in monitoring these challenges and providing the tools to address them.

GeoAI has been successfully applied in a range of planetary health-related areas:

- **Climate Change Monitoring**: GeoAI helps track changes in global climate patterns by analyzing satellite data on temperature, precipitation, and atmospheric composition. It can identify the long-term effects of climate change, such as rising sea levels, and assist in predicting future climate scenarios.

- **Biodiversity Conservation**: By analyzing data from remote sensing and ground-based sensors, GeoAI can detect shifts in ecosystems and species distributions, aiding in biodiversity conservation efforts. Machine learning models can predict areas at risk of species loss, helping prioritize conservation efforts.

- **Disaster Management**: GeoAI is increasingly used in disaster management by analyzing real-time satellite data and other geospatial information to assess damage and predict the potential impacts of natural disasters. It has been particularly useful in monitoring and responding to events like wildfires, hurricanes, and flooding.

Key Advantages of GeoAI

1. **Speed and Scalability**: GeoAI enables the processing of vast amounts of data in real time. Unlike traditional methods, which often require time-consuming manual analysis, AI-driven systems can analyze complex datasets rapidly, providing real-time insights

for decision-makers.

2. **Predictive Modeling**: GeoAI's ability to forecast future trends based on historical data is a major advantage. Predictive models can forecast climate changes, natural disasters, or shifts in biodiversity, helping governments and organizations make proactive decisions.

3. **Increased Accuracy**: By utilizing advanced algorithms, GeoAI improves the accuracy of environmental predictions. Deep learning models, for instance, are capable of recognizing patterns in satellite images with higher precision than traditional image analysis methods.

4. **Handling Big Data**: Earth observation data, especially from satellites, has been growing exponentially in recent years. GeoAI has the ability to manage and analyze these large datasets, extracting meaningful insights that were previously hidden due to data volume.

1.4 Overview of Earth Observation (EO) Technologies

Earth observation technologies are integral to the collection of geospatial data used in GeoAI. EO encompasses a wide range of tools, from satellites and airborne sensors to ground-based monitoring systems.

What is Earth Observation?

Earth observation is the process of gathering information about the Earth's physical, chemical, and biological systems through the use of remote sensing technologies. This data is then analyzed to monitor environmental changes, assess natural resources, and manage ecosystems.

EO data is typically collected by various platforms, each with distinct advantages and limitations. Satellites, for example, provide global coverage and long-term monitoring capabilities, while drones and UAVs offer high-resolution imagery for specific locations. Ground-based sensors provide detailed, real-time data on environmental conditions, such as air quality or soil moisture.

Satellite Remote Sensing

Satellite remote sensing is one of the most widely used EO technologies, providing valuable data for environmental monitoring. Satellites equipped with optical, infrared, and radar sensors can capture high-resolution imagery and measurements of the Earth's surface. Examples of satellite missions include NASA's Landsat series and the European Space Agency's Copernicus program, which provide free and open access to satellite data.

One of the main applications of satellite remote sensing in GeoAI is land use/land cover mapping. Satellites can capture imagery at regular intervals, which allows GeoAI algorithms to detect changes over time. This is crucial for tracking deforestation, urban sprawl, and other significant environmental changes.

Terrestrial Sensors and UAVs

In addition to satellite-based systems, ground-based sensors and UAVs play a critical role in EO. Terrestrial sensors are typically placed in strategic locations to monitor specific environmental parameters, such as air quality, water levels, or soil health. Drones and UAVs can be used to capture high-resolution imagery and monitor ecosystems at a local scale.

The combination of satellite data, UAV data, and sensor networks provides a more comprehensive and detailed picture of Earth's ecosystems, which can then be analyzed using GeoAI methods to identify trends and make predictions.

Big Data and EO

The volume of data produced by Earth observation technologies has been growing exponentially. For example, the Landsat program alone has generated over 30 petabytes of data since its launch in 1972. This data is not only large in volume but also diverse, coming from a range of sensors and platforms.

GeoAI is essential for managing and processing this data. Traditional data analysis methods are ill-equipped to handle the scale and complexity of modern EO datasets. GeoAI, however, can quickly analyze large volumes of satellite imagery, sensor data, and other geospatial information to extract insights in real-time.

1.5 Planetary Health: Importance and Challenges

Planetary health is a concept that recognizes the profound relationship between human health and the health of the Earth's ecosystems. As human activities continue to degrade the environment, the ability of ecosystems to support human life is being undermined. GeoAI offers a powerful tool to address these interconnected challenges and help preserve planetary health.

Defining Planetary Health

Planetary health is a holistic approach to understanding how environmental degradation impacts human well-being. It considers the health of ecosystems, biodiversity, and the climate, recognizing that the deterioration of natural systems has direct consequences for human populations.

Challenges like climate change, deforestation, pollution, and resource depletion threaten the stability of Earth's ecosystems, which in turn jeopardizes human health. For example, the loss of biodiversity affects food security, while rising global temperatures increase the frequency and severity of natural disasters, such as heatwaves and floods.

Global Environmental Challenges

The world faces several urgent environmental challenges, including:

- **Climate Change**: Rising global temperatures, shifting weather patterns, and increased frequency of extreme events threaten both ecosystems and human societies.

- **Biodiversity Loss**: Habitat destruction, pollution, and climate change are causing species extinctions at an unprecedented rate.

- **Pollution**: Air, water, and soil pollution are harming both human and ecological health, contributing to a range of health issues, from respiratory diseases to contaminated water supplies.

- **Resource Depletion**: Overuse of natural resources, such as water, land, and forests, is threatening the ability of ecosystems to regenerate and provide essential services to humanity.

The Role of GeoAI in Addressing These Challenges

GeoAI plays a critical role in monitoring, managing, and mitigating these environmental challenges. By integrating geospatial data with advanced AI methods, GeoAI can help track changes in ecosystems, predict the effects of human activities, and guide conservation efforts. For example, GeoAI can be used to map areas of high biodiversity and prioritize them for protection, or to monitor deforestation in near real-time.

1.6 GeoAI in Monitoring and Managing Earth's Ecosystems

GeoAI offers tremendous potential for monitoring and managing ecosystems, particularly in the context of conservation and environmental management.

Applications in Ecosystem Monitoring

GeoAI is increasingly used to track changes in ecosystems. For example, the Amazon rainforest has been under threat from illegal logging, agriculture, and mining. GeoAI models can analyze satellite imagery to detect illegal deforestation activities, enabling authorities to respond more quickly. Similarly, GeoAI can be used to monitor coral reefs, tracking changes in their health and identifying areas at risk of bleaching due to rising sea temperatures.

Predictive Modeling for Ecosystem Health

GeoAI's ability to create predictive models is invaluable for ecosystem health. For example, by analyzing historical climate and environmental data, GeoAI can predict areas at high risk of desertification or flooding. This allows for proactive planning and mitigation strategies, such as the restoration of degraded lands or the establishment of early warning systems for natural disasters.

Conservation and Restoration

GeoAI is also playing a crucial role in conservation and restoration efforts. By identifying areas of high biodiversity or vulnerable ecosystems, GeoAI helps prioritize conservation initiatives. In addition, AI-driven models can optimize restoration efforts by predicting the most effective methods for rehabilitating ecosystems.

1.7 Conclusion

This chapter has introduced the fundamental concepts of GeoAI and its significance in monitoring and managing Earth's ecosystems. We have explored the core components of GeoAI, its applications in planetary health, and the role of Earth observation technologies in enhancing environmental monitoring. GeoAI is poised to revolutionize the way we address global environmental challenges by offering faster, more accurate, and scalable solutions for ecosystem management, conservation, and climate change mitigation.

As we move forward, GeoAI will continue to play a vital role in protecting planetary health. However, there remain challenges in terms of data accessibility, the need for interdisciplinary collaboration, and the ethical implications of AI-driven decision-making. These are important questions that will need to be addressed as the field evolves, ensuring that GeoAI can reach its full potential in safeguarding the future of our planet.

Chapter 2: The Evolution of Earth Observation Technologies

2.1 Introduction

The evolution of Earth observation (EO) technologies represents a significant leap forward in how we understand and monitor our planet's health. From the early days of aerial photography to the development of modern satellite constellations, these technologies have revolutionized our ability to track environmental changes, manage resources, and respond to natural disasters. This chapter explores the history of EO technologies, highlighting key advancements in satellite and sensor technology and how they have contributed to the development of GeoAI—the integration of geospatial data with artificial intelligence to enhance data processing and analysis.

In recent years, the sophistication of EO technologies has skyrocketed. Modern EO platforms provide real-time data streams, multi-spectral imagery, and global coverage, empowering decision-makers across various sectors—from environmental protection to disaster response. GeoAI has emerged as a critical tool in harnessing the power of this data, providing automated analysis and predictive insights that were once inconceivable. This chapter will trace the evolution of these technologies, from their origins to the cutting-edge systems we rely on today.

2.2 Early Earth Observation: Aerial Imagery and Ground-Based Surveys

The roots of Earth observation trace back to the mid-20th century, when the world first began using aerial imagery and ground-based surveys to study the planet's surface. These early methods laid the foundation for more sophisticated satellite and sensor technologies.

Aerial Photography

Before satellites, aerial photography was the primary method for capturing images of Earth from the sky. The first aerial surveys were conducted using balloons and kites, which carried rudimentary cameras into the atmosphere. These methods were relatively limited in scope and resolution but marked the beginning of using airborne perspectives to map and study the Earth's surface.

In the early 20th century, advancements in aviation technology enabled aircraft to fly at higher altitudes, providing more detailed and expansive views of the landscape. During World War I and II, military reconnaissance efforts saw a surge in aerial photography as a way to map enemy territory and gather intelligence. This use of aerial imagery significantly advanced the field of cartography and resource management. In addition to military applications, early aerial surveys were used to monitor urban growth, track forest cover, and assess agricultural productivity.

By the 1940s and 1950s, commercial aerial photography became increasingly common, especially in mapping and surveying projects. These methods were used to track land use, assess environmental conditions, and develop topographical maps. However, the images captured were still static and required manual interpretation, limiting the speed and scale at which information could be processed.

Ground-Based Sensors

Alongside aerial imagery, ground-based sensors played a crucial role in early Earth observation efforts. Weather stations, soil moisture sensors, and other terrestrial instruments provided valuable data on environmental conditions. These sensors were especially important in climate and agricultural monitoring, offering detailed insights into weather patterns, precipitation levels, and soil health.

Although these ground-based systems offered accurate and localized data, they lacked the ability to provide comprehensive, large-scale insights into global environmental changes. They also faced challenges in remote or inaccessible areas, where it was difficult to install and maintain equipment. Thus, the need for more expansive and automated methods of environmental monitoring became clear, eventually leading to the rise of satellite technology.

2.3 The Rise of Remote Sensing and Satellite Technology

First Satellites for Earth Observation

The launch of Earth observation satellites in the 1960s marked a pivotal moment in the development of EO technologies. These early satellites opened up entirely new possibilities for observing the Earth on a global scale, providing continuous, wide-area coverage.

The first Earth observation satellite was **TIROS-1**, launched by NASA in 1960. This satellite was designed to monitor weather patterns, providing the first real-time satellite images of cloud cover. Although the images were relatively low resolution by today's standards, TIROS-1 demonstrated the potential of space-based observation.

The next major milestone came with the launch of **Landsat 1** in 1972. Landsat 1 was the first satellite dedicated to Earth observation, with the primary goal of capturing multispectral imagery of the planet's surface. Equipped with a multispectral scanner (MSS), Landsat 1 captured images in four bands of the electromagnetic spectrum—visible and infrared wavelengths—which significantly improved the ability to distinguish between different land cover types. The launch of Landsat 1 marked the beginning of a continuous Earth observation program that would provide invaluable data for environmental monitoring, agriculture, forestry, urban planning, and more.

Over the next several decades, numerous satellites joined the ranks, each equipped with more advanced sensors. Satellites like **NOAA's Geostationary Operational Environmental Satellite (GOES)**, launched in 1975, provided real-time weather monitoring. In the 1980s and 1990s, advancements in sensor technology allowed for the capture of more detailed and higher-resolution imagery, as well as more spectral bands, enabling deeper analysis of Earth's surface and atmosphere.

Early Remote Sensing Satellites

Remote sensing technology in its early form was largely focused on passive sensors that captured reflected light from the Earth's surface. The **Soviet Union's Meteor** series and the **NOAA** satellites in the 1970s to 1980s were pioneers in remote sensing, capturing weather data and environmental conditions across vast regions. However, they were limited in terms of spatial resolution, and the data they provided was often more useful for weather forecasting than for detailed land cover analysis.

While these early satellites were crucial for monitoring weather patterns and atmospheric conditions, the technology had significant limitations in its ability to capture detailed surface-level information. The resolution of early satellite images was relatively low, and interpreting these images required manual labor and significant expertise. Furthermore, the amount of data collected was far less than what modern systems can produce today.

2.4 Modern Satellite Constellations and the Advancement of Sensor Technology

The Concept of Satellite Constellations

Satellite constellations represent a significant leap forward in Earth observation technology. Rather than relying on a single satellite to provide coverage over vast areas, satellite constellations consist of multiple satellites working together to provide continuous, global data coverage.

One of the most well-known examples of satellite constellations is the **Copernicus Sentinel** missions. Operated by the European Space Agency (ESA), the Sentinel satellites are part of the Copernicus program, designed to monitor Earth's environment. The **Sentinel-1** constellation, for example, uses Synthetic Aperture Radar (SAR) to monitor the Earth's surface, enabling the detection of changes such as subsidence, deforestation, and flood patterns, regardless of weather conditions. Sentinel-2 focuses on optical and infrared imagery for land and vegetation monitoring.

Similarly, commercial companies like **Planet Labs** have created constellations of small satellites that provide high-resolution imagery at an unprecedented frequency. These satellites capture images of the entire Earth every day, enabling real-time monitoring of global changes, from urban expansion to the health of forests and oceans. Planet Labs, with its fleet of over 200 small satellites, provides the commercial sector with rapid, detailed imagery that supports applications in agriculture, natural resource management, and disaster response.

Advancements in Sensor Technology

The development of satellite constellations has been closely followed by advancements in sensor technology, which have enabled even more detailed and accurate Earth observations. These advancements have resulted in better spatial resolution, spectral resolution, and temporal resolution—the three key parameters that determine the quality of satellite imagery.

- **Multispectral and Hyperspectral Imaging**: Multispectral sensors capture data across a few select bands of the electromagnetic spectrum (e.g., visible and infrared), while hyperspectral sensors capture hundreds or even thousands of spectral bands. This enables scientists to identify a broader range of materials on the Earth's surface, from soil composition to plant health, and even detect pollutants or other harmful substances in the atmosphere or water.

- **Synthetic Aperture Radar (SAR)**: SAR sensors emit microwave signals to the Earth's surface and measure the return signals, enabling high-resolution imaging in any weather conditions. SAR has proven invaluable for monitoring surface deformation, land subsidence, and detecting changes in the environment that may be masked by cloud cover, such as flood events or deforestation.

- **LiDAR (Light Detection and Ranging)**: LiDAR technology uses laser pulses to measure distances to the Earth's surface, creating precise 3D maps of the landscape. This technology has been particularly valuable for mapping forests, monitoring coastal areas, and assessing topography for urban planning and infrastructure development.

- **Thermal Infrared and Microwave Sensors**: Thermal infrared sensors capture temperature variations on the Earth's surface, providing critical data on environmental processes such as vegetation health, ocean currents, and energy fluxes. Microwave sensors, which penetrate cloud cover and are unaffected by daylight, provide valuable data on soil moisture, snow cover, and atmospheric composition.

The integration of multiple sensor types on a single satellite platform allows for a comprehensive understanding of Earth's systems, enabling more accurate and timely environmental monitoring. The availability of high-resolution data from these advanced sensors has made satellite-based Earth observation an indispensable tool for managing natural resources, responding to disasters, and mitigating the effects of climate change.

2.5 Advancements in Data Collection and Processing

The explosion of Earth observation data in recent years has led to significant advancements in data collection and processing techniques. Modern EO satellites produce vast amounts of data daily, creating both challenges and opportunities for data management and analysis.

Big Data and Earth Observation

The scale of data generated by modern satellite constellations has grown exponentially. For example, the Copernicus Sentinel satellites generate

terabytes of data every day, while commercial satellite companies like Planet Labs produce even more. Managing, storing, and processing this "big data" has become one of the primary challenges for the EO community.

To handle these large datasets, new methods for data storage and processing have been developed. Cloud computing platforms, such as Amazon Web Services (AWS) and Google Earth Engine, have become essential tools for storing and analyzing EO data. These platforms allow users to access and process satellite data at scale, providing unprecedented computational power for real-time analysis.

Data Fusion and Integration

Data fusion refers to the process of integrating information from different sources to create more comprehensive datasets. For example, combining satellite imagery with ground-based sensor data, drone-captured images, and social media data can provide a more holistic understanding of environmental conditions.

GeoAI plays a critical role in data fusion, enabling the integration of various data streams and the extraction of meaningful insights. By applying machine learning algorithms to these integrated datasets, GeoAI can detect patterns, predict future changes, and automate the analysis of large volumes of data.

2.6 GeoAI's Role in Enhancing Earth Observation Technologies

As Earth observation (EO) technologies have advanced, the sheer volume and complexity of data generated by modern satellites have created new challenges in terms of data processing and analysis. To address these challenges, **GeoAI** (Geospatial Artificial Intelligence) has emerged as a transformative tool. GeoAI integrates geospatial data with advanced machine learning algorithms, enabling the automation of data analysis and the generation of predictive insights. This section explores how GeoAI is being used to enhance EO technologies and provide more accurate, timely, and actionable insights.

The Integration of AI and Remote Sensing

GeoAI brings together the power of artificial intelligence (AI) and remote sensing technologies to enhance the capabilities of EO satellites and sensors.

AI models, particularly machine learning (ML) and deep learning (DL) algorithms, have been adapted to handle the vast amounts of complex data collected by EO satellites. These algorithms can identify patterns and trends in satellite imagery that would be impossible for human analysts to detect manually.

- **Automated Image Classification**: One of the most significant applications of GeoAI is in the automated classification of satellite imagery. Traditional methods of image analysis required labor-intensive manual interpretation of raw satellite images. With GeoAI, machine learning algorithms can be trained to automatically classify various land cover types, such as urban areas, forests, bodies of water, and agricultural fields, from satellite imagery. These algorithms can process thousands of images in a fraction of the time it would take human analysts, enabling real-time monitoring of Earth's surface.

A case in point is the use of GeoAI to monitor deforestation. The Amazon rainforest, for example, is continuously monitored using satellite imagery and AI-driven image classification models. These models can detect signs of illegal logging, land clearance, and forest degradation at a much higher speed and accuracy than traditional methods.

- **Change Detection**: GeoAI is also crucial in change detection, which involves identifying and analyzing changes in the Earth's surface over time. By comparing satellite images taken at different times, machine learning algorithms can detect subtle changes that may indicate environmental or anthropogenic activities, such as deforestation, urbanization, or the effects of natural disasters.

For example, after the 2010 earthquake in Haiti, satellite images were analyzed using GeoAI to assess the extent of damage to buildings, roads, and infrastructure. By automatically detecting changes between pre- and post-event images, these algorithms provided immediate insights that were critical for directing emergency response efforts.

- **Predictive Modeling and Forecasting**: Another powerful application of GeoAI is in predictive modeling. By leveraging historical satellite data, machine learning models can forecast future changes in the environment. For example, AI models can be trained to predict crop yields, based on historical data on weather patterns, soil conditions, and satellite images of crop health. These models are particularly valuable for agricultural management, allowing farmers to optimize irrigation, anticipate harvests, and minimize resource waste.

In the case of agriculture, the **NASA Harvest Program** uses satellite data combined with machine learning algorithms to improve food security predictions, particularly in developing countries. These AI-driven models help forecast crop yields in regions where ground-based data is scarce, enabling better resource allocation and early interventions.

Applications of GeoAI in Earth Observation

GeoAI is increasingly being applied across a wide range of sectors, offering solutions for monitoring and managing natural resources, disaster response, urban planning, and environmental protection.

- **Disaster Management**: One of the most critical applications of GeoAI is in disaster management. Natural disasters like floods, wildfires, and hurricanes cause widespread damage, and quick response times are crucial to saving lives and minimizing damage. GeoAI can analyze satellite images and other geospatial data to provide real-time assessments of disaster impacts, helping first responders and decision-makers allocate resources more effectively.

After the 2015 Nepal earthquake, GeoAI was used to rapidly assess damage by comparing pre- and post-earthquake satellite imagery. The automated analysis enabled teams to identify areas in need of immediate relief, such as collapsed buildings and blocked roads, significantly speeding up the emergency response.

- **Agriculture**: In agriculture, GeoAI is revolutionizing the way farmers monitor crop health, predict yields, and optimize irrigation. Satellite data, combined with AI models, can identify patterns in soil moisture, temperature, and vegetation health, providing farmers with real-time insights that help them make more informed decisions.

For instance, **Microsoft's AI for Earth** program uses satellite data and machine learning to help farmers in Africa optimize irrigation practices and increase crop yields. By combining weather data with real-time satellite images, the program predicts which areas of the farm need water, reducing water waste and improving crop productivity.

- **Biodiversity and Conservation**: GeoAI is also being applied in biodiversity conservation efforts, helping to monitor and protect endangered species and ecosystems. For example, AI algorithms are used to process satellite imagery and track habitat loss, identify illegal poaching activities, and monitor changes in biodiversity over time.

A notable example is the use of AI to monitor the **Great Barrier Reef**. Researchers use satellite images to track coral bleaching and other threats to the reef's ecosystem. AI models analyze these images to identify areas of the reef most affected by climate change, helping to prioritize conservation efforts.

- **Urban Planning and Infrastructure**: GeoAI is also reshaping urban planning by providing city planners with the tools to monitor urban sprawl, assess the environmental impact of new construction, and optimize the placement of infrastructure. By analyzing satellite images, GeoAI can identify land use patterns, predict future urban growth, and recommend solutions to mitigate congestion and environmental degradation.

The European Space Agency's Copernicus program provides vital satellite data for monitoring urban development, helping city planners to assess land cover changes, track building expansion, and plan for sustainable development.

2.7 Future Directions and Emerging Trends in Earth Observation

As the field of Earth observation continues to evolve, new technologies and approaches are emerging that will further enhance our ability to monitor and protect the planet. The future of EO is characterized by advancements in satellite capabilities, the integration of new data sources, and the continuous improvement of AI and machine learning models. This section explores some of the key trends and future directions in the field.

The Role of Commercial and Private Sector Innovations

The commercial sector is playing an increasingly important role in advancing Earth observation technologies. Companies like **SpaceX**, **Planet Labs**, and **OneWeb** are developing new satellite constellations and providing data as a service. These private-sector innovations are driving down the cost of satellite launches and making high-resolution imagery more accessible to businesses, governments, and researchers alike.

Small satellite companies, in particular, are revolutionizing the field by providing low-cost, high-frequency Earth observation data. **Planet Labs**, for example, operates the largest fleet of small satellites, which capture daily images of the Earth's surface at a resolution of 3 to 5 meters. These satellites enable continuous monitoring of key regions, such as urban areas, agricultural fields, and disaster-prone zones.

New Satellite Technologies

Miniaturization and advancements in sensor technology are enabling the development of more powerful and compact satellites. **CubeSats**—small, low-cost satellites—are becoming increasingly popular for Earth observation, providing affordable alternatives to larger, traditional satellites.

The launch of **Swarm Technologies' CubeSats** is an example of how miniaturized satellites can offer high-frequency, real-time data at a fraction of the cost of conventional satellites. These small satellites are equipped with various sensors to monitor Earth's surface, atmosphere, and even space weather, contributing to a broader understanding of planetary health.

Integration with Other Emerging Technologies

As Earth observation technologies continue to evolve, they will increasingly integrate with other emerging technologies such as the Internet of Things (IoT), blockchain, and 5G networks. These technologies will allow for the creation of more connected, real-time systems for monitoring environmental conditions, sharing data, and improving decision-making.

For example, IoT devices embedded in environmental monitoring stations or agricultural systems will complement satellite data, providing ground-truth measurements that can be used to validate and refine AI models. Similarly, blockchain technology may be used to ensure the integrity and transparency of satellite data, particularly in fields like supply chain management and disaster relief.

Challenges and Opportunities in EO

While the future of Earth observation looks promising, several challenges remain. Data privacy and security are growing concerns, especially as satellite imagery becomes more accessible to the public. Sensitive information about infrastructure, environmental conditions, and political boundaries must be protected to prevent misuse.

Ethical considerations also play a critical role in the development of EO technologies. The widespread use of satellite imagery raises questions about surveillance, consent, and the potential for exploiting geographic data for political or economic gain. Ensuring that EO technologies are used responsibly will be crucial for their continued success and acceptance.

2.8 Conclusion

The evolution of Earth observation technologies has been a journey from rudimentary aerial photography to sophisticated, multi-sensor satellite constellations that provide continuous, high-resolution data. GeoAI has emerged as a key enabler of this transformation, automating data analysis, improving predictive capabilities, and enabling real-time decision-making across various sectors. From agriculture to disaster management and urban planning, the applications of GeoAI in Earth observation are vast and continue to grow.

Looking to the future, advancements in satellite technology, the integration of new data sources, and innovations in AI will continue to drive the field forward. The challenges of managing and processing the ever-expanding volume of Earth observation data remain, but the potential for enhancing planetary health and addressing global environmental challenges is immense.

As these technologies continue to evolve, it will be essential to balance the benefits of real-time, global monitoring with ethical considerations and responsible data use. The next frontier in Earth observation will not only be about capturing more data but also about ensuring that the data is interpreted and applied in ways that promote sustainability, resilience, and planetary well-being.

Chapter 3: Fundamentals of GIS and Remote Sensing

Introduction

Geographic Information Systems (GIS) and Remote Sensing (RS) are cornerstone technologies in modern Earth observation. They enable the collection, processing, and analysis of spatial and temporal data on Earth's environment, resources, and human activity. This chapter explores the basic principles behind these technologies, their essential components, and how they work together to provide powerful insights into planetary health and management. As we move further into the era of big data, their combined applications are critical in addressing some of the world's most pressing challenges, including climate change, resource management, and disaster response.

The significance of GIS and remote sensing lies in their ability to capture and interpret vast amounts of geospatial data, allowing decision-makers to monitor, analyze, and predict changes in the environment. From the monitoring of urban sprawl to tracking forest health and detecting natural hazards, GIS and remote sensing are indispensable tools in managing the Earth's ecosystems.

3.1 Basic Principles of GIS

Definition of GIS: Geographic Information Systems (GIS) is a technology designed for capturing, storing, analyzing, managing, and presenting spatial and geographic data. Essentially, GIS allows us to create, analyze, and interpret maps and models, transforming data into actionable insights for informed decision-making. GIS integrates data from multiple sources to represent spatial phenomena, making it easier to visualize trends, relationships, and patterns that would be difficult to detect through other methods.

Components of GIS: A GIS is composed of several interrelated components that work together to process and analyze spatial data:

- **Hardware**: The physical equipment used to input, store, and display geographic data, such as computers, servers, and GPS devices.

- **Software**: The tools used for creating, analyzing, and visualizing geospatial data. Popular GIS software includes ArcGIS, QGIS, and Google Earth Engine.

- **Data**: The spatial and attribute data that form the foundation of GIS. Spatial data includes the geographic coordinates or the locations of features, while attribute data describe the characteristics of those features (e.g., population density, land use).

- **People**: GIS professionals and users who design, manage, and interpret GIS datasets and outputs.

- **Methods**: The processes and techniques used to manipulate and analyze the data, such as spatial analysis, modeling, and visualization.

Data Models in GIS: There are two primary data models used in GIS:

- **Raster Data**: Represents geographic features as a grid of cells or pixels, each containing a value. Raster data is ideal for continuous data types like elevation, temperature, and vegetation.

- **Vector Data**: Represents geographic features as discrete points, lines, and polygons. Vector data is suitable for representing discrete features like roads, buildings, and political boundaries.

Spatial Analysis in GIS: Spatial analysis involves the manipulation and interpretation of spatial data to reveal patterns, relationships, and trends. Some common operations include:

- **Buffering**: Creating zones around a geographic feature, such as a river or road, to analyze the surrounding area.

- **Overlay Analysis**: Combining multiple layers of spatial data to examine relationships between features. For example, overlaying land use data with transportation networks to plan new roads.

- **Proximity Analysis**: Determining the nearest features to a given location, such as finding the closest hospital to a rural area.

Applications of GIS: GIS is widely used across various fields, including urban planning, agriculture, environmental monitoring, and disaster management. For instance, in urban planning, GIS is used to model traffic patterns, assess land suitability, and manage infrastructure. In environmental monitoring, it helps track deforestation, analyze water quality, and monitor biodiversity. In disaster management, GIS is used to assess the damage from hurricanes, floods, and wildfires.

3.2 Fundamentals of Remote Sensing

Definition of Remote Sensing: Remote sensing refers to the acquisition of information about objects or areas from a distance, typically using satellites or airborne sensors. Unlike traditional surveying methods that require direct contact with the subject, remote sensing gathers data via electromagnetic radiation (such as visible light, infrared, and radar), which is then analyzed to interpret various surface and atmospheric properties.

Types of Remote Sensing: There are two main categories of remote sensing:

- **Passive Remote Sensing**: Involves capturing naturally emitted or reflected energy, such as sunlight. Satellites and sensors detect this radiation, which is then processed to form images. Examples of passive remote sensing include visible and infrared imagery.

- **Active Remote Sensing**: Involves sending a signal (typically microwave or laser) from a sensor to the Earth's surface and measuring the reflected signal. An example of active remote sensing is radar and LiDAR (Light Detection and Ranging).

Key Remote Sensing Platforms: Remote sensing data can be collected from several platforms:

- **Satellites**: Provide global coverage, ideal for large-scale monitoring. Examples include the Landsat series, the European Space Agency's Sentinel missions, and commercial satellites like Planet Labs.

- **Aircraft**: These offer high-resolution images and are useful for localized, detailed analysis. Examples include manned aircraft with multispectral sensors or drones equipped with various types of sensors.

- **Drones**: Increasingly used for specific tasks, such as vegetation mapping or disaster response, drones offer high flexibility and resolution.

Spectral Resolution: Spectral resolution refers to the ability of a sensor to distinguish between different wavelengths of light. The higher the spectral resolution, the more bands a sensor can capture. For instance, sensors may capture data in visible light, near-infrared, and thermal infrared bands, allowing for detailed analysis of land cover and vegetation health.

Temporal Resolution: Temporal resolution refers to the frequency at which a sensor collects data over the same area. Satellites like Landsat revisit a given location every 16 days, while commercial satellites like Planet Labs' fleet provide daily imagery. High temporal resolution is crucial for monitoring dynamic phenomena like vegetation growth or urban development.

Spatial Resolution: Spatial resolution refers to the size of the smallest object that can be detected by a sensor. Higher spatial resolution means finer detail in the imagery. For example, a satellite with 1-meter resolution can distinguish objects as small as 1 meter in size, while a satellite with 30-meter resolution may not distinguish features smaller than 30 meters.

3.3 Satellite Imagery in Remote Sensing

Overview of Satellite Systems: Satellite-based remote sensing provides global-scale observations with frequent revisits. Key satellite systems include:

- **Landsat**: One of the oldest and most widely used satellite series for Earth observation. Landsat provides medium-resolution imagery (30 meters) with a focus on land use/land cover classification.

- **Sentinel**: A part of the European Space Agency's Copernicus program, Sentinel satellites offer both multispectral and synthetic aperture radar (SAR) imagery with high temporal resolution.

- **SPOT**: A commercial satellite system known for its high-resolution imagery, particularly used in urban monitoring and disaster management.

Image Acquisition Process: Satellite sensors capture electromagnetic radiation reflected or emitted from Earth's surface, which is then transmitted to Earth stations for processing. The data is typically pre-processed to correct for atmospheric conditions, sensor calibration, and geometric distortions before being analyzed.

Applications of Satellite Imagery: Satellite imagery plays a crucial role in various applications:

- **Agriculture**: Monitoring crop health, detecting pest infestations, and managing irrigation systems using multispectral and hyperspectral imagery.

- **Forestry**: Tracking deforestation, forest degradation, and biodiversity conservation efforts.

- **Urban Planning**: Analyzing urban sprawl, land use change, and infrastructure development.

- **Disaster Response**: Mapping flood, wildfire, and earthquake damage to aid in rapid response and recovery efforts.

3.4 Remote Sensing Sensors and Technologies

Remote sensing sensors are essential tools for capturing Earth's surface data, and they vary in terms of their technical characteristics and application.

Optical Sensors: Optical sensors capture visible and near-infrared (NIR) radiation reflected from the Earth's surface. These sensors are essential for vegetation analysis, land cover classification, and water body monitoring. A widely known example is the Landsat OLI (Operational Land Imager), which captures imagery in multiple bands, including visible, NIR, and short-wave infrared.

Thermal Infrared Sensors: Thermal infrared sensors detect emitted radiation in the thermal infrared range, typically between 8 and 14 micrometers. These sensors are critical for monitoring heat distribution, land surface temperatures, and urban heat islands. An example is the **MODIS (Moderate Resolution Imaging Spectroradiometer)**, which is used for global temperature and vegetation health monitoring.

Radar Sensors (SAR): Synthetic Aperture Radar (SAR) sensors are active sensors that emit microwaves and measure the reflected signals from the Earth's surface. These sensors can operate in all weather conditions, providing key insights into areas affected by cloud cover or darkness. Applications include topographic mapping, land subsidence detection, and disaster monitoring.

LiDAR (Light Detection and Ranging): LiDAR is a laser-based sensor that measures distances by bouncing laser pulses off the Earth's surface. LiDAR data provides highly detailed, three-dimensional point clouds, which are invaluable for creating topographic maps, vegetation structure analysis, and urban modeling. Applications include flood risk assessment, forest canopy analysis, and infrastructure monitoring.

3.5 Data Types in Remote Sensing

Multispectral Data: Multispectral sensors capture data across a limited number of broad spectral bands (e.g., visible light, near-infrared). This type of data is widely used in land cover classification, vegetation health monitoring, and water quality assessments. A well-known example is the **Landsat** series, which provides multispectral imagery for monitoring land use/land cover changes.

Hyperspectral Data: Hyperspectral sensors capture data in hundreds or even thousands of narrow spectral bands. This finer spectral resolution enables detailed analysis of various materials on the Earth's surface. Hyperspectral data is used in applications such as mineral exploration, environmental contamination detection, and vegetation stress monitoring. One example of hyperspectral remote sensing is the **AVIRIS** (Airborne Visible/Infrared Imaging Spectrometer), which captures high-resolution spectral data for various environmental monitoring applications.

LiDAR Data: LiDAR produces high-resolution, 3D point clouds that are useful for mapping elevation, vegetation height, and urban infrastructure. LiDAR data is invaluable for creating detailed topographic maps, detecting surface changes, and modeling flood risk. A prominent example of LiDAR data use is in forestry, where it is used to map forest structure and estimate biomass.

3.6 Data Processing and Analysis in Remote Sensing

The raw data captured by remote sensing platforms often require significant processing and analysis to extract useful information. This process includes steps like image preprocessing, classification, feature extraction, and change detection. The ability to analyze remotely sensed data effectively is crucial for accurate environmental monitoring and decision-making.

Preprocessing of Remote Sensing Data

Before remotely sensed data can be analyzed, it undergoes several preprocessing steps to correct errors and ensure consistency.

- **Radiometric Correction**: This corrects the data for sensor irregularities, atmospheric interference, and variations in sunlight. It helps ensure that the data is consistent over time and that measurements are accurate. For example, adjustments for atmospheric scattering can make sure that the reflectance of land surfaces is measured correctly.

- **Geometric Correction**: Geometric correction involves aligning the satellite images with a map or a known coordinate system. Due to Earth's curvature, sensor motion, and other factors, the images may be distorted. Geometric correction ensures the data can be accurately integrated into GIS and compared with other datasets.

- **Atmospheric Correction**: This step removes atmospheric interference (like clouds, dust, and humidity), which can distort the data collected from satellite sensors. By correcting for these factors, the reflectance values of the surface features can be retrieved more accurately.

Image Classification Techniques

Once preprocessing is complete, the next step is to classify the data. Classification refers to the process of categorizing pixels based on their spectral characteristics. There are two main types of classification:

- **Supervised Classification**: This technique requires prior knowledge of the classes to be identified in the image. The user provides sample areas, called training data, for each class (e.g., water, forest, urban). The algorithm then uses these samples to classify the entire image. Popular algorithms include Maximum Likelihood Classification (MLC) and Support Vector Machines (SVM).

○ *Example*: In monitoring deforestation, supervised classification can be used to identify areas where forest cover has been lost by comparing current satellite imagery with past data.

● **Unsupervised Classification**: In this approach, the algorithm automatically groups pixels into clusters based on their spectral similarities without any prior knowledge. The user then interprets the clusters and assigns them to classes. This method is particularly useful when there is limited ground-truth data.

○ *Example*: Unsupervised classification can be applied to map land cover types in a region where the specific class labels are not readily available.

Feature Extraction from Remote Sensing Data

Feature extraction refers to the process of identifying and quantifying specific features from remote sensing data. These features might include vegetation, water bodies, built structures, and roads. Feature extraction can be pixel-based, where individual pixels are analyzed, or object-based, where groups of pixels (objects) are analyzed.

● **Object-Based Image Analysis (OBIA)**: This method segments the image into homogeneous regions (objects) and classifies these regions based on their spatial, spectral, and contextual properties. OBIA is especially useful for detecting complex features like urban areas and forest canopies, where traditional pixel-based analysis may fail.

● **Applications**: OBIA has been effectively applied in urban monitoring, where the task is to identify buildings, roads, and green spaces. In agricultural monitoring, OBIA can be used to delineate crop fields and detect signs of pest infestation.

Change Detection Techniques

Change detection is a vital process in monitoring the Earth's dynamic environment. It involves comparing images of the same area taken at different times to detect and quantify changes, such as deforestation, urban expansion, or changes in vegetation health.

- **Image Differencing**: This method involves subtracting the pixel values of one image from another. The difference is then analyzed to identify areas that have changed.

  ○ *Example*: In coastal management, image differencing can be used to detect changes in shoreline position over time.

- **Post-Classification Comparison**: This approach involves classifying two or more images independently and then comparing the resulting classified maps to identify areas of change.

- **Time-Series Analysis**: By analyzing a series of images taken over time, time-series analysis can help track the evolution of certain features, such as the seasonal variations in vegetation health or the progress of land degradation.

3.7 Integration of GIS and Remote Sensing

One of the key advantages of GIS and remote sensing is their ability to work together to provide more comprehensive analysis and insights. GIS provides the spatial tools necessary for analyzing and managing geographic data, while remote sensing delivers the data needed to inform that analysis.

GIS for Spatial Analysis

GIS allows users to visualize, analyze, and interpret remote sensing data. By combining remotely sensed imagery with vector and tabular data, GIS makes it possible to carry out complex spatial analysis. Common applications include:

- **Overlay Analysis**: Combining layers of spatial data to analyze relationships between different features. For example, overlaying a vegetation map with soil data can help identify areas most suitable for farming.

- **Buffer Zones**: Buffering allows users to create zones around features, such as roads, rivers, or protected areas, to assess impacts or make management decisions. This technique is commonly used in environmental protection, where buffer zones around protected areas are used to monitor and manage human activities.

- **Suitability Modeling**: GIS can be used to combine multiple layers of spatial data (e.g., soil type, slope, precipitation) to identify the most suitable locations for specific activities, such as agriculture, mining, or conservation.

Remote Sensing in GIS

Remote sensing plays a critical role in providing the raw data needed for GIS analysis. Remote sensing images can be imported into GIS systems, where they can be analyzed, classified, and integrated with other spatial datasets. By linking remote sensing data with other data sources (such as population density, land use, or administrative boundaries), GIS enables powerful spatial decision-making tools.

- **Case Study**: In flood management, GIS can combine remote sensing data on land elevation and rainfall patterns to model flood risks, and spatial analysis tools in GIS can help identify the most vulnerable areas.

3.8 Applications of GIS and Remote Sensing in Earth Observation

The integration of GIS and remote sensing opens up numerous possibilities for monitoring, managing, and protecting Earth's ecosystems. Below are some of the primary applications in various fields.

Environmental Monitoring

- **Deforestation**: Remote sensing can monitor forest cover loss over time, and GIS can help map areas at risk of deforestation. This combination is often used by organizations like the World Resources Institute (WRI) to track forest cover changes globally.

- **Water Quality Monitoring**: Remote sensing data, such as satellite imagery from MODIS or Sentinel, can be used to monitor water quality by analyzing parameters like chlorophyll concentration, turbidity, and suspended sediments. GIS can map these features to identify regions affected by pollution or sedimentation.

Agriculture and Land Use Management

- **Precision Agriculture**: Remote sensing helps in monitoring crop health, water usage, and soil conditions, providing farmers with real-time data for precision agriculture. GIS then analyzes this data to create management strategies, such as optimizing irrigation schedules or predicting crop yields.

- **Land Use Change**: GIS and remote sensing together can track land use changes, such as urban expansion or agricultural conversion, and help in land management planning.

Disaster Management and Climate Change

- **Wildfire Detection**: Remote sensing can detect wildfires using infrared imagery, while GIS helps to map fire spread and assess potential impacts on nearby communities.

- **Flood Management**: Remote sensing provides real-time imagery of flood-prone areas, while GIS enables flood modeling and risk assessment to optimize disaster response.

3.9 Challenges and Future Directions in GIS and Remote Sensing

Despite the powerful capabilities of GIS and remote sensing, there are several challenges that need to be addressed:

Challenges in Remote Sensing Data Collection

- **Cloud Cover and Atmospheric Interference**: Satellites can have difficulty acquiring clear images due to clouds, haze, or smoke. To overcome this, newer technologies such as radar (SAR) and drones are increasingly used in remote sensing applications.

- **Data Resolution**: While high-resolution imagery provides more detailed data, it also leads to larger datasets, which can be difficult to store and process.

Challenges in GIS

- **Data Integration**: Integrating data from diverse sources (e.g., remote sensing, ground surveys, social media) can be challenging due to differences in data formats, scales, and accuracy.

Emerging Technologies

- **Miniaturization of Sensors**: With the development of small, affordable sensors, remote sensing can become even more accessible and widespread. Small satellite constellations, such as Planet Labs, now provide high-frequency imagery at a lower cost.

- **Real-Time Data Integration**: The integration of real-time data streams, such as IoT and crowdsourced data, with remote sensing and GIS systems has the potential to revolutionize monitoring and response strategies.

The Role of GeoAI

GeoAI (Geospatial Artificial Intelligence) is emerging as a transformative tool in the analysis of GIS and remote sensing data. By using machine learning and deep learning models, GeoAI can automate image classification, anomaly detection, and predictive modeling. It allows for real-time data processing, which is critical for applications like disaster management and climate monitoring.

- **Case Study**: Google Earth Engine uses machine learning to analyze large satellite datasets for deforestation monitoring, while also predicting the future trajectory of forest loss, all in near real-time.

3.10 Conclusion

GIS and remote sensing are indispensable tools for modern Earth observation. Together, they enable the collection, processing, and analysis of spatial data across vast areas, providing critical insights into environmental, agricultural, urban, and disaster management issues. With advancements in technology and integration of GeoAI, the capabilities of these tools will only continue to expand, making them even more valuable for understanding and protecting our planet's ecosystems.

In the future, there will be a greater focus on improving data accuracy, integrating real-time data, and leveraging machine learning to automate analysis. The ability to combine remote sensing data with social and economic data in a GIS framework will provide a more holistic understanding of planetary health and help guide sustainable development.

Chapter 4: Machine Learning in GeoAI for Earth Observation

4.1 Introduction to Machine Learning in GeoAI for Earth Observation

Machine learning (ML) has become an indispensable tool in the field of Earth observation (EO). With the advent of advanced sensor technologies and the increasing availability of satellite imagery, the volume and complexity of Earth observation data have skyrocketed. Traditional methods of processing and analyzing this data have proven inadequate, driving the adoption of machine learning techniques. These techniques allow for the automation of data analysis, enabling faster and more accurate extraction of meaningful information.

GeoAI, a combination of geographic information systems (GIS), remote sensing, and artificial intelligence (AI), leverages ML to provide deeper insights into Earth's systems. The integration of machine learning with Earth observation data is enhancing our ability to monitor, model, and manage planetary health by automating complex tasks, such as land cover classification, disaster monitoring, and environmental change detection.

Machine learning's role in GeoAI for Earth observation extends far beyond simple data analysis. By using algorithms capable of learning from data, ML can detect patterns, make predictions, and identify anomalies within vast datasets that would be impossible for humans to process manually. In doing so, ML is transforming the way we analyze and understand Earth's ecosystems and human activities.

This chapter will explore the various machine learning techniques applied in GeoAI, focusing on supervised and unsupervised learning, as well as deep learning methods. It will also highlight real-world applications, case studies,

Unsupervised Learning

In unsupervised learning, models are trained without labeled data. Instead, the algorithm tries to find inherent patterns or groupings in the data. This approach is particularly useful in situations where labeled data is scarce or unavailable.

Applications in Earth Observation:

1. **Clustering**: Unsupervised learning can be used to cluster similar data points, such as grouping pixels in satellite imagery based on spectral similarities. For example, clustering algorithms can help identify areas of similar vegetation types or distinct geological features.

○ **Example**: K-means clustering has been used to identify patterns in satellite imagery related to urban growth, where different clusters represent different stages of urbanization.

2. **Anomaly Detection**: Unsupervised algorithms can detect outliers or unusual patterns in EO data. These anomalies could be indicative of environmental disturbances, such as forest fires, oil spills, or illegal mining activities.

○ **Example**: A study on wildfire detection used unsupervised learning to analyze thermal imagery and identify areas with unusual heat patterns, providing early warning signs of fire outbreaks.

3. **Dimensionality Reduction**: Techniques like Principal Component Analysis (PCA) are used to reduce the complexity of high-dimensional datasets (e.g., hyperspectral images), while retaining the most important information.

○ **Example**: PCA has been used to analyze multispectral satellite imagery, reducing the number of variables while preserving key features, which helps in faster and more efficient classification.

Common Algorithms in Unsupervised Learning:

● **K-means Clustering**: A popular algorithm used to divide data into K groups based on similarities.

● **DBSCAN (Density-Based Spatial Clustering of Applications with Noise)**: An algorithm used for detecting dense regions in data, useful for identifying spatial patterns in EO data.

● **PCA (Principal Component Analysis)**: A dimensionality reduction technique that helps in handling large datasets by transforming them into fewer dimensions while preserving variance.

Reinforcement Learning

Although less common, reinforcement learning (RL) has significant potential for real-time decision-making in Earth observation, particularly in dynamic environments where continuous data collection and analysis are required.

Applications in Earth Observation:

1. **Optimal Sensing Strategies**: RL can be used to optimize satellite observations in real-time, deciding the best areas to monitor based on evolving conditions (e.g., disaster management, deforestation monitoring).

○ **Example**: RL could be used in satellite constellations to determine the optimal times and locations for capturing high-resolution images, maximizing the value of limited sensor resources.

2. **Disaster Response**: In real-time disaster scenarios, RL could optimize the deployment of resources such as drones or satellites for monitoring damage, guiding the decision-making process for emergency responders.

○ **Example**: During the aftermath of a natural disaster, RL models could prioritize areas with the most significant damage for immediate assessment using satellite data.

4.3 Deep Learning in GeoAI for Earth Observation

Deep learning (DL), a subset of machine learning, has emerged as a transformative technology in the Earth observation domain. Deep learning models, particularly deep neural networks (DNNs), are able to automatically learn hierarchical features from raw data, enabling them to perform tasks with minimal human intervention. These models have proven particularly effective for high-dimensional data such as satellite imagery, offering significant improvements in accuracy and efficiency.

What is Deep Learning?

Deep learning involves the use of neural networks with many layers—referred to as "deep" networks. These networks are capable of learning complex patterns in large datasets without explicit programming for each task. The most common deep learning architectures in EO are Convolutional Neural Networks (CNNs), Recurrent Neural Networks (RNNs), and their variants.

Applications of Deep Learning in Earth Observation:

1. **Satellite Image Classification**: CNNs, in particular, have revolutionized image classification tasks by automating the

extraction of features from raw satellite images. These models excel at detecting complex patterns and are used to classify land cover, urban areas, and vegetation types with high accuracy.

○ **Example**: A deep learning model trained on Landsat or Sentinel imagery was able to classify urban and rural areas, distinguishing between different types of buildings, infrastructure, and vegetation, at a level of accuracy that traditional methods could not achieve.

2. **Object Detection and Mapping**: CNNs can be used for object detection, identifying and classifying individual objects within satellite imagery, such as buildings, roads, and trees. This has significant applications in urban planning, disaster monitoring, and infrastructure development.

○ **Example**: A CNN-based model was used to detect and map new buildings in rapidly growing urban areas, aiding in urban planning and resource management.

3. **Change Detection**: Deep learning models can be trained to detect changes in satellite imagery over time, which is crucial for monitoring environmental changes, deforestation, or the impact of natural disasters.

○ **Example**: A U-Net architecture has been applied to identify changes in forest cover, helping to track deforestation in the Amazon over several years.

4. **Time-Series Analysis**: Recurrent Neural Networks (RNNs) and Long Short-Term Memory (LSTM) networks are particularly suited for time-series analysis, where the goal is to predict trends or detect anomalies over time, such as monitoring vegetation health or predicting crop yields.

○ **Example**: LSTM networks were used to predict the seasonal growth of crops, providing valuable information for farmers to optimize irrigation and fertilization strategies.

Advantages of Deep Learning in EO:

● **Automation of Feature Extraction**: Unlike traditional machine learning, deep learning does not require manual feature engineering. The model automatically learns the important features from raw data, simplifying the process.

● **Improved Accuracy**: Deep learning models have achieved state-of-the-art performance in many EO applications, outperforming traditional methods.

● **Scalability**: Deep learning models can handle large volumes of data, making them suitable for big Earth observation datasets.

4.4 Image Classification in Earth Observation

Image classification is one of the fundamental tasks in Earth observation, allowing for the categorization of pixels in satellite images based on their spectral properties. Machine learning and deep learning models are increasingly being used for this purpose, offering more accurate and automated methods for analyzing Earth observation data.

Supervised Image Classification:

Supervised image classification involves training a model with labeled data to classify each pixel in an image into predefined categories. These categories could represent different land cover types (e.g., forest, water, urban).

● **Example**: In a supervised classification of a tropical rainforest, the model could be trained on labeled images to distinguish between areas of dense forest, deforested land, and urban development.

Unsupervised Image Classification:

Unsupervised classification, on the other hand, groups pixels based on similarities in their spectral signatures without the need for labeled data. This is particularly useful when ground truth data is unavailable or expensive to obtain.

- **Example**: Unsupervised classification might be used to cluster areas in an image with similar vegetation types, providing an initial categorization that can be refined with further analysis.

Deep Learning for Image Classification:

CNNs, as mentioned, are particularly effective for image classification in Earth observation. These models are able to automatically learn features from raw satellite data, enabling them to classify images with minimal human intervention.

- **Example**: A CNN model was applied to classify crops in satellite imagery, achieving a high degree of accuracy in identifying different types of crops across large agricultural areas.

4.5 Challenges and Limitations of Machine Learning in GeoAI for Earth Observation

While machine learning has revolutionized Earth observation, there are still significant challenges that researchers and practitioners must overcome.

Data Quality and Availability:

One of the key challenges in applying ML to Earth observation is the variability and quality of satellite data. Cloud cover, atmospheric conditions, and sensor calibration issues can all affect the quality of the data, leading to inaccurate predictions or classifications.

Model Interpretability:

Many machine learning models, particularly deep learning models, are often considered "black boxes," meaning it is difficult to understand how they arrive at specific predictions. This lack of transparency can be problematic, especially in decision-making scenarios that require trust and accountability.

Scalability:

As the volume of Earth observation data continues to grow, the computational power required to process and analyze these datasets increases. Efficient algorithms and infrastructure are needed to scale machine learning methods for large-scale Earth observation applications.

4.6 Future Directions and Innovations in Machine Learning for Earth Observation

The future of machine learning in GeoAI for Earth observation is promising, with several exciting developments on the horizon:

1. **Integration with Big Data**: As more satellite constellations and IoT devices are deployed, the amount of Earth observation data will increase exponentially. Machine learning techniques will need to evolve to handle this big data and extract insights in real-time.
2. **Explainable AI (XAI)**: To address the interpretability challenge, there is growing research into developing explainable AI models that provide insight into how and why predictions are made, especially in high-stakes applications like environmental monitoring.
3. **Federated Learning**: This is a new approach where machine learning models are trained across decentralized data sources without the need to share raw data. This could enhance privacy and security while enabling collaborative learning across global networks.

4.7 Conclusion

Machine learning has become an integral component of GeoAI, enabling the processing, analysis, and extraction of insights from Earth observation data. By leveraging supervised and unsupervised learning techniques, deep learning models, and advanced image classification methods, machine learning is transforming the way we monitor and manage Earth's ecosystems. From land cover classification to disaster response, ML is helping to address global challenges related to climate change, resource management, and planetary health.

As technology evolves, the integration of machine learning with Earth observation will continue to provide more accurate, scalable, and real-time solutions for planetary health monitoring. However, challenges such as data quality, model interpretability, and scalability remain, and overcoming these hurdles will be key to fully realizing the potential of machine learning in Earth observation.

Chapter 5: Integrating AI with Remote Sensing Data

5.1 Introduction to AI and Remote Sensing Integration

Earth observation (EO) has transformed how we understand our planet, providing valuable insights into everything from climate change to disaster response. Remote sensing data—collected from satellites, drones, and other sensors—offers a bird's-eye view of our world, capturing a wealth of information about land cover, weather patterns, ecosystems, and urban development. However, the true potential of this data can only be unlocked with the help of advanced analytical techniques. Enter Artificial Intelligence (AI).

AI, particularly machine learning (ML) and deep learning (DL), has revolutionized how remote sensing data is processed and analyzed. Traditionally, remote sensing data required manual interpretation, often relying on expert knowledge and time-consuming analysis. With the integration of AI, this process has become more automated, accurate, and scalable, making it possible to process vast volumes of data in a fraction of the time.

AI's ability to automate feature extraction, enhance data fusion, and improve classification accuracy has made it indispensable in many Earth observation applications. The use of AI allows for more efficient monitoring of environmental changes, quicker response to disasters, and deeper insights into the health of our ecosystems.

In this chapter, we will explore the integration of AI with remote sensing data, focusing on key AI-driven methodologies such as data fusion, feature extraction, and classification. Additionally, we will examine real-world applications where AI has already demonstrated its value, alongside case studies that highlight the transformative impact of AI on Earth observation.

5.2 Data Fusion in Remote Sensing

Data fusion is a critical component of remote sensing, as it involves integrating information from multiple sources to create a more comprehensive and accurate representation of the Earth's surface. In the context of remote sensing, data fusion typically refers to the combination of different types of sensor data—such as optical, radar, and thermal data—or even data from different times or locations.

What is Data Fusion?

Data fusion involves the merging of data from various sources to enhance the quality of analysis. For instance, remote sensing satellites may collect optical data, which provides detailed information on surface features, and radar data, which is valuable for detecting surface movement or changes, even through cloud cover. By combining these data types, we obtain a more holistic view of the region being studied.

AI enhances this process by using machine learning algorithms to automatically detect patterns and relationships between the different datasets. This reduces the reliance on manual processing and allows for the extraction of insights that might not be possible with a single data source.

Types of Data Fusion

1. **Sensor Fusion**: This involves combining data from different types of sensors. For example, data from optical and radar sensors can be fused to create images that provide both high-resolution surface details and the ability to detect features under cloud cover. Radar data can penetrate through clouds and provide structural information about the Earth's surface, while optical data can provide detailed color information.

   o **Example**: A typical example of sensor fusion is the combination of Synthetic Aperture Radar (SAR) data with optical imagery from platforms such as Landsat or Sentinel-2. SAR is especially useful for detecting ground displacement in disaster management, while optical imagery can provide clear, detailed information on vegetation, land cover, or urban development.

2. **Multispectral and Hyperspectral Fusion**: Remote sensing satellites like Landsat and Sentinel-2 collect multispectral data, capturing images across a limited number of bands. Hyperspectral sensors, however, capture much broader ranges of spectral data, offering more detailed information about material properties. By combining multispectral and hyperspectral data, researchers can gain a deeper understanding of surface properties, such as vegetation health or mineral composition.

○ **Case Study**: In the agriculture sector, the fusion of multispectral and hyperspectral data has been used to monitor crop health. Multispectral data from Sentinel-2 is combined with hyperspectral data from aircraft or drones to create more accurate vegetation indices, allowing farmers to detect stress, disease, or nutrient deficiencies in crops.

3. **Temporal Fusion**: Temporal fusion refers to the integration of data from multiple time points. This technique is essential for monitoring dynamic changes on the Earth's surface, such as urban expansion, deforestation, or the progression of natural disasters. By comparing images of the same location taken at different times, we can track how the environment evolves.

○ **Example**: In monitoring deforestation in the Amazon rainforest, temporal fusion techniques are employed to combine satellite images from various years, enabling researchers to quantify changes in forest cover and identify areas of illegal logging activity.

Techniques for Data Fusion

- **Pixel-Level Fusion**: At the pixel level, data from different sensors or sources are merged directly at the individual pixel level. This approach typically involves combining the raw data from various sensors to form a composite image that maximizes the amount of useful information at each pixel.

  ○ **Example**: In disaster monitoring, combining radar and optical imagery at the pixel level allows for more accurate assessments of flood or wildfire damage, especially in areas with cloud cover or smoke that might obscure optical imagery.

- **Feature-Level Fusion**: Instead of merging raw data, feature-level fusion involves extracting features (e.g., vegetation indices, texture, or edges) from each data source and combining these extracted features before performing any analysis.

  ○ **Example**: In urban planning, feature-level fusion can combine information on building heights (extracted from LiDAR data) with land cover classifications (from optical imagery) to assess urban sprawl and infrastructure development.

- **Decision-Level Fusion**: This fusion technique involves combining the output from different models or analyses rather than combining raw data. For example, the output from different machine learning classifiers (one based on optical data and one based on radar data) might be merged to produce a more robust classification result.

  ○ **Example**: In flood mapping, decision-level fusion could combine outputs from different AI models that classify water bodies, detect flood damage, and assess infrastructure impacts.

Case Studies of Data Fusion in EO

1. **Agriculture**: Satellite data fusion has been instrumental in precision agriculture. By fusing data from optical satellites like Landsat with ground sensor data, farmers can monitor crop health, soil moisture levels, and irrigation needs. This fusion approach helps improve crop yields and reduce resource consumption.

2. **Disaster Response**: Following a natural disaster, satellite data fusion has been used to rapidly assess damage. For instance, combining SAR and optical imagery has allowed responders to quickly evaluate areas affected by floods, hurricanes, or wildfires. In one case, fusion of radar and optical imagery helped assess flood damage in the aftermath of Hurricane Katrina, providing emergency teams with critical information for rescue and recovery operations.

3. **Forest Monitoring**: The combination of optical imagery and LiDAR data is widely used to monitor forest cover, detect illegal logging, and assess biodiversity. LiDAR data helps determine forest canopy height and structure, while optical imagery provides information on vegetation types and health. The fusion of these two data sources has improved the accuracy of deforestation monitoring programs.

5.3 Feature Extraction in Remote Sensing with AI

Feature extraction is a crucial step in remote sensing data processing, where we identify key patterns and structures in raw data. Traditionally, feature extraction has relied on manual or semi-automated techniques, but AI, particularly machine learning and deep learning algorithms, has dramatically improved this process by automating and enhancing feature extraction, allowing for the extraction of more complex features and patterns that might be overlooked in manual processes.

What is Feature Extraction?

Feature extraction involves identifying and isolating important information from raw remote sensing data, such as identifying vegetation types, land cover classifications, water bodies, and built-up areas. Traditional methods of feature extraction relied heavily on human expertise and were often limited by the complexity of the data, such as the resolution of satellite imagery or atmospheric conditions.

With AI, feature extraction is now more efficient and scalable. Deep learning models, especially convolutional neural networks (CNNs), have proven to be highly effective at extracting hierarchical features from raw images, making them ideal for tasks such as land cover classification, object detection, and change detection.

Traditional Methods of Feature Extraction

1. **Principal Component Analysis (PCA)**: PCA is a linear dimensionality reduction technique used to transform multispectral or hyperspectral data into principal components that capture the maximum variance of the data. This is particularly useful when dealing with high-dimensional data, like hyperspectral images, which can have hundreds of bands.

○ **Example**: In vegetation mapping, PCA can be applied to multispectral data from Landsat to extract the principal components that best represent the distribution of vegetation types.

2. **Texture Analysis**: Texture analysis involves extracting patterns or structures from satellite images based on the spatial arrangement of pixel intensities. Methods like Gray Level Co-occurrence Matrix (GLCM) are often used to identify texture features, which can then be used to classify land cover.

○ **Example**: In urban studies, texture features extracted from high-resolution satellite imagery can be used to differentiate between urban areas, water bodies, and agricultural land.

3. **Edge Detection**: Techniques like the Sobel or Canny edge detectors are used to identify boundaries in an image, which can help delineate different land cover types, such as forests, bodies of water, and urban areas.

AI-Driven Feature Extraction

AI, particularly deep learning, automates and enhances feature extraction in ways that were previously not possible. Deep learning models, especially CNNs, can automatically learn hierarchical representations of features, from basic edges and textures to complex shapes and objects. These features can be used to classify or analyze land cover, vegetation, or built-up areas in satellite images.

1. **Deep Learning for Feature Extraction**:

○ CNNs, which are particularly adept at image classification tasks, have been successfully used for remote sensing feature extraction. In the case of land cover classification, CNNs learn to detect features like roads, buildings, trees, and water bodies by analyzing patterns in raw satellite images.

○ **Example**: A CNN model trained on a large dataset of satellite images from Google Earth or Landsat can automatically extract features such as roads, rivers, and vegetation types, without human intervention.

2. **Semantic Segmentation**: Semantic segmentation is a deep learning approach where each pixel in an image is labeled with a specific class (e.g., water, forest, building, etc.). This approach enables highly detailed and accurate feature extraction from

satellite imagery, as the model assigns labels to each pixel based on its spatial characteristics.

○ **Example**: In forest monitoring, semantic segmentation can be used to classify individual pixels as forest or non-forest, distinguishing between different types of vegetation and identifying areas impacted by deforestation.

3. **Transfer Learning**: Transfer learning allows models trained on large, well-annotated datasets (such as ImageNet) to be applied to remote sensing data. The idea is to take a pre-trained model and fine-tune it on a specific remote sensing task, which is useful for reducing the amount of labeled data required.

○ **Example**: A pre-trained CNN model developed for image classification on natural images can be fine-tuned on satellite images to detect specific features like urban areas, agricultural land, or bodies of water, without needing a large labeled dataset for remote sensing.

Case Studies of Feature Extraction in EO

1. Forest Mapping with AI:

○ Using CNNs for feature extraction, AI models have been able to distinguish between various types of forests, such as tropical rainforests, temperate forests, and urban areas. These models can even detect deforestation by analyzing changes in the images over time.

○ **Example**: A study in the Amazon rainforest used AI-driven feature extraction to identify illegal logging activities by detecting subtle changes in forest structure, which were invisible to traditional methods of analysis.

2. Urban Monitoring:

○ AI algorithms, particularly CNNs, are also employed in urban monitoring to extract features like building footprints, road networks, and other urban infrastructure. These models can process high-resolution imagery from satellites like WorldView or Sentinel to detect urban sprawl and analyze land use changes over time.

○ **Example**: Researchers used deep learning to extract building footprints from high-resolution satellite images, mapping urban expansion in rapidly growing cities like Lagos, Nigeria.

3. Disaster Monitoring:

○ Feature extraction techniques have also been used in disaster response. AI models can automatically identify flooded areas, damaged infrastructure, and other disaster-related features in satellite imagery.

○ **Example**: Following the 2011 Japan earthquake and tsunami, AI models were employed to automatically detect and classify areas affected by the tsunami, providing vital information for response teams.

5.4 AI Classification Algorithms in Remote Sensing

Classification is one of the primary tasks in remote sensing, where pixels in an image are categorized into distinct classes, such as vegetation, water, urban, or barren land. The process typically involves using training data to "teach" an algorithm how to categorize unknown pixels based on the features extracted from the data.

Overview of Classification Techniques

AI has introduced a range of advanced classification techniques that significantly improve the accuracy and scalability of remote sensing applications. These methods rely on machine learning algorithms, particularly supervised and unsupervised learning techniques, to classify land cover types from remote sensing data.

Supervised Classification with AI

Supervised classification requires a labeled dataset where the class of each sample is known. Machine learning algorithms are trained on these labeled samples to learn the relationship between the features (such as pixel intensity or texture) and the class labels. Once trained, the model can classify new, unseen data.

1. **Support Vector Machines (SVM)**: SVM is a widely used machine learning technique for remote sensing classification. It finds the hyperplane that best separates different classes in the feature space. SVMs are particularly effective when dealing with non-linear data, which is often the case in remote sensing images.

o **Example**: SVMs have been successfully used in land cover classification, such as distinguishing between urban areas, forests, and water bodies in satellite imagery.

2. **Random Forest**: Random Forest is an ensemble machine learning method that uses a collection of decision trees to classify remote sensing data. It is robust to overfitting and works well with high-dimensional datasets, such as hyperspectral data.

o **Example**: Random Forest has been employed in agricultural land use classification, accurately identifying different crop types from multispectral satellite imagery.

3. **Deep Learning for Classification**: Deep learning models, especially CNNs, have become increasingly popular for classification tasks in remote sensing. These models automatically learn relevant features from the data and can classify complex patterns that are challenging for traditional algorithms to recognize.

○ **Example**: CNNs have been used to classify urban and rural areas, monitor deforestation, and detect agricultural crops, all from high-resolution satellite imagery.

Unsupervised Classification

Unsupervised classification does not require labeled data. Instead, the algorithm groups the data into clusters based on inherent similarities, and each cluster is then assigned to a specific class.

1. **K-Means Clustering**: K-Means is a simple and widely used clustering algorithm in remote sensing. It partitions data into K clusters, with each cluster representing a different land cover type.

○ **Example**: K-Means has been used in vegetation classification, where pixels are grouped based on spectral similarity to detect forests, grasslands, and other vegetation types.

2. **Self-Organizing Maps (SOMs)**: SOMs are a type of neural network that uses unsupervised learning to map high-dimensional data into a lower-dimensional grid. They are particularly useful for clustering complex remote sensing data, such as hyperspectral images.

○ **Example**: SOMs have been applied to hyperspectral data to classify different mineral types in geological surveys.

Hybrid Classification Methods

Hybrid methods combine the strengths of multiple algorithms to improve classification accuracy. For instance, combining deep learning for feature extraction with traditional classifiers such as decision trees or Random Forest can lead to more robust and accurate results.

- **Example**: A hybrid approach that combines deep CNNs for feature extraction with Random Forest for classification has been used in land cover classification tasks, particularly for mapping forests, wetlands, and agricultural land.

Case Studies of AI Classification in EO

1. **Vegetation Mapping**: AI-based classification algorithms, particularly CNNs, have been used to classify vegetation types from remote sensing data, providing detailed information about biodiversity and land use. These methods have been used to monitor forest health and detect changes in vegetation cover due to deforestation or urbanization.

2. **Urban Mapping**: In urban environments, AI models are applied to classify land cover types like roads, buildings, and green spaces. Deep learning algorithms have enabled accurate mapping of urban sprawl and infrastructure development, which is crucial for sustainable urban planning.

1. **Disaster Response**: AI classification models have been employed in disaster management to rapidly assess the impact of events like floods, wildfires, and earthquakes. For example, AI algorithms have been used to classify flood-affected areas, identify damaged infrastructure, and map post-disaster recovery efforts.

5.5 Summary and Future Directions

The integration of AI with remote sensing data is transforming the way we process, analyze, and interpret Earth observation data. AI-driven techniques, such as data fusion, feature extraction, and classification, have enabled the automated processing of vast amounts of remote sensing data, making it possible to monitor and manage Earth's ecosystems with unprecedented speed and accuracy.

The future of AI in remote sensing holds exciting possibilities. With the continued advancement of machine learning and deep learning techniques, we can expect even more sophisticated AI models capable of handling the growing volumes and complexities of EO data. In particular, advances in generative AI, reinforcement learning, and AI-enabled edge computing will likely open new frontiers in real-time data processing, disaster management, and climate change monitoring.

However, challenges remain. The need for large, high-quality datasets for training AI models is a significant hurdle, as is the interpretability of AI models, particularly deep learning models, which are often seen as "black boxes." Additionally, ensuring that AI models are generalizable across different geographical regions, sensor types, and temporal scales remains an ongoing challenge.

As we move forward, the integration of AI with remote sensing will continue to play a pivotal role in solving some of the world's most pressing environmental challenges, from biodiversity conservation to climate change mitigation and disaster response.

Chapter 6: GeoAI for Climate Change Monitoring and Mitigation

Introduction to Climate Change Monitoring and GeoAI

Climate change is one of the most pressing global challenges of the 21st century, influencing ecosystems, economies, and human societies at an unprecedented rate. The monitoring of climate change indicators, such as temperature fluctuations, sea level rise, and greenhouse gas concentrations, is crucial for understanding its impacts and developing mitigation strategies. The role of technology, particularly GeoAI, has become increasingly vital in enabling large-scale, efficient monitoring of environmental changes.

GeoAI combines geospatial data with advanced artificial intelligence (AI) techniques, such as machine learning (ML) and deep learning (DL), to process, analyze, and interpret vast volumes of Earth observation (EO) data. Through the integration of EO data from satellite imagery, weather models, and ground-based sensors, GeoAI enhances our ability to track climate change trends, predict future scenarios, and devise effective strategies for mitigation.

This chapter explores the role of GeoAI in monitoring and mitigating climate change, focusing on the key indicators of climate change, AI-driven predictive models, and the various ways GeoAI can assist in mitigating its impacts. Real-world case studies will illustrate the effectiveness of GeoAI in addressing climate change issues, from sea level rise to carbon emissions and beyond.

6.1 Climate Change Indicators and Data Sources

6.1.1 Understanding Climate Indicators

Climate change is defined by long-term changes in temperature, precipitation, and other atmospheric conditions. Understanding the various indicators of climate change is essential for evaluating its impacts and planning mitigation strategies. Key indicators include:

- **Temperature Variations**: Rising global temperatures are perhaps the most significant marker of climate change. Long-term temperature data is crucial in assessing the rate of warming and its implications for ecosystems, agriculture, and human health. GeoAI plays a pivotal role in identifying temperature anomalies from satellite and ground data, allowing for the monitoring of warming trends at regional and global scales.

- **Sea Level Rise**: Melting ice caps and glaciers, combined with the thermal expansion of seawater, contribute to rising sea levels. This indicator is particularly important for understanding the risks to coastal cities, small island nations, and low-lying regions. GeoAI techniques are increasingly used to model and predict sea level rise and assess the vulnerability of coastal ecosystems and infrastructure.

- **Carbon Emissions and Greenhouse Gases**: The concentration of greenhouse gases (GHGs) like carbon dioxide (CO_2) and methane (CH_4) in the atmosphere drives global warming. Monitoring and managing emissions is crucial for climate change mitigation. AI-driven models can identify emission hotspots, track trends, and provide data to inform climate policy.

- **Glacial Retreat and Ice Cover**: The retreat of glaciers and ice sheets is one of the most visible consequences of climate change. Monitoring these changes is vital for understanding their contribution to sea level rise and assessing the health of polar ecosystems. GeoAI techniques are employed to process satellite imagery and track changes in ice cover over time.

6.1.2 Data Sources for Climate Monitoring

GeoAI relies on various data sources to monitor climate change indicators. These data sources include satellite imagery, in-situ measurements, and climate models. Key sources for climate monitoring include:

- **Satellites and Remote Sensing**: Satellites such as Landsat, Sentinel, and MODIS provide critical data on global temperatures, vegetation cover, sea levels, and carbon emissions. The vast amount of satellite imagery and remote sensing data collected daily offers a unique opportunity to monitor climate change in real-time.

- **Ground-Based Sensors**: In addition to satellite data, ground-based sensors (e.g., weather stations, ocean buoys, and air quality sensors) provide localized measurements of climate parameters. Combining ground sensor data with satellite imagery allows for more accurate climate models and improved monitoring of regional variations.

- **Climate Models**: Numerical climate models predict how various factors (e.g., emissions, land use, and aerosols) will influence climate systems. AI can help improve the accuracy of these models by optimizing their predictions and integrating diverse data sources.

While these data sources provide invaluable insights into climate change, challenges related to data quality, spatial and temporal resolution, and data accessibility remain. Nonetheless, the ability to combine these data sources using AI technologies provides unprecedented opportunities for more precise climate monitoring.

6.2 Role of AI in Analyzing Climate Change Indicators

6.2.1 Temperature Variations

Monitoring global temperature variations is essential for understanding the pace and magnitude of climate change. Satellites and weather stations record temperature data over long periods, but these datasets are often large and complex. AI techniques, especially machine learning, play an essential role in processing and analyzing this data.

- **Deep Learning for Temperature Anomaly Detection**: Deep learning algorithms can identify patterns and anomalies in temperature data, such as spikes or sudden drops that might indicate extreme events like heatwaves or cold spells. For instance, convolutional neural networks (CNNs) have been used to analyze satellite imagery and temperature data to detect regional temperature changes, particularly in sensitive areas like the Arctic, which is warming faster than the global average.

- **Case Study: Arctic Warming**: A study conducted by researchers from the University of Alaska applied machine learning models to track temperature anomalies in the Arctic using data from the NOAA and NASA. The models showed significant warming trends in the Arctic region, particularly during the winter months, which are contributing to permafrost thawing and changes in ecosystems.

6.2.2 Sea Level Rise and Coastal Monitoring

Sea level rise is a direct consequence of climate change, caused by the melting of glaciers and thermal expansion of seawater. Monitoring this phenomenon is essential to assess the risks to coastal communities and infrastructure.

- **AI in Monitoring Coastal Changes**: AI models process satellite data, such as altimeter readings from missions like

NASA's Jason series, to track changes in sea level. Machine learning algorithms can identify trends in sea level rise and analyze the impact on coastal ecosystems, such as wetlands and mangroves, which act as natural buffers against storm surges.

- **Case Study: Miami's Coastal Vulnerability**: AI models have been used to analyze the effects of rising sea levels on coastal cities like Miami. By combining satellite data with AI-driven models, researchers have been able to predict areas at risk of flooding by 2050, helping urban planners develop strategies to protect vulnerable populations.

6.2.3 Carbon Emissions and Greenhouse Gases

Monitoring carbon emissions is a critical aspect of climate change mitigation. Traditionally, carbon emissions have been tracked using ground-based measurement stations and emission inventories. However, GeoAI enhances this process by analyzing satellite data to identify emission sources and track trends over time.

- **AI in Emission Source Detection**: AI models can process data from satellites such as NASA's OCO-2 and the Japan Aerospace Exploration Agency's GOSAT, which monitor atmospheric CO_2 concentrations. Machine learning algorithms identify emission hotspots, track emission trends, and help pinpoint areas where mitigation efforts are most needed.

- **Case Study: Monitoring Methane Emissions**: AI is also used to detect methane emissions, which have a much higher global warming potential than CO_2. A collaboration between the European Space Agency (ESA) and the startup GHGSat has led to the deployment of AI to analyze satellite data for methane leaks from oil and gas facilities. These AI models have been successfully used to identify leaks and assist companies in reducing emissions.

6.2.4 Glacial Retreat and Ice Cover Changes

Monitoring the retreat of glaciers and changes in ice cover is vital for understanding their contribution to sea level rise and assessing their impact on global ecosystems.

- **AI in Ice Mass Loss Detection**: Machine learning algorithms are increasingly used to process satellite imagery from missions like NASA's ICESat-2, which measures ice thickness, and ESA's CryoSat-2, which tracks changes in ice volume. These models detect changes in ice mass and predict future trends based on past data.

- **Case Study: Greenland Ice Sheet**: A study by researchers at the University of Cambridge used deep learning techniques to analyze changes in the Greenland Ice Sheet using satellite data. The AI model identified significant ice loss in specific regions and predicted future melting rates based on historical patterns, contributing to more accurate climate models and sea-level projections.

6.3 Predictive Modeling and Climate Scenario Forecasting with GeoAI

6.3.1 Climate Models and GeoAI

AI plays a crucial role in improving the accuracy and efficiency of climate models, which are used to predict future climate scenarios. Traditional climate models rely heavily on numerical simulations, which can be computationally expensive and require vast amounts of data.

- **AI-Enhanced Climate Modeling**: GeoAI can optimize these models by using machine learning to process large datasets and identify patterns that might be overlooked by traditional methods. For example, AI can help integrate data from various sources, such as satellite imagery, weather stations, and atmospheric data, to improve the predictions of climate models.

- **Case Study: CMIP6 Model Enhancements**: The Coupled Model Intercomparison Project (CMIP6) provides a standard set of climate model projections. AI-driven enhancements to these models have helped improve the resolution and accuracy of regional climate projections, particularly in understanding localized climate impacts, such as temperature extremes or precipitation patterns.

6.3.2 Time-Series Analysis and Trend Detection

GeoAI-driven time-series models, such as RNNs and LSTMs, are increasingly used for analyzing temporal climate data. These models can process data from satellites, ground stations, and other sources over time to detect patterns, trends, and anomalies, offering insights into the progression of climate change.

- **Analyzing Seasonal and Yearly Variations**: Climate change often manifests as shifts in seasonal patterns and long-term trends. Time-series models can analyze seasonal variations in temperature, precipitation, and other indicators, identifying changes that may suggest long-term shifts in climate. By examining historical data, these models can forecast future trends, allowing scientists and policymakers to better understand potential scenarios for the coming decades.

- **Case Study: Predicting Drought Patterns**: In a study on drought forecasting, researchers used time-series analysis to predict drought conditions in the U.S. Southwest based on historical precipitation and temperature data. AI models processed data from multiple sources to create predictive drought maps, helping agricultural planners and water resource managers take proactive measures to mitigate the impact on agriculture and water supply.

6.3.3 Scenario Analysis for Future Climate Outcomes

GeoAI models are invaluable in generating various climate scenarios, examining the potential outcomes of different climate change trajectories. By analyzing large datasets from climate simulations and historical data, AI-based models can create scenario-based projections for temperatures, sea level rise, and other critical indicators.

- **Using AI to Generate Climate Scenarios**: AI-enhanced climate models can generate scenarios that explore the implications of varying levels of greenhouse gas emissions, land use changes, and other factors. By integrating satellite data, ground observations, and climate models, GeoAI offers refined insights into potential outcomes across different regions and timeframes.

- **Case Example: Regional Climate Projections**: For example, GeoAI was applied to model potential climate outcomes in the Amazon rainforest under different deforestation rates. By comparing scenarios with high deforestation rates to those with reforestation efforts, GeoAI revealed significant differences in regional rainfall and temperature patterns, underscoring the vital role of forest conservation in climate resilience.

6.4 GeoAI in Climate Change Mitigation Efforts

In addition to monitoring climate change indicators, GeoAI plays a crucial role in mitigating climate change through strategies that reduce greenhouse gas emissions and enhance carbon capture. Here, we explore some of the most promising applications of GeoAI in climate mitigation.

6.4.1 Forest Monitoring and Carbon Sequestration

Forests act as critical carbon sinks, absorbing CO_2 from the atmosphere and storing it in biomass and soil. However, deforestation and forest degradation reduce this capacity. GeoAI aids in forest monitoring and conservation, promoting carbon sequestration and helping mitigate climate change.

- **GeoAI for Forest Biomass Estimation**: Machine learning models are used to estimate forest biomass based on satellite imagery and LiDAR data. By accurately estimating biomass, GeoAI can provide insights into how much CO_2 forests are storing, making it possible to monitor changes in carbon sequestration over time.

- **Case Study: Amazon Forest Conservation**: In the Amazon rainforest, GeoAI models are employed to detect deforestation hotspots and track reforestation efforts. By analyzing high-resolution satellite imagery, GeoAI can identify areas of illegal logging and forest fires, supporting enforcement actions and conservation policies. These efforts help preserve one of the world's largest carbon sinks, which is essential for mitigating global warming.

6.4.2 Renewable Energy Resource Assessment

GeoAI aids in the planning and optimization of renewable energy projects, such as solar and wind farms. By analyzing geospatial data, climate conditions, and energy demand patterns, AI can identify optimal locations for renewable energy installations, thereby reducing reliance on fossil fuels.

- **AI in Solar and Wind Potential Mapping**: GeoAI applications analyze solar radiation data, wind patterns, and terrain characteristics to assess renewable energy potential. These assessments are crucial for selecting locations that maximize energy generation and minimize environmental impact.

- **Case Study: Solar Mapping in India**: In India, GeoAI has been used to identify potential sites for solar farms by analyzing satellite data on solar irradiance, land cover, and temperature. This AI-driven approach helps developers avoid environmentally sensitive areas and prioritize regions with high solar potential, accelerating India's transition to renewable energy sources.

6.4.3 Agricultural Practices for Carbon Reduction

Agriculture is both a contributor to and a potential mitigator of climate change. GeoAI helps monitor sustainable farming practices that reduce the agricultural sector's carbon footprint. For instance, precision agriculture techniques allow farmers to minimize inputs, such as water and fertilizers, which can reduce emissions from agricultural fields.

- **Precision Agriculture with GeoAI**: Using satellite imagery and AI, farmers can monitor soil health, crop growth, and nutrient levels, allowing for optimized resource use. This minimizes the emissions associated with excessive fertilization and irrigation, promoting sustainable agriculture.

- **Case Study: Carbon Sequestration in Soils**: In the U.S., GeoAI has been applied to monitor soil carbon levels, tracking practices like crop rotation and no-till farming that increase carbon sequestration in soils. By combining satellite and soil sensor data, AI models help quantify the carbon sequestration potential of different agricultural practices, informing strategies to mitigate emissions from agriculture.

6.5 Case Studies of GeoAI for Climate Change Monitoring and Mitigation

6.5.1 Arctic and Antarctic Climate Observations

The polar regions are among the most affected by climate change, experiencing rapid warming and significant ice loss. GeoAI applications in polar regions have provided valuable insights into temperature trends, ice cover changes, and ecosystem impacts.

- **GeoAI in Polar Ice Monitoring**: AI models process satellite imagery to monitor changes in sea ice and glacier mass. These models can detect trends in ice loss and help predict future melting rates, which are crucial for projecting sea level rise and understanding its implications for global climate.

- **Case Study: Antarctic Ice Sheet**: Researchers at NASA have used AI-driven models to analyze satellite data from the Antarctic ice sheet. By studying trends in ice thickness and volume, they have identified areas most vulnerable to melting, contributing to more accurate predictions of sea level rise.

6.5.2 Deforestation and Land Use Change in the Amazon

The Amazon rainforest, often referred to as the "lungs of the Earth," plays a crucial role in regulating global CO_2 levels. GeoAI has been instrumental in monitoring deforestation and land use changes in this region, supporting conservation efforts and climate mitigation.

- **AI for Deforestation Detection**: By processing satellite imagery, GeoAI detects deforestation and illegal logging activities in real-time. Machine learning algorithms analyze land cover changes and alert authorities, enabling rapid response and enforcement.

- **Case Study: Amazon Deforestation Monitoring**: The Brazilian National Institute for Space Research (INPE) uses GeoAI to monitor deforestation in the Amazon basin. Through machine learning models, they can identify deforestation hotspots and predict future land use trends, supporting policies to protect the Amazon and maintain its carbon storage capacity.

6.5.3 GeoAI in Urban Climate Resilience

Urban areas are particularly vulnerable to climate change impacts, such as urban heat islands and air pollution. GeoAI is used to monitor these challenges and develop climate resilience strategies for cities.

- **AI for Urban Heat Island Analysis**: GeoAI applications analyze thermal satellite imagery to identify heat island hotspots in cities. This information helps urban planners prioritize areas for cooling measures, such as green roofs and increased vegetation.

- **Case Study: Resilience Planning in Los Angeles**: The city of Los Angeles has used GeoAI to map heat islands and assess vulnerability to extreme heat. By identifying areas with limited vegetation and high building density, city planners are implementing initiatives to increase green spaces and reduce urban temperatures, contributing to improved climate resilience.

6.6 Summary and Future Directions in GeoAI for Climate Change

Key Insights from GeoAI Applications in Climate Monitoring

GeoAI has transformed the way we monitor and mitigate climate change. Through the use of machine learning and remote sensing, GeoAI enables the efficient analysis of complex climate data, helping to track indicators such as temperature changes, sea level rise, and deforestation. These technologies are also essential for assessing climate risks, modeling future scenarios, and implementing mitigation strategies across sectors.

Emerging Trends and Technologies

Several emerging trends are likely to further enhance GeoAI's role in climate action:

- **Improved Climate Models**: Advances in AI models, particularly deep learning and generative models, are expected to further improve climate forecasting accuracy.

- **Edge Computing for Real-Time Monitoring**: With the rise of edge computing, it will be possible to analyze satellite and sensor data in real-time, enabling more responsive climate monitoring.

- **Multi-Sensor Data Fusion**: Integrating data from multiple sensors, including those on drones and autonomous vehicles, will allow GeoAI applications to capture environmental data at finer spatial and temporal resolutions.

Challenges and Opportunities for GeoAI in Climate Change Mitigation

While GeoAI offers vast potential, several challenges remain:

- **Data Quality and Accessibility**: The effectiveness of GeoAI depends on high-quality, accessible data. Efforts to improve data sharing and standardization across agencies and nations will be essential.

- **Ethical and Privacy Concerns**: The use of geospatial data raises ethical issues related to privacy and surveillance, particularly in sensitive areas.

- **Collaboration Across Disciplines**: Tackling climate change requires collaboration between AI researchers, climate scientists, policymakers, and industry stakeholders. Fostering these interdisciplinary efforts will be key to maximizing the impact of GeoAI.

GeoAI is positioned to play a transformative role in combating climate change, helping us understand, predict, and mitigate its effects. The integration of GeoAI into global climate efforts holds promise for creating a sustainable future, with ongoing research and innovation paving the way for increasingly impactful applications.

Chapter 7: GeoAI for Disaster Management and Response

7.1 Introduction to GeoAI in Disaster Management

7.1.1 Defining Disaster Management and the Role of GeoAI

Disaster management refers to the systematic approach to managing and mitigating the effects of natural and man-made disasters. It involves preparedness, response, recovery, and mitigation efforts to reduce disaster impacts. In the context of natural disasters, effective management is key to saving lives, protecting property, and minimizing long-term environmental damage.

GeoAI, the integration of geospatial data with artificial intelligence (AI), plays a transformative role in disaster management. By combining satellite imagery, sensors, machine learning algorithms, and real-time data, GeoAI enhances disaster prediction, response, and recovery efforts. It enables decision-makers to access timely, actionable insights, improving preparedness and resilience.

Traditional methods of disaster management often rely on manual processes and limited data sources. GeoAI bridges this gap by enabling real-time, data-driven decision-making through automated analysis of vast datasets, which can include satellite imagery, weather patterns, and ground-level sensor data.

7.1.2 Importance of GeoAI for Disaster Preparedness and Resilience

GeoAI is essential for improving the efficiency and effectiveness of disaster management across all stages—before, during, and after a disaster. In the preparedness phase, GeoAI helps identify at-risk areas, allowing communities to plan more effectively. For instance, predictive models powered by AI can forecast the likelihood of a disaster occurring in a given region, facilitating early warning systems. These models are continually improved through machine learning, enabling them to provide more accurate predictions as they process more historical and real-time data.

In the response phase, GeoAI facilitates rapid damage assessment, guiding emergency responders to critical areas. AI models process satellite images and sensor data to quickly determine which regions have been most affected and to assess damage, aiding in prioritizing resources and evacuation efforts.

During recovery, GeoAI continues to provide vital insights by monitoring the long-term impacts of disasters and assessing environmental changes, allowing governments and organizations to develop strategies for rebuilding and improving resilience to future disasters.

7.2 GeoAI in Disaster Prediction and Early Warning Systems

7.2.1 Predictive Modeling and Risk Assessment

GeoAI's predictive modeling capabilities allow scientists and decision-makers to assess disaster risks based on various factors, such as weather patterns, geological features, and historical data. These models utilize machine learning algorithms to identify patterns in data that are often too complex for traditional models to discern.

For example, flood risk models use historical rainfall and river level data combined with machine learning algorithms to predict flood events in real-time. By analyzing patterns from past storms and floods, these models can estimate the severity and timing of potential future floods.

In earthquake-prone regions, GeoAI models can analyze geological features, historical seismic data, and current tectonic activities to assess the likelihood of future earthquakes. While predicting earthquakes with complete accuracy remains a challenge, AI models help improve risk assessments and can give early warnings about other hazards like landslides triggered by seismic activity.

7.2.2 GeoAI for Weather-Related Early Warning Systems

GeoAI plays a crucial role in weather-related disaster prediction and early warning systems. Machine learning models integrate real-time weather data from satellites, ground sensors, and other sources to monitor the development of severe weather events such as hurricanes, cyclones, and tornadoes.

For example, AI models have been applied to track hurricanes, predicting their path, intensity, and potential landfall zones. These models analyze vast datasets of atmospheric conditions, ocean temperatures, and wind patterns. Through advanced machine learning techniques like deep learning, the models can continuously learn from new data, improving the accuracy of their predictions.

In regions vulnerable to flooding, GeoAI systems combine weather forecasts, river gauge data, and satellite imagery to generate flood models. These models can provide forecasts for river levels and flood risk areas up to several days in advance, enabling authorities to issue timely flood warnings to at-risk populations.

7.2.3 Case Study: Cyclone Early Warning System in South Asia

A prime example of GeoAI's role in disaster prediction and early warning is the Cyclone Early Warning System (CEWS) implemented in South Asia. The region, particularly countries like India, Bangladesh, and Sri Lanka, is highly vulnerable to cyclones and storm surges. GeoAI-driven models use a combination of satellite imagery, sea surface temperature data, and atmospheric pressure readings to forecast the trajectory of cyclones.

One notable success was the 2019 Super Cyclone Fani, which struck India and Bangladesh. Thanks to advanced early warning systems powered by AI, authorities were able to evacuate over 1.2 million people in advance, minimizing casualties. AI models continuously refined the cyclone's predicted path, helping decision-makers allocate resources and deploy emergency teams in real time.

This case demonstrates the value of GeoAI in not only predicting disasters but also ensuring that communities are adequately prepared, and lives are saved through proactive measures.

7.3 Monitoring and Real-Time Detection of Natural Disasters with GeoAI

7.3.1 Using Satellite Imagery for Disaster Detection

GeoAI enhances disaster detection by analyzing satellite imagery in real time. Satellites equipped with high-resolution cameras and sensors can capture vast amounts of data, which AI models then process to detect changes in land cover, temperature, and other environmental factors that signify disaster events. This capability is especially useful for monitoring natural disasters such as wildfires, floods, and hurricanes.

For example, satellite sensors can detect the thermal signatures of wildfires in remote or forested areas. GeoAI systems analyze the imagery to identify fire hotspots, assess the size and spread of the fire, and even predict its future movements based on wind patterns and topography.

Similarly, during hurricanes, satellites track cloud formation, rainfall, and wind speeds, while AI algorithms analyze this data to generate real-time maps of the hurricane's intensity and trajectory. Such tools allow emergency responders to prepare for evacuation and provide support where it's most needed.

7.3.2 Real-Time Data Processing and AI Integration

Real-time data processing is a core strength of GeoAI systems. Traditionally, the time required to process satellite images and extract actionable information has been a bottleneck in disaster response. However, AI models can now process these data sets almost instantaneously, enabling faster decision-making and immediate action.

AI models use deep learning techniques such as convolutional neural networks (CNNs) to identify patterns in images, classify disaster types, and evaluate the extent of damage. For example, during the 2020 Australian wildfires, satellite imagery was processed through AI models to assess the damage in real time. The ability to process imagery in near real-time allowed emergency responders to identify the most severely affected areas, allocate firefighting resources efficiently, and direct evacuation efforts.

7.3.3 Case Study: Wildfire Detection and Monitoring in California

California has been a hotspot for wildfires, with devastating impacts on communities, wildlife, and the environment. GeoAI has been increasingly used to detect and monitor these fires. The National Aeronautics and Space Administration (NASA) and the European Space Agency (ESA) use AI-driven models to analyze satellite data from their respective Earth-observing satellites.

For example, in 2020, the use of AI for wildfire monitoring helped to map fire progression in California, enabling real-time situational awareness for firefighting teams. AI models were used to predict the spread of fires based on weather data, terrain, and other environmental factors. By rapidly processing satellite data, these AI systems helped to guide firefighting strategies and evacuation orders, contributing to saving lives and minimizing property damage.

7.4 GeoAI for Specific Disaster Types

This section covers the application of GeoAI across various types of natural disasters, each with unique characteristics and challenges.

7.4.1 Hurricanes and Tropical Storms

GeoAI has revolutionized the monitoring and prediction of hurricanes and tropical storms. Satellites such as NASA's GOES series and NOAA's Geostationary Operational Environmental Satellite System provide valuable data on atmospheric conditions and storm intensity. AI models use this data to track storm movement, predict landfall, and estimate potential damage.

In addition to tracking hurricanes, GeoAI can also assist in post-disaster damage assessments by analyzing before-and-after satellite images to identify flooded areas, damaged infrastructure, and areas requiring urgent relief efforts.

7.4.2 Wildfires

Wildfires are another natural disaster where GeoAI provides significant value. AI models analyze satellite imagery and sensor data to detect fire hotspots, monitor fire spread, and assess damage. These models work in conjunction with other systems like fire detection networks and on-the-ground sensors to provide a comprehensive view of wildfire activity in real time.

7.4.3 Flooding and Coastal Storm Surges

Flooding is one of the most common and destructive natural disasters. GeoAI models help by forecasting river levels and potential flooding zones based on real-time rainfall and soil moisture data. During coastal storm surges, AI models analyze tides, wind patterns, and water temperature to predict flooding events. Such predictive capabilities enable early evacuations and infrastructure protection strategies.

7.4.4 Earthquakes and Tsunamis

GeoAI's application to earthquake and tsunami monitoring remains a challenge, primarily due to the unpredictability of seismic events. However,

AI can assist in post-event damage assessments by analyzing satellite imagery and ground-based sensor data to identify affected areas and estimate the scale of destruction.

7.5 Real-Time Damage Assessment and Post-Disaster Recovery

7.5.1 Importance of Rapid Damage Assessment

The immediate aftermath of a disaster is critical for saving lives and minimizing economic losses. One of the most time-sensitive aspects of disaster management is damage assessment, which informs the allocation of resources, evacuation plans, and emergency services. Traditionally, post-disaster damage assessments relied heavily on human resources and ground surveys, which were slow and sometimes inaccurate.

GeoAI, however, enables faster and more precise damage assessment by utilizing satellite imagery, drones, and other geospatial data. AI models analyze before-and-after imagery, detecting changes in land cover, building structures, vegetation, and infrastructure. The ability to quickly quantify and assess the extent of disaster damage allows emergency response teams to prioritize interventions in the most affected areas.

7.5.2 AI-Driven Damage Detection and Classification

GeoAI models use computer vision algorithms and deep learning techniques, such as convolutional neural networks (CNNs), to detect and classify damage from satellite images. These AI algorithms can identify damaged buildings, collapsed bridges, inundated areas, and other infrastructure in a matter of hours. By processing high-resolution satellite data or drone footage, these models can generate detailed damage maps that guide response efforts.

For example, after the 2015 Nepal earthquake, AI-driven algorithms were used to assess the level of destruction in urban and rural areas. The system automatically classified damaged and undamaged buildings based on satellite images, significantly speeding up the assessment process. This allowed authorities to quickly allocate resources to the most severely impacted regions.

Moreover, these AI-based systems can also estimate the cost of damage, helping governments and organizations allocate funding more effectively. In large-scale disasters, where ground-level assessments are logistically difficult or dangerous, GeoAI provides an invaluable tool for remote, real-time damage evaluation.

7.5.3 Case Study: Hurricane Harvey Damage Assessment

In 2017, Hurricane Harvey devastated the Houston area, causing widespread flooding and damage. GeoAI played a crucial role in the rapid damage assessment following the storm. The European Space Agency's Copernicus program used satellite data to monitor the extent of the flooding, while AI algorithms processed the imagery to identify inundated areas and assess damage to buildings and infrastructure.

By comparing pre- and post-event satellite imagery, AI models helped responders quickly map flood zones and prioritize emergency services. Additionally, AI models helped estimate the number of homes affected and the potential displacement of residents. This information was used to allocate resources efficiently and support recovery efforts.

7.6 GeoAI in Crisis Communication and Decision Support

7.6.1 Enhancing Crisis Communication with GeoAI

Effective communication during and after a disaster is essential for coordinating relief efforts and informing the public about ongoing threats. GeoAI helps improve crisis communication by providing real-time geospatial data that can be integrated into public-facing dashboards, social media feeds, and emergency notifications.

For example, AI-powered platforms can track the movement of wildfires or hurricanes and push alerts to affected populations with evacuation instructions. By combining real-time data with geospatial maps, these systems provide a more accurate and timely picture of disaster impacts, allowing authorities to update the public as conditions evolve.

Moreover, GeoAI models can be used to analyze social media posts, such as tweets or Facebook updates, to gauge public sentiment and track real-time information about disaster events. This helps authorities understand the on-the-ground situation more accurately and adjust their responses accordingly.

7.6.2 Decision Support Systems in Disaster Response

GeoAI is increasingly being integrated into decision support systems (DSS) for disaster management. These systems combine geospatial data, AI models, and expert input to assist decision-makers in choosing the best course of action during a disaster.

For example, in the case of a flood, DSS can use AI to analyze data on rainfall, river levels, and floodplain maps. Based on this analysis, the system can generate real-time recommendations on evacuation routes, flood defense measures, and emergency shelter locations. By incorporating the expertise of emergency managers and policymakers, these systems enhance decision-making and improve the efficiency of disaster response.

7.6.3 Case Study: GeoAI in the 2011 Japan Earthquake and Tsunami

In 2011, Japan was struck by a powerful earthquake and tsunami, resulting in widespread destruction and the Fukushima nuclear disaster. GeoAI played a critical role in both the immediate response and the recovery efforts that followed.

After the tsunami, satellite images were quickly processed by AI algorithms to map the extent of the destruction. These AI systems were able to detect and classify damage to buildings, roads, and infrastructure, providing emergency responders with up-to-date information on the hardest-hit areas. In the case of the Fukushima nuclear plant, GeoAI was used to monitor radiation levels, track the movement of contaminants, and assess the impact on surrounding regions.

The integration of AI into Japan's disaster response and recovery operations allowed for more efficient use of resources and helped the nation rebuild more rapidly after the devastation.

7.7 Challenges and Limitations of GeoAI in Disaster Management

7.7.1 Data Availability and Quality

One of the key challenges in integrating GeoAI into disaster management is the availability and quality of geospatial data. While satellite imagery and sensor data are abundant, these data sources may not always be timely, high-resolution, or accurate enough for certain disaster scenarios. For example, cloud cover or smoke from wildfires can obstruct satellite sensors, hindering the acquisition of reliable imagery.

GeoAI models rely heavily on high-quality data to make accurate predictions and assessments. In regions with limited satellite coverage or outdated sensors, AI models may struggle to provide actionable insights.

Moreover, data privacy concerns and the need for secure access to sensitive information can complicate data sharing and integration across multiple agencies or countries during disaster response.

7.7.2 AI Model Limitations

While AI models have made significant advances, they still face limitations, especially in complex and unpredictable disaster scenarios. For instance, predicting the exact location and intensity of earthquakes remains difficult, as AI models struggle with the chaotic nature of tectonic processes. Similarly, while AI has improved the accuracy of weather-related predictions, there is still room for improvement in forecasting extreme events like tornadoes or volcanic eruptions.

AI models also require continuous training on large datasets, which can be resource-intensive. Ensuring that models are well-calibrated and capable of handling a variety of disaster scenarios is crucial for their effective use.

7.7.3 Ethical Considerations

As with any AI application, the use of GeoAI in disaster management raises ethical questions. Decisions made based on AI models—such as the allocation of resources or prioritization of certain areas for evacuation—can have life-altering consequences. It is essential that AI systems are transparent, unbiased, and accountable to ensure that they are used ethically and in the best interests of all affected populations.

7.8 Future Directions in GeoAI for Disaster Management

7.8.1 Enhanced Data Fusion and Real-Time Processing

The future of GeoAI in disaster management lies in the enhanced fusion of data from multiple sources, including satellites, drones, ground sensors, and social media platforms. By integrating these data streams, AI models will be able to provide more accurate, real-time insights into disaster scenarios.

For example, combining satellite data with real-time weather data from ground-based sensors could enable more precise flood forecasts, or integrating drone footage with satellite imagery could allow for better wildfire detection and damage assessment.

Real-time processing will also continue to evolve, reducing the time required to process satellite images and provide actionable information. As computational power increases and AI models become more advanced, we can expect near-instantaneous insights, enabling faster responses and saving more lives.

7.8.2 AI-Driven Autonomous Disaster Response Systems

Looking forward, AI-driven autonomous systems could play a larger role in disaster response. Drones, robots, and autonomous vehicles equipped with AI algorithms could be deployed to areas affected by natural disasters to conduct damage assessments, deliver supplies, or search for survivors. These systems could work alongside human responders, improving efficiency and reducing the risk to human lives.

For example, AI-powered drones equipped with thermal imaging could be used in search-and-rescue operations during wildfires or earthquakes, autonomously navigating disaster zones to locate survivors or assess damage in areas that are otherwise inaccessible.

7.8.3 Collaboration and Global Disaster Management Networks

The future of GeoAI in disaster management will likely involve closer collaboration between governments, private companies, and international organizations. Global disaster management networks will be strengthened by AI-powered platforms that facilitate the sharing of data, resources, and expertise. Collaborative models will allow for more coordinated responses, ensuring that disaster relief is faster, more efficient, and more equitable.

7.9 Conclusion

GeoAI is rapidly transforming disaster management by enabling more accurate predictions, faster responses, and efficient recovery. The integration of AI with remote sensing data has proven invaluable in natural disaster scenarios, from tracking hurricanes to assessing flood damage and monitoring wildfires. As AI technologies continue to evolve, their potential for enhancing disaster resilience and saving lives will only grow.

Despite the challenges—such as data limitations, AI model accuracy, and ethical considerations—the future of GeoAI in disaster management looks promising. With advancements in real-time data processing, data fusion, and autonomous systems, GeoAI will continue to revolutionize how we respond to and recover from natural disasters.

Chapter 8: Land Use and Land Cover Change Monitoring with GeoAI

8.1 Introduction to Land Use and Land Cover Change Monitoring

Land Use and Land Cover (LULC) changes are among the most significant indicators of human impact on the environment. These changes influence numerous ecological processes such as biodiversity, climate regulation, and water cycles, and they shape socioeconomic structures globally. For example, urban sprawl, agricultural expansion, and deforestation are prime examples of land use changes that have profound environmental and societal impacts. LULC monitoring is therefore critical for sustainable environmental management, policy formulation, and urban planning.

Traditionally, LULC monitoring involved time-consuming methods like manual surveys, aerial photography, and ground-based observation. While these methods were valuable, they were limited by spatial and temporal constraints, as well as human error. However, the advent of remote sensing technologies and GeoAI (Geospatial Artificial Intelligence) has revolutionized the process of monitoring LULC changes. Remote sensing allows for the collection of vast amounts of data over large areas, while GeoAI leverages machine learning and deep learning algorithms to analyze this data efficiently, enabling timely and accurate change detection.

This chapter explores the role of GeoAI in LULC change monitoring, examining how satellite imagery, machine learning techniques, and data fusion methods are utilized to understand and predict land cover shifts. Furthermore, it delves into the specific applications of GeoAI for monitoring key drivers of LULC change, such as urbanization, deforestation, and agricultural expansion.

8.2 Importance of Tracking Land Use and Land Cover Changes

Land use and land cover changes are primarily driven by economic activities, population growth, technological development, and climate conditions. The effects of these changes on ecosystems and society are profound. Urbanization, for instance, often leads to habitat loss, soil sealing, and increased pollution, while deforestation results in diminished carbon sequestration and biodiversity loss. On the other hand, the expansion of agriculture can degrade soils, alter water cycles, and increase the pressure on local ecosystems.

1. **Urbanization**: The rapid growth of cities, driven by increasing populations and economic opportunities, often leads to significant changes in land cover. As cities expand, they replace natural habitats with built environments, significantly affecting local climates, air quality, and water cycles. For example, urban heat island effects, where cities become significantly warmer than surrounding rural areas, are a result of large-scale urbanization. GeoAI is instrumental in detecting urban sprawl through satellite imagery and predicting future growth patterns to assist in urban planning.

○ **Case Study**: In the context of China, rapid urbanization has led to massive land transformations. Researchers used GeoAI to monitor and predict urban expansion in cities like Beijing and Shanghai. Satellite imagery paired with machine learning models enabled precise mapping of urban growth trends, aiding in sustainable city planning.

2. **Deforestation**: The ongoing deforestation in tropical regions like the Amazon and Southeast Asia has severe implications for biodiversity, climate change, and the livelihoods of indigenous communities. By monitoring forest cover over time, GeoAI helps

track deforestation rates, identify illegal logging activities, and predict future forest loss.

○ **Case Study**: GeoAI has been used to monitor deforestation in the Amazon rainforest. Researchers applied machine learning algorithms to satellite imagery (e.g., Landsat) to detect changes in forest cover and track illegal logging activities in near real-time. This approach has been used to enforce conservation policies and promote reforestation efforts.

3. **Agricultural Expansion**: As the global population grows, the need for food production has driven the expansion of agricultural land. However, this often comes at the cost of natural ecosystems, contributing to soil degradation, loss of biodiversity, and altered hydrological cycles. GeoAI plays a critical role in monitoring agricultural land expansion, assessing crop health, and optimizing irrigation practices to ensure sustainable land use.

○ **Example**: In India, a combination of satellite-based remote sensing and AI-powered data analysis has helped track the conversion of forested areas into agricultural lands. The use of multispectral imagery and machine learning models has enhanced land classification accuracy, allowing for the detection of illegal land conversions.

4. **Environmental and Social Implications**: LULC changes are not just about the loss of forests or the expansion of cities; they also impact local communities, economies, and global ecosystems. For instance, the expansion of urban areas leads to population displacement, changes in local economies, and shifts in cultural landscapes. GeoAI aids in evaluating the social dimensions of land use changes by providing decision-makers with actionable insights into land resource management.

○ **Example**: In Sub-Saharan Africa, GeoAI has been used to track land use patterns, specifically in relation to agricultural land expansion. These insights have been critical in assessing the impact of land transformations on food security, resource availability, and local economies.

8.3 GeoAI for Urbanization Monitoring

Urbanization is one of the most visible and impactful forms of land use change. It involves the conversion of rural and natural landscapes into built environments, including roads, buildings, and industrial complexes. Urban areas are often hotspots for increased carbon emissions, resource consumption, and waste production, making urban monitoring a top priority for sustainable development.

1. **Tracking Urban Sprawl**: GeoAI enables the tracking of urban sprawl through satellite imagery, where changes in land cover are detected over time. Machine learning techniques such as supervised classification (e.g., Random Forest, Support Vector Machines) and unsupervised classification (e.g., k-means clustering) allow for the extraction of urban features from remote sensing data. Temporal analysis using time-series data further enhances our understanding of urban growth patterns.

○ **Example**: In the United States, researchers have used satellite data to monitor urban sprawl in cities like Los Angeles and New York. By using machine learning algorithms on Landsat imagery, they tracked changes in urban land cover over several decades, helping policymakers plan for sustainable growth.

2. **Predicting Future Urban Growth**: GeoAI models can be used to predict future urbanization trends by analyzing historical land use patterns, population growth rates, and socio-economic data. These predictive models can guide urban planners in making informed decisions about infrastructure development, zoning laws, and resource allocation.

○ **Case Study**: In India, AI-driven models have been used to forecast urban growth in cities like Bengaluru and Hyderabad. These models take into account demographic factors, economic growth, and historical land use data to predict the expansion of urban areas and recommend sustainable urban planning strategies.

3. **Urban Heat Island Effect**: As cities expand, they often experience localized temperature increases due to the concentration of buildings, roads, and other impervious surfaces. The urban heat island (UHI) effect can exacerbate heat stress, increase energy consumption, and worsen air quality. GeoAI, when combined with thermal satellite data, helps map UHI patterns and predict areas at risk, which can inform mitigation strategies such as green roofs, urban forests, and reflective surfaces.

○ **Example**: In cities like New York and Tokyo, GeoAI has been employed to assess the UHI effect using thermal infrared imagery. The models have been used to predict heat vulnerability hotspots and recommend areas for urban greening initiatives.

8.4 GeoAI for Deforestation Monitoring

Deforestation remains one of the most critical environmental issues, contributing to habitat loss, carbon emissions, and climate change. GeoAI has emerged as a powerful tool for monitoring forests, detecting illegal logging activities, and tracking forest degradation.

1. **Detecting Deforestation**: Satellite-based remote sensing techniques such as MODIS, Landsat, and high-resolution imagery (e.g., WorldView) are used to monitor forest cover over large regions. Machine learning algorithms, particularly deep learning approaches like Convolutional Neural Networks (CNNs), are increasingly applied to these datasets to detect subtle changes in land cover, such as the transition from forest to agricultural land or urban areas.

○ **Case Study**: GeoAI has been used to monitor deforestation in the Amazon rainforest. Deep learning models were trained on multi-temporal satellite imagery to automatically identify areas of deforestation and illegal logging activities. These models can detect changes in land cover within days of occurrence, providing timely insights for enforcement and policy interventions.

2. **Mapping Forest Degradation**: Deforestation is not always characterized by total tree loss but can also involve degradation, such as thinning, logging, or fire damage. GeoAI models can analyze multi-spectral and multi-temporal data to assess degradation patterns and monitor changes in forest density, which are crucial for understanding the health of forest ecosystems.

○ **Example**: In Southeast Asia, GeoAI has been used to map forest degradation in Indonesia, where illegal logging and forest fires are common. The AI models detect even subtle signs of degradation, enabling governments and NGOs to target conservation efforts effectively.

8.5 GeoAI for Agricultural Expansion Monitoring

The expansion of agriculture has been a dominant driver of land use change, particularly in regions where economic growth relies heavily on agriculture for food production, resource extraction, and livelihoods. GeoAI plays a crucial role in monitoring agricultural land expansion, understanding its environmental impacts, and optimizing land use for sustainable practices.

1. **Detecting Agricultural Land Expansion**: Agricultural expansion often leads to the conversion of natural habitats, forests, and wetlands into cropland or pasture. This process can be tracked using satellite imagery combined with machine learning algorithms. The detection of land use change, particularly from forest to agriculture, can be done using supervised classification methods, which assign pixels of satellite images to predefined land

cover classes. GeoAI models can analyze multi-temporal satellite data to track the dynamics of agricultural expansion over time.

○ **Case Study**: In the Amazon region, satellite imagery has been used to track the conversion of forested land to agricultural areas, particularly for soy cultivation and cattle ranching. By applying machine learning models to Landsat imagery, researchers were able to detect changes in land cover and provide actionable insights for environmental monitoring and policy enforcement.

2. **Precision Agriculture**: Beyond monitoring the expansion of agricultural land, GeoAI is instrumental in optimizing agricultural practices, ensuring efficient use of land and resources. Machine learning algorithms are used to analyze satellite data to predict crop yields, detect pests and diseases, and optimize irrigation. This is a crucial aspect of GeoAI's role in enhancing food security while minimizing environmental degradation.

○ **Example**: In countries like India and Brazil, farmers are using GeoAI-powered tools to monitor crop health and optimize fertilizer application through satellite data. Machine learning models can predict crop growth patterns based on historical data, weather forecasts, and real-time satellite imagery, enabling farmers to make more informed decisions.

3. **Sustainable Land Use Practices**: One of the biggest challenges in monitoring agricultural land expansion is ensuring that it is done sustainably. GeoAI enables the identification of areas that are more suitable for agriculture, based on environmental variables such as soil quality, water availability, and slope. This assists in promoting sustainable farming practices and reduces the encroachment on ecologically sensitive areas.

○ **Example**: In Africa, where agricultural expansion often leads to deforestation and land degradation, GeoAI has been applied to guide land use planning by identifying areas with high agricultural potential while minimizing environmental impacts. Through land suitability analysis using AI models, countries can better allocate agricultural lands, reduce the destruction of natural ecosystems, and protect biodiversity.

8.6 Data Analysis Techniques in LULC Monitoring

Effective land use and land cover monitoring using GeoAI involves processing vast amounts of geospatial data. The role of data analysis techniques cannot be overstated, as these methods help in interpreting satellite images, identifying land cover classes, and detecting changes over time. The integration of machine learning and advanced data processing techniques is essential for making accurate predictions and assessments.

1. **Data Fusion for Enhanced Analysis**: Data fusion involves combining different types of data from multiple sources to enhance the accuracy of land classification and change detection. For example, combining optical satellite imagery with radar data (SAR) allows for the identification of features that are otherwise difficult to detect, such as land cover types in areas with frequent cloud cover.

○ **Example**: The European Space Agency's Copernicus Sentinel satellites offer a variety of data products, including optical and radar imagery. By using data fusion techniques, GeoAI models can provide a more comprehensive view of land cover and changes, helping in areas such as flood monitoring, forest management, and urban growth tracking.

2. **Temporal Analysis for Change Detection**: The ability to analyze temporal changes in land cover is critical for monitoring long-term trends in LULC. Temporal analysis involves comparing satellite images taken at different times to detect changes in land cover. This can be done using various machine learning techniques, including change vector analysis (CVA) and deep learning models that detect even subtle shifts in land cover.

○ **Case Study**: In the case of wildfire monitoring, temporal analysis using GeoAI can detect changes in vegetation cover before, during, and after fires. AI models, trained on multi-temporal data, can identify burned areas and track recovery rates over time, which is valuable for both disaster management and ecological restoration.

3. **Spectral Analysis for Feature Extraction**: Spectral analysis involves examining the electromagnetic spectrum captured by satellite sensors. Different land cover types reflect and absorb light in distinct patterns across various wavelengths. For example, vegetation typically reflects more light in the near-infrared spectrum, while urban areas absorb more visible light. By using machine learning algorithms to analyze spectral data, GeoAI can extract features that are indicative of land cover types.

○ **Example**: In monitoring urban areas, spectral analysis can distinguish between different types of built environments, such as roads, buildings, and industrial zones. For instance, the WorldView satellites' high-resolution imagery, combined with machine learning algorithms, enables the identification of various urban features, including the detection of informal settlements and infrastructure development.

8.7 Land Classification and GeoAI Techniques

Land classification is a key process in monitoring land use and land cover changes, as it involves categorizing pixels in satellite imagery into different land cover types. Accurate classification is essential for assessing the extent and nature of land cover changes. GeoAI has significantly enhanced the accuracy of land classification through the application of advanced machine learning techniques.

1. **Supervised vs. Unsupervised Classification**: In supervised classification, the user provides a set of labeled data, or "training samples," which are used to train a machine learning model to

classify land cover. In unsupervised classification, the model groups data into clusters based on similarities, with little to no prior labeling. Both methods have their advantages, with supervised classification being more accurate but requiring a larger dataset of labeled samples, while unsupervised methods are more flexible but may produce less precise results.

○ **Case Study**: In the monitoring of deforestation in Central Africa, supervised classification using Random Forest algorithms has been applied to classify forested and non-forested areas, helping policymakers track changes in forest cover. Unsupervised methods, on the other hand, have been used to classify diverse vegetation types in tropical rainforests, where distinct boundaries between classes are not always easily identifiable.

2. **Deep Learning for Advanced Land Classification**: Deep learning, particularly Convolutional Neural Networks (CNNs), has brought a revolution in land classification. CNNs are able to learn complex patterns in data and can classify land cover types with high accuracy, even in heterogeneous landscapes or under challenging conditions like cloud cover.

○ **Example**: In India, deep learning algorithms have been applied to classify agricultural land use from satellite images, detecting even small-scale changes in land cover, such as the conversion of land from forest to crops. By using CNNs trained on large datasets, the system can detect subtle changes and even predict future trends based on historical data.

8.8 GeoAI in Sustainable Land Management

Sustainable land management (SLM) is an integrated approach to managing land resources in a way that promotes sustainable agricultural practices, protects ecosystems, and ensures long-term environmental health. GeoAI supports sustainable land management by providing the tools necessary for assessing land suitability, monitoring land degradation, and optimizing land use practices.

1. **Land Suitability Analysis**: GeoAI can help determine the most suitable areas for specific land uses, such as agriculture, forestry, or urban development. By analyzing environmental factors like soil type, water availability, and topography, GeoAI models can identify optimal land uses that minimize environmental impacts.

○ **Example**: In Mexico, GeoAI has been used to identify areas most suitable for sustainable agriculture by assessing factors such as soil fertility, climate conditions, and water availability. This analysis has led to the implementation of agroforestry systems, where crops and trees are grown together to improve soil health and reduce deforestation.

2. **Monitoring Land Degradation**: Land degradation, often driven by overuse or climate change, is a critical issue for sustainable land management. GeoAI helps monitor land degradation by identifying changes in vegetation cover, soil quality, and water resources. Machine learning models can process satellite images to detect signs of desertification, soil erosion, and deforestation.

○ **Case Study**: In parts of sub-Saharan Africa, GeoAI has been used to monitor desertification and land degradation caused by drought and overgrazing. By analyzing time-series satellite data, machine learning models detect shifts in vegetation cover and provide early warnings of land degradation, which allows for timely intervention and restoration.

3. **Ecosystem Services Monitoring**: GeoAI can also be used to assess the provision of ecosystem services, such as carbon sequestration, water regulation, and biodiversity support. These services are essential for maintaining healthy ecosystems and

supporting human well-being. By combining remote sensing data with AI models, GeoAI can track changes in ecosystem services over time and inform management strategies.

○ **Example**: In the Amazon, GeoAI has been used to monitor changes in forest biomass and carbon storage. This information is vital for understanding the role of forests in global carbon cycles and for implementing conservation strategies aimed at mitigating climate change.

8.9 Conclusion and Future Directions

In conclusion, GeoAI has revolutionized the way we monitor and manage land use and land cover changes. By leveraging machine learning algorithms, satellite data, and AI-powered analysis techniques, we can now track and predict land use changes with unprecedented accuracy and efficiency. This capability is crucial for addressing environmental challenges like urbanization, deforestation, and agricultural expansion, all of which contribute to global environmental stress.

Looking ahead, the future of GeoAI in LULC monitoring holds tremendous potential.

With advancements in AI and remote sensing technologies, we can expect even more accurate and granular analyses, leading to better decision-making for sustainable land management. Further integration of GeoAI with other emerging technologies, such as blockchain for land rights management and IoT for real-time data collection, will also enhance the effectiveness of LULC monitoring systems.

As we move forward, it will be crucial to address challenges such as data privacy, algorithm transparency, and the need for global cooperation to ensure that GeoAI applications are both ethical and equitable. Nevertheless, the role of GeoAI in land use and land cover change monitoring will continue to grow, shaping the future of environmental management and sustainable development.

Chapter 9: Biodiversity Monitoring with GeoAI

Introduction:

Biodiversity, the variety of life on Earth, is essential for maintaining ecosystem services that sustain humanity. Healthy ecosystems provide vital services like clean water, pollination of crops, regulation of climate, and protection against natural hazards. However, biodiversity is increasingly under threat due to human activities such as deforestation, urbanization, climate change, and poaching. Effective monitoring of biodiversity is crucial for conservation efforts and to track the health of ecosystems globally.

The rapid advancements in Artificial Intelligence (AI) and GeoAI—AI technologies applied to geospatial data—are transforming biodiversity monitoring. Through the integration of AI with remote sensing and GIS (Geographic Information Systems), it is now possible to track species movements, monitor habitats, and predict changes in biodiversity with unparalleled accuracy. This chapter explores how GeoAI is revolutionizing biodiversity monitoring, focusing on habitat mapping, wildlife tracking, and the assessment of habitat health, alongside how these tools support conservation efforts.

9.1 The Importance of Biodiversity Monitoring

Definition of Biodiversity and Its Importance

Biodiversity refers to the variety of life forms on Earth, spanning genetic diversity within species, the variety of species themselves, and the range of ecosystems in which they exist. The health of biodiversity is an indicator of the overall well-being of the planet. Species diversity contributes to ecosystem stability, resilience, and the ability to adapt to environmental changes, while genetic diversity ensures populations can evolve and survive over time.

Biodiversity is fundamental to human survival as it provides essential services:

- **Ecosystem Services**: Biodiversity supports food production, water purification, disease regulation, carbon sequestration, and more.

- **Cultural and Economic Value**: Biodiversity is a source of inspiration, recreation, and direct economic benefits, including from ecotourism, fisheries, and pharmaceuticals.

- **Resilience to Environmental Change**: Diverse ecosystems are more resilient to disturbances such as climate change, extreme weather, and invasive species.

However, biodiversity is increasingly threatened by factors like deforestation, land use changes, pollution, invasive species, and climate change. As a result, effective monitoring of biodiversity is critical to understanding its current state, identifying threats, and informing conservation policies.

Why Monitoring Biodiversity is Crucial

Monitoring biodiversity is vital for several reasons:

- **Early Warning Systems**: Detecting changes in biodiversity—such as population declines or ecosystem degradation—can provide early warnings for impending environmental or ecological crises.

- **Conservation and Resource Management**: Biodiversity monitoring helps conservationists prioritize areas for protection, restoration, or intervention, ensuring resources are allocated efficiently.

- **Tracking Ecosystem Health**: Understanding changes in biodiversity can indicate broader environmental shifts, such as habitat degradation, climate change impacts, and the spread of invasive species.

Real-time and accurate biodiversity monitoring is essential for informing decisions that can help mitigate biodiversity loss and guide restoration efforts. GeoAI, which combines spatial data and machine learning techniques, offers unprecedented capabilities in this regard.

9.2 Methods for Habitat Mapping Using GeoAI

Overview of Habitat Mapping

Habitat mapping is a crucial tool in biodiversity conservation, as it helps identify and classify ecosystems based on their composition, structure, and ecological functions. By understanding the distribution and condition of habitats, conservationists can assess threats, prioritize areas for protection, and track the effectiveness of restoration efforts.

Traditionally, habitat mapping was done manually through field surveys and aerial photography, but these methods were limited in their spatial coverage and temporal resolution. With GeoAI, habitat mapping has evolved into a more dynamic, scalable, and real-time process. Satellite imagery, remote sensing technologies, and AI algorithms allow for the continuous monitoring of large areas, making it possible to track habitat changes over time.

Satellite Imagery and Remote Sensing for Habitat Mapping

Satellites and drones equipped with remote sensing instruments are invaluable tools for habitat mapping. They provide high-resolution, spatially detailed images of Earth's surface and can capture data on a variety of environmental variables, such as vegetation cover, soil moisture, water bodies, and land use.

● **Multispectral and Hyperspectral Imagery**: These imaging technologies capture data across multiple wavelengths of light, from visible to infrared. This allows for the classification of different types of vegetation, soil, water, and other habitat components.

● **LiDAR (Light Detection and Ranging)**: LiDAR sensors use laser pulses to measure distances, generating detailed 3D maps of terrain, vegetation canopy structure, and forest height. LiDAR is particularly useful in mapping forested habitats, as it can penetrate tree canopies and reveal the underlying terrain.

These remote sensing technologies are often used in combination with AI techniques to create detailed habitat maps. AI enables the processing of vast amounts of data in real time, offering improved accuracy, efficiency, and scalability compared to traditional methods.

GeoAI Techniques for Habitat Classification and Change Detection

GeoAI techniques allow for sophisticated analysis of habitat data. Machine learning algorithms can process satellite images and classify land cover into different habitat types, such as forests, grasslands, wetlands, and urban areas.

● **Supervised and Unsupervised Classification**: In supervised classification, labeled training data is used to teach the algorithm to identify different habitat types. Unsupervised classification, on the other hand, identifies patterns and clusters in the data without pre-existing labels. Both techniques are commonly used for land use and land cover classification.

● **Deep Learning for Habitat Mapping**: Deep learning models, particularly Convolutional Neural Networks (CNNs), have proven effective in identifying habitat types from satellite images. CNNs are capable of learning hierarchical features, making them ideal for analyzing complex spatial data, such as natural landscapes and habitats.

- **Change Detection**: Change detection algorithms, often powered by AI, can compare satellite images taken at different times to track changes in habitat over time. This is useful for monitoring processes like deforestation, urban expansion, and the degradation of ecosystems due to climate change or human activity.

Case Study: Habitat Mapping in Tropical Rainforests

Tropical rainforests, such as the Amazon, are critical to global biodiversity, yet they face significant threats from deforestation, logging, and agriculture. Remote sensing and GeoAI are being used to monitor the health of rainforests and track deforestation patterns.

For instance, NASA's Earth Observing System Data and Information System (EOSDIS) uses satellites like Landsat to provide high-resolution images of forest cover. These images are analyzed using machine learning algorithms to identify deforestation hotspots, monitor illegal logging activities, and assess the effectiveness of conservation policies.

LiDAR technology has also been used to map the structure of rainforests, providing insights into forest biomass, canopy height, and overall habitat complexity. These metrics are essential for understanding the health of rainforest ecosystems and the species that depend on them.

9.3 Wildlife Tracking and Monitoring with GeoAI

The Need for Wildlife Tracking

Wildlife tracking is a cornerstone of biodiversity monitoring, as it allows researchers to understand the movement patterns, behavior, and population dynamics of species. Tracking also helps in the identification of critical habitats, migration corridors, and areas that require protection.

GeoAI enables the integration of spatial and temporal data to provide a more comprehensive understanding of wildlife behavior. This data is increasingly being used to inform conservation strategies, such as establishing wildlife corridors, protected areas, and sustainable land-use plans.

GeoAI Technologies for Tracking Wildlife

The combination of GPS technology, remote sensing, and AI allows for advanced wildlife tracking. Researchers attach GPS collars, tags, or trackers to animals, which provide real-time location data. AI models can then analyze this data to track animal movements, predict migration routes, and detect changes in behavior.

- **Satellite Tracking**: Some animals, especially migratory species, are tracked using satellite-based GPS collars. These collars transmit data to satellites, which then relay the information back to researchers. AI helps process this data and predict future movements.

- **Acoustic and Camera Sensors**: GeoAI can also process data from acoustic sensors (such as microphones used to detect animal sounds) and camera traps (which automatically capture images of wildlife). Machine learning algorithms can identify animal species, detect anomalies in behavior, and help track populations in areas that are difficult to access.

Deep Learning in Wildlife Image and Video Analysis

Camera traps are widely used to monitor wildlife, particularly in remote areas where human presence is minimal. However, processing the vast number of images captured by camera traps is labor-intensive. AI-driven deep learning algorithms, particularly Convolutional Neural Networks (CNNs), are now being used to automate the identification of species and analyze wildlife behavior.

- **Automatic Species Identification**: AI can automatically classify images, identifying species and tracking their movements over time. For example, AI models can be trained to identify endangered species like tigers, lions, or elephants, ensuring that no sightings are missed and reducing the risk of human error.

- **Behavioral Analysis**: AI can also analyze animal behavior, such as identifying mating activities, feeding habits, or territorial movements. These insights are essential for understanding species ecology and improving conservation strategies.

Case Study: Tracking Migratory Species with GeoAI

Migratory species, such as monarch butterflies, sea turtles, and wildebeest, follow long and often complex migration routes that span thousands of kilometers. GeoAI is used to track these species by integrating satellite tracking, remote sensing, and AI models to predict migration patterns and identify key habitat areas along the way.

For example, the use of GPS tags and satellite imagery has allowed researchers to track the migration routes of monarch butterflies across North America. AI algorithms analyze this data

to predict how climate change may affect migration patterns in the future and identify potential risks to their migratory routes.

9.4 Assessing Habitat Health Using GeoAI

Measuring Ecosystem Health

Ecosystem health is a reflection of the state of biodiversity and the ability of ecosystems to provide essential services. GeoAI can assess the health of habitats by analyzing environmental indicators such as vegetation cover, water quality, soil conditions, and species diversity.

- **Vegetation Health**: Remote sensing data is often used to monitor vegetation health. AI models can analyze data from multispectral and hyperspectral imagery to calculate vegetation indices such as NDVI (Normalized Difference Vegetation Index), which helps assess plant health and monitor stress caused by droughts, diseases, or pests.

- **Water Quality and Wetland Health**: Wetlands and freshwater ecosystems are highly sensitive to environmental changes. GeoAI can monitor water quality parameters, such as temperature, salinity, and nutrient levels, and assess the health of aquatic habitats.

GeoAI for Coral Reef Monitoring and Ocean Health

Coral reefs, often referred to as the "rainforests of the sea," are crucial to marine biodiversity but are facing severe threats from climate change, pollution, and overfishing. GeoAI is helping monitor coral reef health by analyzing remote sensing data to track coral cover, assess bleaching events, and predict future risks to coral ecosystems.

For instance, researchers use satellite imagery and machine learning algorithms to map coral reefs and monitor changes in reef composition. AI can identify areas at risk of coral bleaching due to rising sea temperatures and help prioritize conservation actions.

9.5 Supporting Conservation Efforts with GeoAI

Real-Time Data and Decision Making

One of the greatest advantages of integrating AI with biodiversity monitoring is the ability to provide real-time insights. Traditional methods of data collection and analysis often have time lags, limiting their utility for urgent conservation decisions. With GeoAI, conservationists can access up-to-date information on species populations, habitat conditions, and potential threats, enabling timely responses to emerging challenges.

For example, GeoAI can monitor areas affected by illegal logging, poaching, or habitat encroachment in real-time using satellite imagery, drones, and sensor data. AI models process this data and highlight areas of concern, enabling quicker interventions and enforcement of conservation policies.

AI for Predicting and Preventing Extinctions

AI's ability to process vast amounts of data also makes it a powerful tool for predicting the future of endangered species and their habitats. Machine learning models can predict population trends based on historical data and environmental factors, such as habitat loss, climate change, and human activities. These predictions are invaluable for prioritizing conservation efforts and identifying at-risk species before they reach the brink of extinction.

- **Population Modeling**: AI models are used to predict the future population dynamics of endangered species. By analyzing environmental variables, human impact, and genetic data, these models can forecast how populations will evolve under different conservation strategies.

- **Habitat Suitability Modeling**: AI can also be used to assess habitat suitability for different species based on factors such as climate, vegetation, and human disturbances. This helps conservationists identify new areas where endangered species might thrive and helps to protect or restore critical habitats before they degrade further.

Case Study: GeoAI in Elephant Conservation

Elephants are a keystone species whose presence is vital to the health of their ecosystem. However, they are heavily threatened by poaching and habitat loss. In Africa and Asia, conservation efforts have been greatly enhanced by GeoAI tools.

For example, in Kenya, researchers use GPS-enabled collars to track elephant movements and analyze their migration patterns. GeoAI models process the GPS data alongside environmental data from satellite imagery to detect potential threats, such as the expansion of human settlements or changes in vegetation that may impact elephant habitats. In areas with increased poaching activity, GeoAI models help prioritize patrol routes for anti-poaching units, allowing for faster intervention.

The use of AI in identifying "hotspots" for illegal activities also extends beyond elephants to other endangered species, such as rhinos and tigers, by processing vast amounts of environmental and behavioral data in real time.

9.6 Case Studies: GeoAI in Action for Biodiversity Monitoring

Case Study 1: Monitoring Endangered Species in the Amazon Rainforest

The Amazon rainforest, often referred to as the "lungs of the Earth," is a biodiversity hotspot that harbors millions of species, many of which are yet to be discovered. The region is also facing rapid deforestation, driven by agriculture, logging, and mining.

GeoAI is playing a key role in monitoring the biodiversity of the Amazon. Researchers use a combination of satellite imagery, drone data, and ground-based sensors to track deforestation and its impact on wildlife habitats. Machine learning models help to classify habitat types, detect land-use changes, and predict the movement of species across the landscape.

In particular, AI is being used to monitor endangered species like jaguars, which rely on large, uninterrupted tracts of forest for their survival. Using camera traps and GPS tracking, AI algorithms analyze movement patterns and track population trends, helping researchers design more effective conservation strategies and identify areas that require urgent protection.

Case Study 2: Monitoring Coral Reef Health with GeoAI

Coral reefs are among the most biodiverse ecosystems on the planet, yet they are highly vulnerable to climate change, particularly through the phenomenon of coral bleaching caused by rising ocean temperatures. Coral reefs also face pressure from pollution, overfishing, and coastal development.

GeoAI is being used to monitor coral reefs and assess their health. Using satellite imagery, AI models analyze reef composition and identify areas suffering from coral bleaching. Deep learning algorithms process multispectral satellite images to detect changes in coral cover and provide early warnings of bleaching events. This real-time monitoring allows conservationists to intervene quickly, prioritizing restoration efforts in the most affected areas.

AI is also helping to map and monitor marine protected areas (MPAs), ensuring that they are effectively managed. By combining remote sensing data with AI, researchers can assess the success of conservation measures and track the recovery of coral reefs over time.

Case Study 3: Using GeoAI for Biodiversity Hotspot Identification

Biodiversity hotspots are regions that are both rich in species and threatened by human activity. Identifying and prioritizing these areas for conservation is essential for preventing biodiversity loss.

GeoAI is being used to identify biodiversity hotspots globally by combining remote sensing data with AI-driven models. For example, in Southeast Asia, machine learning algorithms process satellite images to identify forested regions that are rich in biodiversity. These regions are then assessed for vulnerability, and conservation actions can be directed toward protecting these critical ecosystems.

In some cases, AI is used to model the effects of climate change on biodiversity hotspots. By predicting how species distribution may change in the future under different climate scenarios, GeoAI helps prioritize conservation efforts to safeguard ecosystems at risk.

9.7 Future Directions in Biodiversity Monitoring with GeoAI

Advancements in Real-Time Wildlife Monitoring

While current wildlife tracking and monitoring systems provide valuable insights, they often rely on periodic data collection and analysis. The future of biodiversity monitoring lies in real-time systems that continuously collect and analyze data. With advances in IoT (Internet of Things) devices and sensor technologies, researchers will be able to monitor wildlife habitats and animal populations in near real time, providing immediate insights into changes in species behavior, migration, and ecosystem health.

Integration of Multi-Source Data

The integration of multiple data sources, including satellite imagery, drone data, acoustic sensors, and environmental data, will continue to improve the accuracy and comprehensiveness of biodiversity monitoring efforts. AI models that can process diverse types of data, from visual images to acoustic signals and environmental variables, will provide richer insights into biodiversity dynamics.

AI for Predicting Biodiversity Trends Under Climate Change

As climate change continues to impact biodiversity, there is an increasing need for AI models that can abdict how sapcies and ecosystems will respond to future climate scenarios. By incorporating climate models with species distribution models, AI can help predict how ecosystems will evolve, guiding conservation strategies to mitigate potential losses.

Enhancing Public Participation in Conservation with GeoAI

One promising future direction is the integration of citizen science with GeoAI. Tools that allow the public to contribute biodiversity data through mobile apps, camera traps, or other technologies will democratize conservation efforts and enable more comprehensive monitoring across larger areas. GeoAI can help process and analyze this crowd-sourced data, providing valuable information for researchers and conservationists.

Ethical Considerations in AI for Biodiversity Monitoring

As AI continues to play a larger role in biodiversity monitoring, it is important to consider the ethical implications of these technologies. Ensuring privacy in data collection, transparency in AI decision-making, and the responsible use of AI tools will be essential to maintain public trust and support for biodiversity conservation efforts.

9.8 Conclusion: GeoAI's Role in Biodiversity Conservation

GeoAI represents a transformative leap in biodiversity monitoring and conservation. By leveraging AI's data processing capabilities alongside remote sensing and geospatial technologies, conservationists can gain unprecedented insights into the health of ecosystems, track endangered species, and predict future changes in biodiversity.

Through case studies and real-world applications, it is clear that GeoAI has already made significant contributions to understanding and preserving the natural world. From tracking wildlife migrations to monitoring the health of coral reefs, GeoAI tools are helping conservationists address urgent biodiversity challenges with greater precision and efficiency.

As technology continues to evolve, the future of biodiversity monitoring with GeoAI looks promising. Advances in real-time monitoring, multi-source data integration, and AI-driven predictions will enhance conservation efforts and improve our ability to protect biodiversity for future generations.

Chapter 10: Water Resource Management with GeoAI

10.1 Introduction to Water Resource Management

Water, as one of the planet's most vital resources, plays a crucial role in sustaining life, enabling agriculture, supporting ecosystems, and fueling industrial activities. However, the challenges associated with water resource management are increasingly complex due to rapid population growth, climate change, urbanization, and pollution. With increasing demand and diminishing availability, managing water resources effectively has become one of the central concerns for governments, industries, and communities worldwide.

Water resources management involves a variety of complex processes, including the allocation, distribution, and conservation of water for different uses. This encompasses a variety of tasks: monitoring water availability and quality, forecasting potential shortages, managing water infrastructure, addressing contamination, and planning for future needs. Traditionally, these tasks have relied on extensive monitoring networks, hydrological models, and human judgment. However, with the rapid advancements in technology, particularly in the field of artificial intelligence (AI) and satellite-based Earth observation (EO), the management of water resources has entered a new era.

GeoAI, which integrates AI techniques with Earth observation data, plays a transformative role in water resource management. By leveraging vast datasets collected by remote sensing technologies, AI is enabling more efficient monitoring, predictive modeling, and decision-making in the management of water resources. This chapter explores the multifaceted role of GeoAI in water resource management, including applications in water quality monitoring, drought and flood prediction, agricultural water use, and climate change adaptation.

10.2 GeoAI in Water Quality Monitoring

Water quality is essential for human health, agriculture, and ecosystem sustainability. However, monitoring water quality on a large scale presents numerous challenges. Traditional methods, such as laboratory testing and manual sampling, can be labor-intensive, time-consuming, and not suited for continuous or real-time monitoring, especially in large bodies of water or remote areas.

Remote Sensing for Water Quality

GeoAI has revolutionized the ability to monitor water quality using remote sensing data from satellites and sensors. Earth observation satellites equipped with multispectral and hyperspectral sensors can capture detailed information about water bodies, enabling the monitoring of various water quality parameters such as temperature, pH levels, turbidity, salinity, and chlorophyll concentrations. By analyzing the reflected light from water surfaces, these sensors can detect harmful algae blooms, sediment concentrations, and even pollutants in water bodies.

For example, satellites like NASA's Landsat and ESA's Sentinel series provide continuous global coverage, capturing data that is crucial for monitoring changes in water quality. The data collected is processed and analyzed using machine learning (ML) and deep learning algorithms to detect trends and identify potential contamination or pollution events in real-time. These insights are crucial for managing water resources, preventing environmental damage, and ensuring that water quality meets health and safety standards.

AI-Driven Data Processing

AI plays a significant role in processing and interpreting the large amounts of data collected by satellite sensors. Machine learning algorithms, including supervised and unsupervised learning, can identify patterns in water quality data, allowing for the automatic classification of water conditions across large areas. For example, AI can automatically detect the presence of algae blooms in a water body by analyzing the color signatures captured in satellite imagery. These blooms, which can lead to hypoxic conditions and harm aquatic life, can be predicted and monitored with high precision.

Deep learning algorithms, specifically convolutional neural networks (CNNs), are used to analyze satellite images to classify water bodies based on their quality. These models can be trained on labeled datasets to recognize patterns associated with specific water quality conditions, such as pollution or the presence of contaminants.

Case Studies in Water Quality Monitoring

A prime example of GeoAI in action for water quality monitoring is the use of machine learning in the monitoring of harmful algal blooms (HABs) in freshwater and coastal waters. AI models developed by researchers at the University of California, Santa Barbara, have used satellite imagery to predict the occurrence and extent of HABs in water bodies such as lakes, rivers, and coastal regions. These models analyze historical data along with current environmental conditions to provide early warnings to local authorities and water resource managers, allowing them to take precautionary actions.

Another example is the use of AI-driven satellite monitoring in monitoring water quality in the Great Lakes region. Researchers have applied machine learning techniques to remotely assess the levels of pollutants like phosphorus and nitrogen, which can cause harmful eutrophication. These AI models predict which areas are most likely to experience significant water quality deterioration, enabling better-targeted interventions.

10.3 Predicting and Managing Water Scarcity with GeoAI

Water scarcity is one of the most pressing challenges facing the world today, with regions such as Sub-Saharan Africa, parts of Asia, and the Middle

East experiencing increasing levels of water stress. The ability to predict and manage water scarcity is essential to ensure that water resources are used efficiently and equitably. GeoAI can help by forecasting water availability, optimizing the use of water resources, and identifying areas at risk of water shortages.

Drought Prediction

GeoAI has been instrumental in enhancing the prediction of droughts, one of the most severe consequences of water scarcity. AI-driven models that combine satellite data, meteorological data, and soil moisture information can predict the onset of drought conditions with greater accuracy than traditional methods. These models use machine learning algorithms to analyze patterns in climate variables such as precipitation, temperature, and wind speed, as well as long-term trends in water storage and streamflow.

For example, NASA's Earth Observing System Data and Information System (EOSDIS) provides satellite data that is used to monitor drought conditions across the globe. GeoAI models combine this data with historical drought patterns to forecast future drought events, providing valuable lead time for water managers to prepare for water shortages. These forecasts help to direct resources for irrigation, mitigate crop losses, and manage water distribution in times of stress.

Water Stress and Availability

GeoAI models can also assess the vulnerability of specific regions to water stress by evaluating factors such as groundwater depletion, rainfall patterns, and the water demands of local populations and agriculture. In regions where water resources are limited, AI can help optimize water usage by recommending conservation strategies, adjusting irrigation schedules, and prioritizing water use based on critical needs.

For example, AI-based decision support systems have been developed in the southwestern United States to assist in managing water resources in arid regions. These systems combine satellite data, weather forecasts, and hydrological models to make real-time decisions about water distribution. By providing insights into which areas are most at risk, the systems help ensure that available water is allocated efficiently, reducing waste and mitigating the impacts of drought.

Case Study: Drought Prediction in California

One notable case study of GeoAI's application in drought prediction is the use of AI-driven models in California, one of the most water-stressed regions in the United States. Researchers have used satellite data and machine learning algorithms to predict when and where drought conditions are likely to occur in California's Central Valley, a critical agricultural region. By analyzing historical weather patterns and water usage data, AI models have been able to predict water shortages, helping farmers adjust irrigation schedules and reduce water waste.

10.4 Flood Prediction and Management with GeoAI

Flooding is one of the most devastating natural disasters, and with climate change increasing the frequency and intensity of extreme weather events, the need for accurate flood prediction and management has never been greater. GeoAI is proving to be a game-changer in this domain, as it can predict, monitor, and mitigate the impacts of floods.

Flood Monitoring and Detection

GeoAI models leverage satellite data, weather forecasts, and river basin information to detect rising water levels and predict floods in real-time. By analyzing satellite images and sensor data, AI can identify changes in river and lake levels, as well as flooding in urban or rural areas. Machine learning algorithms can also predict how floods will evolve, including the areas that are likely to be inundated, the extent of the damage, and the expected duration of the flooding event.

For instance, AI-based flood prediction models have been developed for cities like Jakarta, Indonesia, which are prone to severe flooding during the rainy season. By analyzing topographic data and real-time rainfall forecasts, these AI systems can predict which neighborhoods are at highest risk and issue early warnings to local authorities and residents.

Flood Risk Assessment

AI can also be used to assess flood risks by combining data from historical flood events, hydrological models, and satellite imagery. This data is used to create flood risk maps that identify flood-prone areas, which can be valuable for urban planning, disaster preparedness, and policy-making.

For example, the European Space Agency (ESA) has used satellite-based AI models to map flood risks in the Danube River Basin. These models use a combination of elevation data, rainfall patterns, and hydrological simulations to predict the likelihood of flooding in different parts of the region. This information helps guide flood protection measures, such as the construction of levees and dams, and informs emergency response strategies.

Real-Time Flood Response

During a flood event, GeoAI can provide real-time insights to help authorities respond effectively. By combining satellite images, weather data, and local sensor networks, AI systems can provide up-to-the-minute updates on flood extent, helping to direct emergency services to the most affected areas. Additionally, AI can assist in the rapid assessment of flood damage, enabling quicker recovery efforts.

One example is the use of machine learning algorithms to analyze satellite data during Hurricane Katrina. Researchers used AI to assess the extent of flood damage in New Orleans, helping rescue teams prioritize their efforts and expedite recovery.

10.5 Conclusion

GeoAI represents a significant breakthrough in the way we manage water resources. By integrating artificial intelligence with Earth observation data, we can better

monitor water quality, predict and manage water scarcity, and prepare for and respond to floods and droughts. As the challenges facing global water resources intensify, GeoAI will play an increasingly central role in ensuring that water is used efficiently, equitably, and sustainably. The future of water resource management lies in the continued development of AI-driven technologies that enable smarter, data-driven decision-making for a more water-resilient world.

Chapter 11: GeoAI for Agriculture and Food Security

11.1 Introduction to Agriculture and Food Security

In a world facing an expanding population, climate change, and environmental degradation, the issue of food security has become more critical than ever. Food security is a multi-dimensional problem encompassing the availability, access, utilization, and stability of food supplies. It is estimated that by 2050, the global population will exceed 9 billion, placing unprecedented pressure on agriculture to meet the demand for food.

Agriculture, as the backbone of the global food system, plays a pivotal role in ensuring food security. However, the challenges facing the sector are enormous. Climate change is altering weather patterns, leading to droughts, floods, and unpredictable growing seasons. Additionally, the expansion of urban areas, soil degradation, and water scarcity further complicate efforts to achieve food security. As traditional farming methods struggle to keep up with these evolving challenges, technology has emerged as a crucial ally. Among these, GeoAI (Geospatial Artificial Intelligence) is proving to be a game-changer in the field of agriculture.

GeoAI leverages satellite imagery, sensor data, and AI algorithms to provide detailed insights into agricultural processes. By integrating geospatial data with machine learning models, GeoAI offers a more precise understanding of farming landscapes, enabling farmers to make data-driven decisions. This chapter explores how GeoAI is reshaping agriculture and contributing to food security. It delves into various applications, from precision agriculture to pest detection, climate resilience, and beyond.

11.2 The Role of GeoAI in Sustainable Agriculture

Sustainable agriculture is critical in ensuring that food production meets the needs of today without compromising the ability of future generations to meet their own needs. GeoAI is a powerful tool that can help make agriculture more sustainable by optimizing resource use, increasing productivity, and minimizing environmental impact.

GeoAI facilitates precision farming, a method that involves monitoring and managing variability in fields to maximize yield while minimizing waste. Using data from satellites, drones, and ground-based sensors, farmers can gain real-time insights into crop health, soil conditions, and weather patterns. AI algorithms then analyze this data to recommend tailored farming practices. For instance, AI can predict the optimal time for planting and harvesting, or suggest adjustments to irrigation systems based on weather forecasts and soil moisture data.

Moreover, GeoAI can reduce environmental impacts by promoting the efficient use of inputs such as water, fertilizers, and pesticides. By providing a detailed picture of crop conditions across large areas, GeoAI helps farmers avoid overuse of these resources, which can lead to soil degradation, water pollution, and other environmental problems. For example, in precision irrigation, AI algorithms can determine when and where water is most needed, thus reducing water consumption and helping mitigate the effects of water scarcity in agriculture.

Case Study: Precision Irrigation in California

In California, a state that faces frequent droughts, farmers are using GeoAI to optimize irrigation. Satellite data and soil moisture sensors provide a detailed picture of the soil's needs. AI models process this data and generate precise irrigation recommendations, helping farmers conserve water while maintaining crop health. This approach has not only helped reduce water usage but also led to better crop yields.

GeoAI is also crucial in reducing waste and improving supply chain efficiency. By analyzing data from harvests, storage facilities, and transportation systems, GeoAI can forecast food demand more accurately, minimizing spoilage and waste. This is particularly important in regions with limited infrastructure, where food often spoils before it reaches consumers.

11.3 Precision Agriculture with GeoAI

What is Precision Agriculture?

Precision agriculture is an approach that uses data-driven technologies to monitor and optimize agricultural practices. It integrates information from various sources, such as satellite imagery, sensors, drones, and climate models, to make more informed decisions about farming activities. The goal is to increase efficiency, reduce costs, and minimize environmental impact, all while maximizing yields.

GeoAI plays a central role in precision agriculture. By combining geospatial data with machine learning algorithms, GeoAI enables farmers to monitor crops at a level of detail that was previously impossible. For example, satellite imagery can provide a broad view of crop conditions, while sensors on the ground can deliver granular data about soil moisture, temperature, and nutrient levels. AI then processes and analyzes this data to identify patterns and predict future trends, allowing farmers to make proactive decisions.

AI Applications in Precision Agriculture

1. **Crop Monitoring:** GeoAI enables farmers to track the health of their crops through satellite images and drone footage. Using image classification algorithms, GeoAI can detect signs of disease, pest infestations, or nutrient deficiencies in crops, allowing farmers to take targeted action before problems spread.

2. **Soil Health Monitoring:** Soil is the foundation of farming, and its health is crucial for productivity. GeoAI helps farmers monitor soil conditions, including its moisture, temperature, and nutrient levels. By combining this data with AI algorithms, farmers can optimize irrigation schedules, apply fertilizers more efficiently, and improve crop rotation practices to maintain soil health.

3. **Irrigation Management:** In regions with limited water resources, efficient irrigation is essential. GeoAI uses weather forecasts, soil moisture data, and satellite imagery to recommend precise irrigation schedules. This ensures that crops receive the right amount of water at the right time, reducing water wastage and improving crop yields.

Case Study: Precision Farming in India

In India, precision farming techniques powered by GeoAI have been employed to improve productivity in water-scarce regions. Farmers in Rajasthan use satellite data to monitor soil moisture levels and predict irrigation needs. With AI recommendations, they are able to optimize water use, improve crop yields, and conserve valuable water resources.

11.4 Crop Monitoring and Yield Prediction

GeoAI has revolutionized crop monitoring and yield prediction by providing farmers with accurate, real-time information about crop conditions and performance. By combining satellite imagery, drone data, and ground-based sensor inputs, AI models can assess factors such as plant health, growth stages, and weather patterns, which are crucial for predicting yields.

Monitoring Crop Health

AI-powered crop monitoring systems can identify early signs of stress in plants, such as disease, pest damage, or water stress. By analyzing images from satellites or drones, machine learning algorithms can detect subtle changes in plant color, texture, and structure that may indicate problems. For example, chlorophyll content in leaves is a good indicator of plant health, and AI models can use this data to assess whether crops are receiving adequate nutrients and water.

Yield Prediction Models

Yield prediction is an essential part of farm management, allowing farmers to estimate their harvest and plan for marketing and storage. AI models predict crop yields by analyzing multiple factors, including historical yield data, current crop health, and weather conditions. These predictions can be made at different scales, from individual fields to entire regions, providing valuable insights for farmers and policymakers.

Case Study: Yield Prediction for Wheat in the United States

In the U.S., GeoAI has been used to predict wheat yields based on satellite imagery and historical data. By analyzing crop health indicators from space, AI models are able to forecast wheat yields with remarkable accuracy. This information is crucial for farmers to decide when to harvest and how to manage their resources effectively.

Benefits of Accurate Yield Predictions

Accurate yield predictions enable farmers to plan their harvests and marketing strategies more effectively. They can also adjust their input usage (e.g., fertilizers, water, pesticides) based on yield forecasts, ensuring that resources are used optimally. Additionally, predictive models help farmers prepare for market fluctuations, allowing them to sell their crops at the best possible prices.

11.5 Pest Detection and Management with GeoAI

Pests are one of the greatest threats to global agriculture, responsible for substantial crop losses each year. GeoAI offers innovative solutions for pest detection and management by enabling early warning systems and precision pest control strategies.

The Problem of Pests in Agriculture

Pests, including insects, rodents, and plant pathogens, cause significant damage to crops, leading to reduced yields and increased costs. Traditional pest management practices, such as blanket pesticide application, are inefficient and environmentally harmful. In contrast, GeoAI helps target pest control efforts more precisely, reducing chemical use and minimizing environmental impact.

GeoAI for Pest Monitoring

GeoAI uses remote sensing data, such as satellite and drone imagery, to monitor crops for signs of pest infestations. AI algorithms analyze these images to detect unusual patterns that could indicate the presence of pests. For example, changes in leaf texture, color, or damage patterns may signal the presence of insects or fungal diseases. Once pests are detected, farmers can apply targeted treatments, reducing the need for widespread pesticide use.

AI for Pest Management

Machine learning models can predict pest outbreaks by analyzing environmental factors such as temperature, humidity, and historical pest data. These models can provide early warnings, allowing farmers to take preventative action before pests cause significant damage.

Case Study: Locust Swarm Detection in Africa

In East Africa, locust swarms have caused devastating crop losses. GeoAI has been used to detect and monitor locust swarms using satellite images and AI algorithms. The system analyzes changes in vegetation health and movement patterns, providing early warnings to farmers and authorities. This early detection allows for swift intervention, helping to mitigate the impact of locust infestations on food security.

11.6 Climate Resilience in Agriculture with GeoAI

As climate change leads to more extreme weather events and shifting growing seasons, agriculture must adapt to new climate realities. GeoAI plays a crucial role in building climate resilience by helping farmers understand and mitigate climate risks.

Impact of Climate Change on Agriculture

Rising temperatures, changing precipitation patterns, and extreme weather events such as droughts and floods are all threatening agricultural productivity. Crops that were once reliable in certain regions may become less viable as climate conditions change, and new pests and diseases may emerge.

GeoAI for Climate Resilience

GeoAI helps farmers adapt to climate change by providing tools for climate risk assessment, crop modeling, and resilience planning. For example, AI can analyze long-term climate data and predict future weather patterns, helping farmers plan their planting and harvest schedules more effectively. Additionally, GeoAI can identify areas at risk of drought or flooding, allowing farmers to take preventative measures.

Case Study: Drought Prediction in Sub-Saharan Africa

In Sub-Saharan Africa, where agriculture is heavily dependent on rain-fed systems, GeoAI has been used to predict drought conditions. By analyzing satellite data and climate models, AI systems can forecast droughts months in advance, giving farmers time to adjust their practices. This early warning system has been crucial in improving food security and reducing the impact of droughts on crop yields.

11.7 GeoAI in Food Security and Global Supply Chains

GeoAI's influence extends beyond individual farms and fields; it is also transforming food distribution and global supply chains. By improving the efficiency of food logistics and predicting demand, GeoAI helps reduce food waste and improve food access.

GeoAI for Food Distribution and Access

GeoAI enables more efficient food distribution by analyzing real-time data on transportation routes, storage conditions, and market demand. By identifying inefficiencies in the supply chain, GeoAI helps ensure that food reaches consumers more quickly, reducing spoilage and waste. This is particularly important in developing countries, where food often spoils before it reaches the market.

Food Insecurity and GeoAI

GeoAI also helps address food insecurity by providing insights into areas at risk of food shortages. By analyzing data on crop yields, weather patterns, and socio-economic conditions, AI models can predict where food insecurity is likely to occur. This allows governments and humanitarian organizations to intervene before food shortages lead to crises.

Case Study: Food Distribution in Conflict Zones

In conflict zones like Syria, where traditional supply chains are disrupted, GeoAI has been used to track food availability and distribution. By combining satellite data with on-the-ground reports, AI systems can assess the location and severity of food shortages, enabling aid organizations to respond more efficiently.

11.8 The Future of GeoAI in Agriculture and Food Security

The future of GeoAI in agriculture and food security holds immense potential. As technology advances, new applications are emerging that promise to further transform the way we approach farming and food security.

Emerging Technologies

The integration of AI with blockchain, autonomous farming systems, and 5G networks will create a new frontier in GeoAI applications. Blockchain technology can provide transparent supply chain tracking, while autonomous vehicles can optimize fieldwork, reducing the need for human labor. With 5G, real-time data transmission from sensors and drones will become even more efficient, providing farmers with instant insights.

Global Adoption of GeoAI

While large-scale farms in developed countries have already adopted GeoAI technologies, there is still a significant opportunity to extend these benefits to smallholder farmers in developing countries. Governments, NGOs, and tech companies must work together to provide affordable solutions and build capacity in these regions.

Policy and Governance

For GeoAI to achieve its full potential, governments and international organizations must provide the right policies, funding, and infrastructure. This includes investments in digital infrastructure, regulatory frameworks that support data sharing, and training programs for farmers.

11.9 Conclusion

GeoAI is revolutionizing agriculture and food security by enabling farmers to make better, data-driven decisions. From precision agriculture to climate resilience and food distribution, GeoAI is enhancing productivity, sustainability, and access to food. As the technology continues to evolve, its potential to transform the agricultural sector grows, offering new solutions to global food security challenges.

By embracing GeoAI, farmers can optimize their practices, reduce environmental impact, and contribute to a more food-secure world. The path forward involves scaling these technologies to benefit smallholder farmers and addressing the broader structural issues that impact food security globally.

Chapter 12: Monitoring Urbanization with GeoAI

12.1 Introduction to Urbanization and Its Challenges

Urbanization is one of the most significant demographic and environmental phenomena of the 21st century. By 2050, it is estimated that nearly 70% of the world's population will live in urban areas, up from about 55% today. This shift is driven by a multitude of factors, including rural-to-urban migration, population growth, and economic development. While urbanization can stimulate economic progress, technological advancements, and improved access to services, it also presents a variety of challenges.

Urbanization contributes to changes in land use, the consumption of natural resources, environmental degradation, and the strain on infrastructure and public services. As cities expand, they must adapt to handle increasing population densities while mitigating the adverse effects on the environment. The need for effective, data-driven planning is more critical than ever.

The rise of GeoAI (Geospatial Artificial Intelligence) provides an opportunity to address these challenges by integrating advanced geospatial data processing with machine learning. This combination enables city planners, environmental scientists, and policymakers to gain a deeper understanding of urbanization patterns and devise more sustainable urban development strategies.

In this chapter, we will explore how GeoAI is revolutionizing urbanization monitoring, with a focus on population growth, infrastructure development, and environmental impacts. We will look at how satellite imagery, machine learning, and AI algorithms are used to analyze urban growth trends, predict future developments, and help cities plan for sustainable growth.

12.2 Urbanization Trends and Drivers

Urbanization is a global phenomenon, but it is most pronounced in regions such as Asia, Africa, and Latin America. According to the United Nations, the global urban population grew by 1.84 billion people between 2000 and 2020, a trend that is expected to continue, particularly in developing countries.

Global Urbanization Trends

The urbanization process has been accelerating since the mid-20th century, driven by factors such as industrialization, improved healthcare, and better educational opportunities. Large-scale migration from rural to urban areas has contributed significantly to the rapid growth of cities. In many developing nations, this shift is spurred by the search for better employment prospects, improved living standards, and access to better healthcare and education.

In Africa, for example, urbanization is happening at a rate faster than any other continent. Cities like Lagos, Nairobi, and Kinshasa are expanding rapidly, creating both opportunities and challenges in terms of infrastructure development and environmental management.

Drivers of Urbanization

Several drivers contribute to urbanization, including:

- **Economic Development**: As countries industrialize, cities become hubs for commerce, employment, and innovation.

- **Technological Advancements**: Improvements in communication, transportation, and infrastructure allow cities to expand and offer better services to larger populations.

- **Rural-to-Urban Migration**: People move from rural areas to cities in search of employment, education, and healthcare, often driven by the limitations of agricultural land and the promise of economic opportunities in urban centers.

Challenges of Rapid Urbanization

While urbanization brings significant opportunities for economic growth, it also presents considerable challenges:

- **Overburdened Infrastructure**: Cities often struggle to provide adequate housing, transportation, and sanitation services for their growing populations.

- **Environmental Degradation**: Urban expansion can lead to the loss of green spaces, increased pollution, and greater strain on natural resources.

- **Social Inequality**: Rapid urban growth can exacerbate inequality, leading to the creation of informal settlements or "slums" where people live without access to basic services.

Given these challenges, it is imperative to monitor urbanization trends effectively to ensure that cities grow sustainably and manage their environmental and social impacts. GeoAI is at the forefront of this effort, enabling data-driven urban planning and decision-making.

12.3 The Role of Satellite Imagery in Urban Monitoring

Satellite imagery is a powerful tool for monitoring urbanization. It provides a bird's-eye view of the Earth, capturing high-resolution images that can be analyzed to detect changes in land use, population density, and infrastructure development. Over the past few decades, advancements in satellite technology have significantly improved the ability to monitor urbanization on a global scale.

Types of Satellite Imagery Used

- **Optical Satellite Imagery**: Optical satellites, such as Landsat and WorldView, capture visible and near-infrared light, providing high-resolution images that reveal changes in land cover and urban sprawl. These images are particularly useful for monitoring urban growth over time, as they allow for the detection of new buildings, roads, and changes in vegetation.

- **Radar Imagery**: Synthetic Aperture Radar (SAR) satellites, such as those used in the Sentinel-1 mission, are able to capture images regardless of weather conditions or time of day. SAR imagery can penetrate through clouds and provide valuable data for detecting ground movement, urban settlements, and infrastructure changes, particularly in regions prone to heavy cloud cover or frequent rainfall.

- **Multispectral and Hyperspectral Imagery**: These types of imagery capture data across multiple wavelengths, including the visible, near-infrared, and thermal infrared spectra. Multispectral and hyperspectral satellites can help monitor vegetation health, land cover changes, and even urban heat islands, providing deeper insights into the environmental impacts of urbanization.

Urban Growth Detection

Satellite imagery plays a crucial role in urban growth detection. By comparing satellite images from different time periods, analysts can track changes in land use and identify areas of rapid urban expansion. This process is known as **change detection** and is one of the primary applications of GeoAI in urbanization monitoring. For example, researchers may compare images of a city over a 10-year period to assess how much urban land has expanded, identify newly developed areas, and predict future growth trends.

Change Detection Algorithms

AI-driven change detection algorithms can automatically identify and classify changes in satellite images. These algorithms typically involve:

- **Image Registration**: Aligning satellite images from different time periods to ensure accurate comparisons.

- **Feature Extraction**: Identifying specific features in the images, such as roads, buildings, and green spaces.

- **Classification**: Classifying the changes in land cover into categories such as urban, agricultural, or forested land.

Machine learning models, such as **Convolutional Neural Networks (CNNs)**, have proven to be highly effective in classifying land cover types and detecting changes between images. These models can be trained on large datasets to recognize urban features and predict future urban growth patterns based on historical data.

12.4 AI Algorithms for Urban Growth Analysis

AI algorithms are essential for processing the vast amounts of data collected from satellite imagery and other geospatial sources. These algorithms help urban planners, environmental scientists, and policymakers analyze urban growth trends, predict future developments, and plan for sustainable growth.

Machine Learning Models in Urban Monitoring

Machine learning (ML) models play a critical role in urban monitoring by providing insights from vast amounts of spatial data. ML algorithms can be applied to satellite images, population data, and infrastructure data to detect patterns and trends that are not immediately obvious to human analysts.

- **Supervised Learning**: In supervised learning, an algorithm is trained on labeled data to classify different land use types, such as urban, agricultural, or forested areas. This can be applied to satellite images to track changes in land cover over time.

- **Unsupervised Learning**: Unsupervised learning is used when there is little or no labeled data. Clustering algorithms, such as k-means, can be used to group similar areas in satellite imagery, revealing underlying patterns of urbanization and land use.

- **Deep Learning Models**: Convolutional Neural Networks (CNNs) and other deep learning models are especially effective in urban growth analysis because they can automatically learn complex features from raw satellite imagery, improving the accuracy of urban detection and classification.

Urban Classification and Segmentation

Urban classification and segmentation are essential for monitoring land use and understanding how urbanization is unfolding. In urban monitoring, segmentation refers to dividing an image into different regions, or segments, based on certain characteristics such as color, texture, or object type. These segments are then classified into categories like residential, commercial, industrial, or green spaces.

Machine learning models can be used to automate the classification and segmentation process, saving time and resources while ensuring greater accuracy. For example, AI models can be trained to distinguish between high-density residential areas and industrial zones based on differences in image features.

Big Data and AI Integration

One of the challenges of urbanization monitoring is dealing with the enormous volume of geospatial data. GeoAI addresses this challenge by integrating various types of data—satellite imagery, IoT sensor data, and social media inputs—into a unified analysis pipeline. Big data analytics and cloud computing enable real-time processing of geospatial data, providing city planners and decision-makers with up-to-date insights into urban development.

12.5 Environmental Impacts of Urbanization and the Role of GeoAI

As urban areas expand, they inevitably exert pressure on the environment. From the destruction of natural habitats to increased pollution, urbanization can have significant long-term effects on the ecosystem. Understanding and mitigating these impacts are essential for promoting sustainable urban development. GeoAI plays a vital role in monitoring these environmental changes by processing satellite data and sensor inputs, allowing policymakers and urban planners to make more informed decisions.

Loss of Natural Habitats

Urban expansion often leads to the destruction or fragmentation of natural habitats, such as forests, wetlands, and grasslands. The conversion of these areas into residential, industrial, or commercial zones reduces biodiversity, affects local wildlife, and disrupts ecosystem services such as water filtration, air purification, and carbon sequestration.

GeoAI can help detect these changes by analyzing land cover data over time. Satellite imagery can be compared to identify areas where natural habitats are being replaced by urban infrastructure. Machine learning algorithms can classify these changes and generate heatmaps that show areas of significant environmental loss. For instance, researchers have used GeoAI to monitor deforestation in the Amazon rainforest, correlating deforestation rates with urban sprawl and the expansion of infrastructure.

Urban Heat Island Effect

One of the most well-documented environmental impacts of urbanization is the urban heat island (UHI) effect. UHI occurs when urban areas become significantly warmer than their rural surroundings due to factors like reduced vegetation, increased impervious surfaces (such as concrete and asphalt), and heat emitted from buildings and vehicles.

GeoAI can be used to monitor and assess UHI by analyzing thermal infrared satellite imagery. AI models process this data to create detailed temperature maps of urban areas, helping identify hotspots where the UHI effect is most pronounced. This information is crucial for urban planners, as it can inform the development of strategies to mitigate UHI, such as increasing green spaces, installing reflective roofing materials, or enhancing urban water management systems.

Pollution Monitoring

Urbanization is often associated with increased levels of pollution, including air, water, and soil contamination. Satellite imagery, combined with AI algorithms, can be used to monitor various types of pollution. For example, AI models can analyze multispectral imagery to detect air pollution in the form of aerosol concentrations or greenhouse gas emissions, providing valuable data for policymakers to implement air quality control measures.

Similarly, AI can be applied to analyze water quality in urban areas by processing remote sensing data from satellites that measure parameters like turbidity, chlorophyll concentrations, and suspended sediments. These analyses can be used to monitor the health of water bodies affected by urban runoff, industrial waste, or wastewater discharges.

Flooding and Stormwater Management

Urbanization often increases the risk of flooding due to the expansion of impervious surfaces, such as roads and buildings, which reduce the natural absorption capacity of soil. Urban flooding can lead to significant damage to infrastructure, displacement of communities, and loss of life.

GeoAI plays an important role in flood risk mapping by integrating remote sensing data (such as precipitation, elevation, and land cover data) with hydrological models to predict flood-prone areas. For example, AI models can process satellite images of urban areas to identify low-lying regions and analyze how changes in land cover affect water flow during heavy rainfall. These predictions can be used to guide flood mitigation strategies, such as the design of green infrastructure, the construction of flood barriers, or the implementation of better stormwater management practices.

12.6 GeoAI in Urban Planning for Sustainable Growth

With rapid urbanization creating complex challenges, sustainable urban planning has become a critical need. GeoAI provides decision-makers with the tools to assess the environmental, economic, and social dimensions of urban development, helping to create cities that are resilient, efficient, and environmentally responsible.

Urban Land Use Planning

Urban land use planning is an essential aspect of sustainable city development. It involves zoning land for various purposes—residential, commercial, industrial, recreational, etc.—in a way that promotes balanced growth and minimizes conflicts. GeoAI can optimize urban land use planning by processing spatial data and generating insights about land availability, population densities, and environmental constraints.

For example, machine learning algorithms can analyze historical growth patterns to predict where new development is likely to occur. Planners can use this information to allocate land more effectively, ensuring that urban expansion does not come at the cost of valuable agricultural land or ecologically sensitive areas.

Infrastructure Development and Optimization

GeoAI can also play a role in optimizing the development of urban infrastructure, such as roads, transportation networks, utilities, and public services. AI algorithms can analyze satellite data to identify areas with the greatest need for infrastructure upgrades or new facilities. Additionally, AI can process real-time data from urban sensors (such as traffic sensors, water meters, and pollution monitors) to optimize the operation of urban systems.

For example, AI-based systems can be used to optimize public transportation routes, reducing congestion and air pollution. Smart grid technologies, powered by AI, can improve energy efficiency in urban areas by predicting demand and adjusting energy distribution accordingly.

Smart Cities and IoT Integration

The concept of "smart cities" refers to urban areas that leverage technology and data to enhance the quality of life for their residents. GeoAI plays a pivotal role in smart city development by integrating satellite data with data from Internet of Things (IoT) sensors placed throughout the city. These sensors collect real-time data on traffic flow, air quality, noise levels, energy consumption, and more.

By analyzing this data with machine learning algorithms, cities can become more responsive to the needs of their inhabitants. For instance, AI can predict traffic congestion and suggest alternative routes for commuters or analyze air quality data to issue health warnings when pollution levels rise.

Sustainable Development Goals (SDGs)

GeoAI can support the achievement of Sustainable Development Goals (SDGs) by providing the data needed to make cities more sustainable, resilient, and inclusive. In particular, GeoAI is instrumental in SDG 11, which aims to "make cities and human settlements inclusive, safe, resilient, and sustainable." By tracking urbanization trends, monitoring environmental impacts, and optimizing resource management, GeoAI contributes to the creation of urban spaces that promote both economic growth and environmental stewardship.

12.7 The Future of GeoAI in Urbanization Monitoring

As urbanization continues to shape the global landscape, the role of GeoAI in urban planning and management will become increasingly important. Advances in machine learning, remote sensing, and big data analytics will enable more precise monitoring and prediction of urban growth, allowing for more effective and sustainable city development.

Integration with Other Technologies

The future of GeoAI lies in its integration with other emerging technologies, such as 5G, autonomous systems, and edge computing. 5G networks will enable faster data transmission, allowing real-time urban monitoring and analysis. Autonomous drones and vehicles could enhance data collection in urban environments, providing new insights into mobility patterns and infrastructure needs. Edge computing could process data closer to the source, reducing latency and improving the efficiency of urban monitoring systems.

AI-Driven Policy Making

AI will play a more prominent role in the development of data-driven policies that respond to the needs of urban populations. As AI algorithms become more sophisticated, policymakers will have access to more granular, real-time data on urban dynamics, which can be used to make informed decisions about land use, infrastructure, housing, and environmental protection.

Urban Resilience to Climate Change

As cities face the impacts of climate change, GeoAI will become an essential tool for building urban resilience. By monitoring changes in climate patterns, predicting extreme weather events, and optimizing resource allocation, GeoAI will help cities adapt to changing environmental conditions. GeoAI's ability to integrate climate models with urban data will support efforts to reduce carbon footprints, manage water resources, and protect vulnerable communities from climate-related risks.

12.8 Conclusion

GeoAI offers a transformative approach to monitoring and managing urbanization, enabling cities to grow sustainably while minimizing negative environmental and social impacts. From detecting urban sprawl to assessing the environmental consequences of development, GeoAI provides the data-driven insights needed for effective urban planning. As urbanization continues to accelerate, the role of GeoAI in shaping the cities of the future will only become more vital.

The integration of satellite imagery, AI algorithms, and big data analytics holds the potential to create smarter, more sustainable cities that can adapt to the challenges of the modern world. Moving forward, continued advancements in GeoAI and related technologies will empower urban planners, policymakers, and researchers to better understand the dynamics of urbanization and make more informed decisions that benefit both people and the planet.

Chapter 13: Air Quality and Pollution Monitoring Using GeoAI

13.1 Introduction to Air Quality Monitoring

Air pollution remains one of the most pressing environmental challenges of the 21st century. With the rapid urbanization and industrialization in many parts of the world, the degradation of air quality has become a critical concern, directly affecting both public health and the environment. Traditionally, air quality monitoring relied on ground-based stations that provided real-time measurements of pollutants like particulate matter (PM2.5), nitrogen oxides (NOx), carbon monoxide (CO), sulfur dioxide (SO2), and ozone (O3). While this method has been useful, it presents limitations in terms of spatial coverage, data resolution, and the ability to monitor continuously across large areas.

GeoAI, a combination of geospatial analysis and artificial intelligence, has revolutionized the way air quality is monitored by integrating satellite data with real-time sensor networks. This chapter explores how GeoAI is transforming the field of air quality monitoring and pollution management, with a particular focus on how AI-powered algorithms help identify pollution sources, predict pollution hotspots, and support policy decisions aimed at improving air quality.

Key Air Pollutants

Air pollution is caused by a variety of pollutants, but the most common ones include:

- **Particulate Matter (PM2.5):** These tiny particles, less than 2.5 micrometers in diameter, can penetrate deep into the lungs, causing respiratory diseases and contributing to cardiovascular problems. They are primarily emitted by vehicles, industrial processes, and wildfires.

• **Nitrogen Oxides (NOx):** These gases, including NO and NO2, are produced from the combustion of fossil fuels, such as in vehicle engines and power plants. NOx contributes to the formation of ground-level ozone and acid rain.

• **Carbon Monoxide (CO):** CO is a colorless, odorless gas produced by the incomplete combustion of fossil fuels. It can cause harmful health effects, especially in high concentrations.

• **Sulfur Dioxide (SO2):** SO2 is released primarily by industrial processes and the burning of coal and oil. It can lead to the formation of acid rain and respiratory problems.

• **Ozone (O3):** Ground-level ozone forms when NOx and volatile organic compounds (VOCs) react in the presence of sunlight. It is a major component of smog and has detrimental effects on human health, particularly on lung function.

13.2 Integration of Satellite and Sensor Data for Pollution Monitoring

Role of Remote Sensing in Air Quality Monitoring

Remote sensing has become an indispensable tool in air quality monitoring. Satellite-based sensors, such as the Moderate Resolution Imaging Spectroradiometer (MODIS), Sentinel-5 Precursor, and TROPOMI, collect data on atmospheric composition, including the concentration of pollutants like nitrogen dioxide (NO2), ozone (O3), and particulate matter (PM2.5). These satellites provide broad coverage, capturing data over vast geographical regions and offering insights into long-term trends in air quality.

For example, the **Sentinel-5P mission**, launched by the European Space Agency, provides detailed measurements of atmospheric pollutants such as NO2 and ozone. Sentinel-5P's TROPOMI sensor is a prime example of how satellite technology has evolved to support air quality monitoring. The data collected by TROPOMI helps scientists track pollution sources, study trends, and predict future pollution patterns on a global scale.

Satellite data, however, has its limitations in spatial resolution and temporal frequency. This is where ground-based sensors and Internet of Things (IoT) technologies come into play, complementing satellite observations with more granular, real-time data.

Ground-Based Sensors and IoT for Real-Time Monitoring

Ground-based air quality monitoring stations provide highly accurate, real-time data on pollutant concentrations in specific locations. These sensors can be deployed in urban, rural, and industrial environments, offering localized insights into air quality. The integration of IoT sensors with cloud computing enables the collection and analysis of vast amounts of environmental data in real time. For example, low-cost air quality sensors, which can be installed in residential areas, schools, and offices, provide critical data that supports health and safety decisions.

An example of this is the **PurpleAir** sensor network, a low-cost sensor network that monitors air quality and provides real-time data through a web interface. By aggregating data from multiple sensors, researchers can obtain hyper-local pollution insights that can inform policy decisions on air quality management.

Data Fusion: Combining Satellite and Ground Data

Combining satellite-based data with ground sensor data, a process known as **data fusion**, enhances the spatial resolution and accuracy of air quality monitoring. While satellite data provides broad coverage, ground sensors offer highly localized, real-time measurements. By integrating these datasets,

GeoAI algorithms can create more detailed pollution maps that reflect both short-term variations and long-term trends.

Data fusion also helps address the challenge of spatial and temporal resolution. For example, the **CAMS (Copernicus Atmosphere Monitoring Service)** uses satellite data along with ground-based measurements to produce detailed air quality forecasts for European cities. This service integrates satellite-derived aerosol optical depth (AOD) data with ground-level sensor data to improve the accuracy of air quality predictions.

13.3 AI Algorithms for Pollution Source Identification

Machine Learning for Source Identification

GeoAI harnesses machine learning (ML) algorithms to identify pollution sources and track their emissions over time. One of the most significant advancements in pollution monitoring is the use of supervised learning techniques to classify air pollution sources. These algorithms are trained on historical pollution data, satellite imagery, and sensor readings to predict pollution sources such as industrial plants, power stations, and transportation networks.

For example, machine learning models can identify the location and intensity of pollution based on temporal and spatial patterns observed in the satellite data. By analyzing emission data from various sources, GeoAI systems can identify whether the pollution stems from vehicle traffic, industrial activities, or natural events like forest fires.

Deep Learning and Neural Networks

Deep learning models, particularly **Convolutional Neural Networks (CNNs)**, have demonstrated remarkable success in image-based pollution monitoring. CNNs can analyze satellite images and automatically detect pollution patterns based on image texture, color, and shape. These models excel in classifying large volumes of satellite imagery and identifying subtle differences in pollution levels that are difficult to detect with traditional methods.

For example, **DeepAir**, a deep learning model developed by researchers in the UK, uses CNNs to analyze satellite images for signs of air pollution. This AI system can differentiate between industrial emissions, vehicle exhaust, and other sources of pollutants, thus aiding in source identification and long-term monitoring.

Predictive Modeling for Pollution Hotspot Identification

AI algorithms can predict future pollution hotspots by analyzing temporal patterns in air quality data. By leveraging historical air quality measurements, machine learning models can forecast which areas will experience high pollution levels, helping governments and organizations take preventive action.

An example is the **AI-powered pollution forecasting system** used in New Delhi, India, where pollution levels often reach hazardous levels due to vehicle emissions and industrial activity. The system uses machine learning to predict which parts of the city will be most affected, providing actionable insights for early intervention.

13.4 GeoAI's Role in Policy Decision-Making and Environmental Regulation

Informing Air Quality Policies

GeoAI plays a pivotal role in shaping air quality policies by providing real-time, accurate data that informs decision-makers. Governments and regulatory bodies can use GeoAI tools to evaluate the effectiveness of air quality regulations, assess emission levels, and identify areas in need of stricter enforcement.

For instance, AI models can predict how different policy interventions—such as banning certain types of vehicles, introducing stricter industrial emission standards, or expanding green spaces—will impact air quality over time. These insights allow policymakers to make data-driven decisions, ensuring that interventions are both effective and sustainable.

Evaluating the Impact of Pollution Control Measures

AI-powered models help assess the effectiveness of existing pollution control measures. By comparing air quality data before and after implementing regulations, GeoAI can quantify the benefits of interventions. For example, after implementing stricter vehicle emission standards in California, AI models could be used to compare the pollution levels in urban areas, revealing improvements in air quality.

Additionally, GeoAI can simulate the effects of new regulations or policies on air quality. This capability allows governments to predict the impact of proposed measures without having to wait for years of data.

13.5 Enhancing Public Health with GeoAI Insights

Health Impacts of Air Pollution

Air pollution is a leading cause of respiratory and cardiovascular diseases, with long-term exposure linked to premature deaths. GeoAI models can identify areas with high pollution levels and correlate them with health data to assess the impact of poor air quality on public health. AI-powered tools also help track the distribution of health effects, identifying vulnerable populations who are most at risk from poor air quality.

For example, in cities like **Beijing** and **Mexico City**, researchers have used GeoAI to correlate pollution data with health statistics, identifying areas with the highest incidence of asthma, heart disease, and other pollution-related health issues.

Public Health Interventions and Awareness

GeoAI tools also play a crucial role in improving public health awareness. Real-time air quality data is accessible to the public through apps and online platforms, helping residents make informed decisions about their health. For instance, the **Air Quality Index (AQI)** is integrated with GeoAI models to provide real-time pollution forecasts and alerts, allowing people to avoid outdoor activities during times of high pollution.

Furthermore, AI can model the health impacts of air pollution, predicting future health crises and enabling early interventions, such as advising vulnerable populations to limit exposure during pollution peaks.

13.6 GeoAI Applications in Urban and Industrial Pollution Management

Urban Air Pollution Monitoring

GeoAI is playing an increasingly important role in managing air pollution in urban areas. By integrating real-time data from both satellites and sensors, GeoAI models can help cities monitor pollution levels, identify sources, and predict future pollution hotspots. For example, in **Los Angeles**, real-time pollution monitoring systems based on GeoAI are used to guide traffic regulations, industrial policies, and health advisories.

GeoAI systems can also be used to model the impact of future urban developments on air quality, helping urban planners make decisions that prioritize sustainable growth and minimize environmental impact.

Tracking Agricultural Pollution

In rural areas, agricultural activities are a significant source of air pollution, particularly from the use of fertilizers, pesticides, and methane emissions from livestock. GeoAI tools help track pollution from agricultural sources, providing insights into its impact on surrounding ecosystems and human health. For instance, in regions like the **Midwest U.S.,** AI models are used to monitor ammonia emissions from farms, helping farmers adopt cleaner practices.

13.7 The Future of GeoAI in Air Quality and Pollution Monitoring

Advancements in AI and Sensor Technology

The future of GeoAI in air quality monitoring will likely see significant advancements in AI algorithms and sensor technology. Emerging sensor networks, including low-cost air quality sensors and drones, will further enhance the resolution and accuracy of pollution data. These technologies, combined with AI, will enable continuous, real-time pollution monitoring on a global scale.

Improvement in International Collaboration

GeoAI has the potential to improve international collaboration in monitoring global air pollution. By integrating global air quality data, AI models can help identify cross-border pollution trends and enable nations to collaborate on pollution reduction strategies.

13.8 Conclusion

GeoAI is transforming the way air quality is monitored and managed, enabling more accurate, timely, and data-driven decision-making. By integrating satellite data, ground-based sensors, and AI algorithms, GeoAI is helping track pollution sources, predict hotspots, and support public health initiatives. As technology advances, GeoAI will continue to play a crucial role in combating air pollution and improving environmental health on a global scale.

Chapter 14: GeoAI and Ocean Health Monitoring

14.1 Introduction to Ocean Health Monitoring

Ocean ecosystems are vital to the health of the planet. They cover about 71% of Earth's surface and are home to an astounding variety of life, from the smallest plankton to the largest whales. Oceans regulate climate, support biodiversity, provide food, and contribute to the global economy. However, human activities—overfishing, pollution, climate change—have significantly impacted these ecosystems. To preserve these vital resources, monitoring ocean health is crucial. Traditional methods of monitoring oceans, such as manual surveys and oceanographic cruises, are costly and logistically challenging. This is where GeoAI comes in.

GeoAI, which combines geographic information systems (GIS), remote sensing, and artificial intelligence (AI), has revolutionized the monitoring and management of ocean health. Through the integration of satellite data, sensor networks, and machine learning, GeoAI provides real-time insights, predictive models, and actionable information to assess ocean health. This chapter will explore how GeoAI is transforming ocean health monitoring, focusing on coral reefs, marine biodiversity, pollution levels, and how AI processes vast amounts of satellite data to assess the state of marine environments.

14.2 GeoAI and Coral Reef Monitoring

Coral reefs are one of the most diverse and productive ecosystems on Earth. However, they are extremely vulnerable to environmental stressors like rising sea temperatures, ocean acidification, and pollution. Monitoring the health of coral reefs is challenging due to their vast and often remote locations.

Importance of Coral Reefs

Coral reefs support nearly 25% of all marine species, provide food and income for millions of people, and protect coastlines from storm surges and erosion. The loss of coral reefs would have devastating consequences for marine biodiversity and the coastal populations that depend on them. Given their importance, tracking coral reef health is a top priority for conservation efforts.

Threats to Coral Reefs

The primary threats to coral reefs include ocean acidification, rising sea temperatures, overfishing, and pollution. Coral bleaching, a phenomenon caused by temperature increases, is one of the most visible signs of reef degradation. As water temperatures rise, corals expel the symbiotic algae that live in their tissues, causing them to turn white and become more susceptible to disease.

AI and Satellite Data for Coral Reef Health

GeoAI uses remote sensing and satellite data to monitor coral reefs at scale. Satellites such as **Sentinel-2** (European Space Agency) provide high-resolution images of coral reef areas, allowing scientists to monitor changes over time. AI models process these images to detect changes in coral health, such as bleaching or damage due to storms. Machine learning algorithms can also detect subtle environmental changes that may indicate stress on the reef, such as changes in water temperature or sediment levels.

Case Study: Great Barrier Reef

One of the most well-known examples of GeoAI's application in coral reef monitoring is the use of AI to monitor the **Great Barrier Reef** in Australia. Researchers have employed AI algorithms to process satellite images and detect coral bleaching events. By analyzing historical data, the models are also able to predict where bleaching is most likely to occur based on environmental factors, allowing early interventions to protect vulnerable areas.

Predicting Reef Degradation

GeoAI models can predict future coral reef degradation by incorporating environmental variables such as sea surface temperature, water quality, and ocean currents. By feeding these variables into deep learning models, researchers can forecast areas where coral reefs are likely to experience bleaching or disease outbreaks. These predictions help conservationists take proactive measures to protect reefs before they reach critical levels of degradation.

14.3 Marine Biodiversity Monitoring with GeoAI

Marine biodiversity is critical for ecosystem health, yet it remains under threat from habitat loss, pollution, and climate change. Monitoring marine species and ecosystems is complex due to the vastness of the ocean and the mobility of marine life.

Importance of Marine Biodiversity

Marine biodiversity contributes to food security, carbon sequestration, and the overall functioning of ocean ecosystems. It also supports industries such as fisheries, tourism, and pharmaceuticals. A decline in marine biodiversity can have cascading effects on ecosystems and economies.

Tracking Marine Species

GeoAI technologies, including satellite imagery, drones, and underwater sensors, allow researchers to track the movement and behavior of marine species. For example, **whale migration** has been monitored using satellite tags and AI algorithms that analyze patterns of movement across large distances. GeoAI models are able to identify the routes whales take during migration and track their behavior in relation to environmental conditions like ocean temperature and salinity.

AI for Habitat Mapping

AI is also used to map marine habitats, such as seagrass beds, mangroves, and kelp forests, which are essential for supporting marine biodiversity. By analyzing satellite data, machine learning algorithms can classify different habitat types and track changes over time. These habitat maps are crucial for conservation efforts and inform policy decisions related to marine protected areas (MPAs).

Case Study: Whale Migration

A notable example of GeoAI in marine biodiversity monitoring is the tracking of whale migration patterns in the Pacific Ocean. By combining satellite imagery, GPS tags, and AI-driven analysis, researchers have been able to map the migration routes of various whale species and understand how environmental variables, such as water temperature, affect their movements. This data is crucial for understanding the impact of climate change on marine life and for developing conservation strategies.

AI for Identifying Biodiversity Hotspots

GeoAI is also used to identify marine biodiversity hotspots, regions that are rich in species and provide crucial ecosystem services. AI algorithms process satellite and sensor data to analyze factors such as water temperature, nutrient availability, and species abundance, helping scientists identify areas that are critical for conservation. By tracking these hotspots over time, GeoAI helps assess the effectiveness of marine conservation efforts.

14.4 Marine Pollution and Pollution Source Detection with GeoAI

Pollution, particularly plastic pollution, is one of the most significant threats to ocean health. Monitoring marine pollution is challenging due to the vastness of the oceans and the dynamic nature of pollutants like plastics and oil.

Types of Marine Pollution

Marine pollution includes plastics, chemicals, oil spills, and agricultural runoff. Plastics are particularly harmful because they persist in the ocean for hundreds of years and can be ingested by marine species, leading to injury or death. Oil spills can have devastating effects on marine ecosystems, coating coral reefs and damaging sensitive habitats.

AI for Pollution Detection

GeoAI is crucial for detecting and monitoring marine pollution. By integrating satellite imagery, sensor data, and machine learning models, researchers can track the movement of pollutants in the ocean. For example, AI algorithms can detect oil spills by analyzing the characteristics of the ocean surface, identifying changes in reflectivity that indicate the presence of oil. Similarly, machine learning models can track the movement of plastic debris using satellite images and ocean current data.

Tracking Ocean Plastics

AI is particularly effective in tracking plastics in the ocean. With the help of satellite imagery, AI models can identify floating plastic waste and track its movement across the ocean's surface. In the **Great Pacific Garbage Patch**, AI algorithms have been used to analyze satellite images and track the spread of plastic debris. By combining data on ocean currents and weather patterns, GeoAI can predict where plastic waste will accumulate, providing insights for clean-up efforts.

Oil Spill Detection and Response

Oil spills are another area where GeoAI plays a critical role. Using satellite images, AI can identify the presence of oil slicks on the ocean's surface. Once detected, AI algorithms can map the extent of the spill and predict its movement based on ocean currents and wind patterns. This information is essential for organizing a rapid response to minimize the environmental impact of oil spills.

Case Study: The Deepwater Horizon Spill

One of the most well-known examples of GeoAI's application in pollution monitoring is the response to the **Deepwater Horizon oil spill** in 2010. Satellite images were analyzed using machine learning algorithms to detect and monitor the oil slick's spread. This real-time data was then used to guide the response efforts, including the use of dispersants and containment booms, and to assess the long-term environmental impacts of the spill.

14.5 Ocean Temperature and Climate Change Impacts

The oceans play a key role in regulating Earth's climate, and changes in ocean temperature have significant implications for marine ecosystems and global weather patterns.

Global Warming and Ocean Health

As global temperatures rise due to climate change, oceans absorb much of the excess heat, leading to rising sea temperatures. This has a range of effects, including coral bleaching, altered migration patterns, and shifts in species distributions. In addition, warming oceans contribute to sea level rise, which threatens coastal communities.

GeoAI for Monitoring Ocean Temperatures

GeoAI is used to monitor ocean temperature changes in real-time. Satellites like **NOAA's GOES** series provide sea surface temperature data, which is processed by machine learning algorithms to identify trends and anomalies. By combining ocean temperature data with other environmental variables, AI can predict the impact of warming oceans on marine ecosystems.

Predicting the Future of Ocean Health

GeoAI models also predict how ocean health will change under different climate scenarios. Using data on ocean temperature, sea level rise, and marine species distributions, AI algorithms can simulate the effects of continued warming on coral reefs, fish populations, and coastal ecosystems. These predictions are essential for developing effective adaptation strategies to protect vulnerable marine environments.

AI for Climate Change Adaptation

AI can help develop strategies for adapting to climate change, such as coral restoration or the establishment of marine protected areas. By analyzing data on ocean health, AI can identify areas that are most vulnerable to climate change and recommend specific actions to mitigate the effects of warming temperatures.

4.6 AI-Driven Models for Predicting Oceanic Changes

AI-driven models are transforming how scientists predict changes in ocean ecosystems. By analyzing historical data and real-time observations, AI models can predict shifts in species distributions, changes in biodiversity, and the impacts of climate change.

Predicting Oceanic Trends

AI models can predict trends in ocean health, such as the spread of coral bleaching or changes in fish populations. By incorporating environmental data such as water temperature, salinity, and ocean currents, machine learning algorithms can forecast future changes in marine ecosystems and help guide conservation efforts.

Deep Learning for Oceanographic Data Analysis

Deep learning techniques are used to analyze vast oceanographic datasets, such as those collected by ocean sensors, satellite imagery, and underwater vehicles. These models can process complex data more efficiently than traditional methods, allowing scientists to identify patterns and make predictions with greater accuracy.

Dynamic Ocean Models

Dynamic ocean models, powered by AI, simulate the interactions between ocean currents, ecosystems, and climate variables. These models help scientists understand how changes in one part of the system, such as rising temperatures, can affect other aspects of ocean health, including biodiversity and fish populations.

14.7 GeoAI in Ocean Conservation and Policy Making

GeoAI is instrumental in supporting ocean conservation and informing policy decisions. By providing accurate, real-time data on ocean health, GeoAI helps guide decisions related to marine protected areas, sustainable fisheries management, and climate adaptation.

AI for Policy Support

GeoAI helps policymakers make informed decisions about ocean conservation. By providing insights into the state of marine ecosystems, AI supports the development of policies that promote sustainable resource use and protect vulnerable areas. For example, AI can identify areas in need of protection based on biodiversity data and ocean health indicators.

Supporting Sustainable Fisheries

AI is used to support sustainable fisheries management by providing data on fish populations, migration patterns, and habitat use. Machine learning algorithms can predict fish stock levels, helping policymakers implement fishing quotas and prevent overfishing.

Conservation Efforts

GeoAI helps assess the effectiveness of conservation programs by monitoring marine protected areas (MPAs) and other conservation initiatives. By tracking biodiversity and ecosystem health over time, AI provides valuable data to evaluate whether conservation efforts are achieving their intended outcomes.

Case Study: The Galapagos Islands

The **Galapagos Islands** are a prime example of how GeoAI supports conservation efforts. AI-driven models have been used to monitor biodiversity and assess the health of marine ecosystems around the islands. By analyzing satellite data, researchers have identified critical habitats for marine species and developed conservation strategies to protect these areas.

14.8 Future Directions and Challenges in GeoAI for Ocean Health

GeoAI is still evolving, and there are many exciting opportunities and challenges ahead. As technology improves, AI's ability to monitor and predict changes in ocean health will continue to grow.

Technological Advancements

The integration of autonomous underwater vehicles (AUVs), drones, and the Internet of Things (IoT) with GeoAI will enable more detailed, real-time monitoring of ocean ecosystems. These technologies will provide continuous data streams, allowing for more precise predictions and quicker responses to environmental changes.

Challenges and Limitations

Despite its potential, GeoAI faces challenges, including the need for more accurate and higher-resolution satellite data, computational limitations, and the complexity of ocean ecosystems. Additionally, access to data can be limited due to cost or political barriers, particularly in regions of the world that are most vulnerable to ocean health issues.

Ethical and Policy Considerations

There are also ethical considerations around the use of GeoAI in ocean monitoring. For example, how can we balance the need for data with concerns about privacy and surveillance? Furthermore, how can GeoAI be used responsibly to ensure it benefits all regions and communities, especially those that are most affected by ocean health issues?

Opportunities for Global Collaboration

Finally, global collaboration is key to advancing GeoAI in ocean health monitoring. By sharing data, resources, and expertise, countries can work together to protect the oceans and ensure sustainable ocean management for future generations.

14.9 Conclusion

GeoAI is revolutionizing the way we monitor and manage ocean health. By combining satellite data, sensor networks, and AI algorithms, GeoAI enables real-time insights into coral reef health, marine biodiversity, pollution levels, and climate change impacts. While challenges remain, the future of ocean health monitoring is promising, with technological advancements and global collaboration offering new opportunities to protect these vital ecosystems.

Chapter 15: GeoAI for Sustainable Development Goals (SDGs)

15.1 Introduction to the United Nations' Sustainable Development Goals (SDGs)

The United Nations' Sustainable Development Goals (SDGs), established in 2015, represent a universal agenda to guide global development towards a more equitable, sustainable, and prosperous future. The 17 SDGs address critical global challenges, from poverty eradication to climate action, and are underpinned by the need for sustainable management of resources and ecosystems. These goals are aimed at improving the quality of life for all, ensuring environmental sustainability, and fostering economic growth that benefits all segments of society.

The role of technology, particularly in the context of **GeoAI**, is pivotal in achieving these goals. GeoAI combines geographic information systems (GIS) with artificial intelligence (AI) to process vast amounts of spatial and environmental data, uncover patterns, and deliver actionable insights. With its ability to monitor real-time conditions, predict future trends, and optimize decision-making, GeoAI has become a powerful tool in advancing the SDGs.

This chapter explores how GeoAI is contributing to the achievement of several of the SDGs, focusing on applications that enhance environmental sustainability, climate resilience, food security, and more. By integrating satellite data, AI algorithms, and machine learning models, GeoAI provides new capabilities for monitoring and addressing challenges on a global scale.

15.2 GeoAI for Affordable and Clean Energy (SDG 7)

SDG 7 aims to ensure access to affordable, reliable, sustainable, and modern energy for all by 2030. With the global energy demand growing, transitioning to renewable energy sources such as solar, wind, and hydroelectric power is essential to mitigate climate change and foster sustainable development.

GeoAI's role in renewable energy planning is particularly impactful. Satellite data, in combination with AI models, is used to identify optimal sites for renewable energy infrastructure. By processing factors such as solar radiation, wind speed, topography, and land use, GeoAI can help identify regions with the highest potential for energy generation.

- **Solar Energy Monitoring**: AI algorithms process satellite imagery to assess solar energy potential across large geographic areas. For instance, AI models can analyze cloud cover patterns and sunlight availability to predict the best areas for solar farm placement. This can be observed in projects like the *Solar Energy Mapping Project* in India, which leverages GeoAI to plan and expand solar infrastructure.

- **Wind Energy**: The integration of wind speed data from satellites and sensor networks with AI models enables precise wind energy predictions. By analyzing patterns of wind velocity, GeoAI can assist in the siting of wind turbines, ensuring efficient energy generation while minimizing environmental and economic costs.

Furthermore, GeoAI models support **energy efficiency initiatives** by analyzing energy consumption patterns, identifying inefficiencies, and optimizing resource allocation. Smart grids and AI-driven demand-response systems can leverage data from satellites and sensors to reduce energy waste and improve distribution networks, particularly in regions with limited infrastructure.

15.3 GeoAI for Life on Land (SDG 15)

SDG 15 focuses on protecting, restoring, and promoting the sustainable use of terrestrial ecosystems. This includes halting deforestation, reversing land degradation, and conserving biodiversity. Given the rapid pace of environmental changes caused by human activities, monitoring and protecting land-based ecosystems is crucial to the achievement of long-term sustainability goals.

GeoAI plays a central role in **monitoring land degradation and deforestation**, leveraging satellite data and machine learning to detect changes in land cover and assess ecosystem health. Remote sensing data, when coupled with AI algorithms, allows for the continuous monitoring of forests, wetlands, and other vital ecosystems.

- **Deforestation and Land Degradation**: By analyzing satellite images over time, GeoAI systems can identify deforestation hotspots and predict areas at risk of land degradation. In the Amazon rainforest, for example, GeoAI has been used to track illegal logging and deforestation, providing real-time data to support enforcement and conservation efforts.

- **Biodiversity Conservation**: GeoAI is used to create detailed maps of biodiversity hotspots and monitor the health of habitats. Machine learning models analyze vegetation cover, wildlife movements, and land use changes, helping to inform conservation strategies and protected area management.

- **Habitat Restoration**: GeoAI is also essential in habitat restoration efforts. By identifying regions impacted by deforestation, soil erosion, or desertification, AI can predict areas where reforestation or land restoration efforts would be most successful. Additionally, GeoAI helps monitor the progress of restoration activities, ensuring that interventions are yielding the desired ecological benefits.

15.4 GeoAI for Responsible Consumption and Production (SDG 12)

SDG 12 emphasizes the need to ensure sustainable consumption and production patterns. This includes reducing waste generation, improving resource efficiency, and fostering environmentally friendly supply chains. GeoAI's ability to process large amounts of data from various sources can drive efficiency and reduce the environmental footprint of industries and households alike.

- **Sustainable Agriculture**: GeoAI contributes significantly to **precision agriculture**, enabling farmers to optimize their resource use. Through satellite imagery and sensor data, AI models can monitor soil health, water usage, and crop growth. These insights help farmers reduce input waste, increase crop yields, and improve resource efficiency. For example, AI-powered irrigation systems use real-time weather data to adjust water usage based on plant needs, minimizing water waste.

- **Waste Management**: GeoAI is also used to monitor waste management processes. By analyzing data from satellite images and IoT devices, AI models can identify areas of high waste generation, track the flow of waste in urban environments, and optimize waste collection routes. For instance, in cities like *San Francisco*, GeoAI systems are used to monitor waste streams and inform recycling programs.

- **Supply Chain Optimization**: GeoAI helps optimize supply chains by analyzing transportation routes, minimizing energy consumption, and reducing emissions. AI models identify inefficiencies in the movement of goods and suggest more sustainable alternatives. GeoAI also assists in tracking the environmental impact of production processes, helping businesses identify areas where they can reduce their carbon footprint.

15.5 GeoAI for Climate Action (SDG 13)

SDG 13 addresses the urgent need to combat climate change and its impacts through mitigation and adaptation strategies. GeoAI plays a crucial role in **climate change monitoring, emission tracking**, and **predicting future climate scenarios**, helping decision-makers better understand the magnitude of climate risks and take timely actions.

- **Climate Change Prediction**: GeoAI models process data from satellites, weather stations, and sensor networks to predict future climate scenarios, including temperature increases, sea level rise, and extreme weather events. For example, the *European Space Agency* (ESA) uses satellite data combined with AI models to predict the effects of climate change in vulnerable regions, such as small island nations and coastal areas.

- **Carbon Emissions Tracking**: Satellite data, enhanced by AI algorithms, can be used to monitor greenhouse gas emissions from industrial facilities, agriculture, and transportation. These data are critical for measuring compliance with international climate agreements and for implementing effective mitigation strategies. In countries like China, GeoAI has been employed to track industrial emissions, providing valuable data to support carbon reduction efforts.

- **Disaster Risk Management**: GeoAI helps predict and mitigate the impacts of climate-induced disasters such as floods, hurricanes, and droughts. By analyzing environmental factors and historical data, AI models provide early warning systems and inform disaster preparedness strategies. For instance, *Google's AI* has been used to predict areas at risk of flooding, improving community preparedness and response.

15.6 GeoAI for Clean Water and Sanitation (SDG 6)

SDG 6 aims to ensure the availability and sustainable management of water and sanitation for all. With growing concerns over water scarcity, contamination, and the impacts of climate change, the need for effective water resource management is more critical than ever.

- **Water Quality Monitoring**: GeoAI models combine satellite data with in-situ sensor networks to monitor water quality in lakes, rivers, and oceans. AI algorithms identify pollutants, measure water temperature, and assess contamination levels, providing actionable insights for water treatment and management systems. For instance, AI-driven systems are used to monitor the water quality of the *Ganges River* in India, where real-time data helps manage pollution levels and inform policy decisions.

- **Water Stress Prediction**: AI models, when combined with satellite data, can predict water shortages in specific regions based on climate, population growth, and water consumption patterns. By assessing current and future water availability, GeoAI helps identify vulnerable areas and supports the development of sustainable water use strategies.

- **Flood and Drought Monitoring**: GeoAI supports **drought and flood prediction systems** by analyzing environmental variables such as precipitation patterns, river discharge, and soil moisture. This enables early warning systems to mitigate the impacts of these events and inform water resource planning.

15.7 GeoAI for Life Below Water (SDG 14)

SDG 14 focuses on conserving and sustainably using the oceans, seas, and marine resoures for sustainable development. With oceans playing a vital role in climate regulation, biodiversity, and the global economy, GeoAI is indispensable in tracking marine health, pollution, and biodiversity.

- **Marine Pollution Monitoring**: GeoAI integrates satellite imagery, sensor data, and oceanographic models to track marine pollution sources, including plastic debris, oil spills, and industrial discharges. For instance, in the Mediterranean Sea, AI-powered systems analyze satellite data to track oil spill movements and predict their impact on coastal ecosystems. This data aids emergency response teams in mitigating damage and improving recovery efforts.

- **Marine Biodiversity and Coral Reef Health**: Monitoring coral reefs, marine ecosystems, and fish populations is crucial for preserving marine biodiversity. Using high-resolution satellite imagery and AI-based image classification techniques, GeoAI models can detect changes in coral cover and other important habitat features. The *Great Barrier Reef* in Australia is an example where GeoAI has been applied to monitor coral bleaching and assess the overall health of the reef. Machine learning algorithms analyze satellite images to map coral reefs, tracking their degradation and helping scientists design restoration efforts.

- **Fisheries Management**: GeoAI can help monitor and regulate fisheries by detecting illegal, unreported, and unregulated fishing activities. Satellite data, combined with AI techniques, can analyze vessel movements, fishing patterns, and environmental factors to track fishing activities. This helps enforce regulations and ensures sustainable fish populations. For instance, AI models are used to monitor fisheries in the *Pacific Ocean*, identifying illegal fishing vessels operating in protected marine areas.

15.8 GeoAI for Sustainable Cities and Communities (SDG 11)

SDG 11 calls for the creation of inclusive, safe, resilient, and sustainable cities. As urbanization continues to rise, the pressure on infrastructure, resources, and ecosystems intensifies. GeoAI can significantly enhance urban planning, disaster management, and resource allocation to create sustainable urban environments.

- **Urban Growth and Land Use Planning**: GeoAI supports city planners by providing detailed, real-time analysis of urban sprawl, infrastructure development, and land use changes. Satellite data, combined with AI algorithms, tracks urban expansion, helping planners identify areas at risk of overdevelopment or environmental degradation. In cities like *Cape Town* and *Singapore*, GeoAI is used to optimize land use and plan infrastructure in alignment with sustainability goals.

- **Smart Cities**: The concept of **smart cities** leverages AI, IoT, and satellite data to enhance urban livability and resource efficiency. GeoAI systems monitor air quality, traffic patterns, and water usage, helping cities manage resources, reduce waste, and enhance quality of life for residents. For example, AI-powered platforms in *Barcelona* analyze real-time data to optimize traffic flows, reduce emissions, and improve public services.

- **Disaster Risk Reduction in Urban Areas**: GeoAI helps cities prepare for natural disasters, such as earthquakes, floods, and hurricanes. Using satellite data, machine learning models, and environmental monitoring systems, AI algorithms predict disaster-prone areas, assess risks, and support evacuation planning. In *Los Angeles*, AI-based systems analyze seismic data and provide real-time alerts about potential earthquakes, helping minimize damage and loss of life.

- **Affordable Housing and Social Inclusion**: GeoAI can also aid in identifying areas for affordable housing development by analyzing socio-economic data, land prices, and infrastructure availability. This promotes equitable urban development and addresses housing shortages in rapidly growing cities.

15.9 GeoAI for Decent Work and Economic Growth (SDG

8)

SDG 8 promotes inclusive and sustainable economic growth, employment, and decent work for all. GeoAI plays a significant role in advancing these goals by enabling data-driven decision-making that fosters job creation, industry development, and economic sustainability.

- **Agriculture and Rural Development**: GeoAI supports the agricultural sector by enhancing productivity and promoting sustainable farming practices, which in turn support rural economic development. Precision agriculture, aided by GeoAI, improves crop yields, reduces costs, and minimizes environmental impact. For example, AI models optimize the use of fertilizers and pesticides, boosting crop productivity while reducing harmful environmental effects.

- **Disaster Recovery and Economic Resilience**: GeoAI helps in assessing the economic impact of natural disasters and developing recovery strategies. By processing satellite data, AI models evaluate damage to infrastructure, agricultural lands, and industrial sectors. This data informs recovery efforts, providing governments and organizations with the necessary insights to restore economic stability. After Hurricane Maria in Puerto Rico, AI algorithms were used to assess the damage to infrastructure, helping in the efficient distribution of relief resources.

- **Optimizing Transportation and Supply Chains**: GeoAI optimizes supply chain management by improving transportation routes, reducing energy consumption, and minimizing emissions. In countries with rapidly developing economies, efficient supply chain management is critical for fostering economic growth. For instance, GeoAI tools are employed in *China* to track container shipping routes, helping businesses reduce costs and environmental impact.

15.10 GeoAI for Reduced Inequality (SDG 10)

SDG 10 seeks to reduce inequalities within and among countries. By enabling data-driven decision-making, GeoAI can help identify inequality patterns, promote social inclusion, and support the fair distribution of resources.

- **Mapping Socioeconomic Inequality**: GeoAI can identify regions suffering from social, economic, and infrastructure inequality by analyzing spatial data such as access to healthcare, education, and clean water. By combining demographic and satellite data, GeoAI can map areas of poverty and social exclusion, providing insights to guide targeted interventions.

- **Healthcare Access**: AI models that analyze geospatial data can also help improve access to healthcare in underserved areas. By mapping healthcare facilities and identifying underserved populations, GeoAI enables more equitable distribution of medical resources. During the COVID-19 pandemic, GeoAI was used in several countries to track the spread of the virus, ensuring that healthcare resources were distributed equitably.

- **Inclusive Education**: GeoAI can identify areas where access to education is limited due to geographical, economic, or infrastructural barriers. By integrating data from satellites, sensors, and local surveys, AI models pinpoint regions where educational infrastructure development is needed. This supports equitable access to education for marginalized communities.

15.11 Challenges and Future Directions

While GeoAI presents vast opportunities for advancing the SDGs, there are several challenges that must be addressed to fully harness its potential. These include issues related to data privacy, model bias, and accessibility.

- **Data Privacy and Ethics**: The use of satellite data, sensor data, and personal information can raise concerns about privacy and surveillance. Ensuring that GeoAI applications comply with data privacy laws and ethical standards is critical.

- **Bias in AI Models**: AI models are only as good as the data they are trained on. Inaccurate, incomplete, or biased data can lead to inaccurate predictions, which may harm marginalized communities. Addressing this challenge involves ensuring the diversity and inclusivity of training data and building transparent, interpretable AI systems.

- **Access to Technology**: In many parts of the world, access to satellite data, advanced computing infrastructure, and AI expertise is limited. As GeoAI becomes more central to achieving the SDGs, ensuring equitable access to these technologies is essential to prevent widening inequalities.

15.12 Conclusion and Path Forward

GeoAI is a transformative tool that can significantly contribute to the achievement of the United Nations' Sustainable Development Goals. By harnessing satellite data, AI, and machine learning, GeoAI enhances our ability to monitor environmental changes, predict future trends, and optimize resource use. As we move forward, continued advancements in GeoAI technology, improved data accessibility, and collaboration across nations and industries will be crucial to achieving a sustainable and equitable future for all.

In the coming years, as more countries adopt GeoAI applications, we can expect to see greater integration of this technology into policymaking, disaster management, environmental conservation, and socioeconomic development. However, it is important that this progress is achieved responsibly, ensuring that the benefits of GeoAI are shared equitably and that the technology is used to promote human well-being and environmental health.

Chapter 16: GeoAI for Carbon Emissions Tracking and Reduction

16.1 Introduction

The impact of carbon emissions on the global climate is one of the most pressing issues of our time. As governments and industries work toward meeting international climate goals, such as the Paris Agreement's target to limit global warming to well below 2°C, it has become increasingly clear that accurate, real-time monitoring of carbon emissions is essential. GeoAI, which integrates geographic information systems (GIS), remote sensing, and artificial intelligence (AI), plays a vital role in this effort by enabling the tracking and reduction of carbon emissions.

GeoAI models leverage a wide range of satellite data, ground-based sensors, and sophisticated machine learning techniques to identify emission sources, quantify their impact, and predict future trends. This chapter will explore how GeoAI is used for carbon emissions tracking, pollution source identification, and carbon sequestration assessments, as well as how it informs policy decisions and strategies for reducing carbon footprints. By examining the integration of AI with remote sensing, this chapter highlights the critical role of technology in achieving global sustainability goals.

16.2 Monitoring Carbon Emissions with GeoAI

16.2.1 Sources of Carbon Emissions

Carbon emissions primarily result from human activities such as the burning of fossil fuels, deforestation, agriculture, and industrial processes. Among these, the largest sources include:

- **Fossil Fuel Combustion**: Power generation, transportation, and industrial activities are major contributors.

- **Agriculture**: Methane emissions from livestock and rice paddies, as well as nitrous oxide from fertilizers, are significant.

- **Deforestation**: Land-use change that reduces the ability of ecosystems to absorb carbon dioxide.

GeoAI can enhance the identification and monitoring of these sources, providing highly accurate, spatially explicit data. Traditional methods of emissions tracking, such as ground-based measurements and emissions inventories, often lack the spatial resolution or global coverage required for comprehensive monitoring. By incorporating satellite imagery and AI-based data processing techniques, GeoAI offers a more dynamic and real-time solution to tracking emissions.

16.2.2 Integration of Satellite Data

GeoAI relies heavily on satellite data for monitoring atmospheric carbon concentrations. Satellites like **Sentinel-5P** and **OCO-2** (Orbiting Carbon Observatory-2) provide critical data on carbon dioxide, methane, and aerosols. These satellites carry sensors that measure concentrations of gases in the atmosphere, offering insights into the geographical distribution of carbon emissions at both global and regional scales.

AI-powered models use these satellite observations to track emissions over time, even in remote or politically challenging areas. For example, **Sentinel-5P**, which is part of the European Space Agency's Copernicus program, provides highly accurate carbon dioxide measurements, detecting emission sources such as power plants, deforestation zones, and urban centers.

Case Study: Researchers at NASA and the California Institute of Technology have used OCO-2 satellite data, combined with machine learning techniques, to map global carbon dioxide concentrations. By focusing on regions like the industrial Midwest of the United States, the AI algorithms can pinpoint large-scale emission hotspots, helping policymakers target reduction efforts.

16.2.3 Ground-Based Sensors and GeoAI

While satellites provide a broad view of carbon emissions, ground-based sensors add crucial data points, particularly in urban areas or regions with frequent emissions events. These sensors measure real-time air quality and trace gas levels, allowing for finer resolution data.

GeoAI models can integrate satellite data with ground sensor networks to improve the accuracy and granularity of emissions estimates. In urban environments, this integration is particularly valuable for monitoring local air quality and quantifying emissions from vehicular traffic, power plants, and other sources.

Example: The **Air Quality Index (AQI)** monitoring system in cities like New York uses both ground-based sensors and satellite data. AI-based algorithms analyze data from thousands of sensors, detecting pollution patterns and providing early warnings for residents and policymakers.

16.2.4 Temporal and Spatial Analysis

One of the strengths of GeoAI is its ability to analyze both temporal and spatial patterns of carbon emissions. Through satellite imagery and AI, it is possible to detect fluctuations in emissions over time—whether due to seasonal changes, economic activities, or specific events (e.g., holidays or industrial accidents). This capability enables governments to monitor emissions dynamically, making it easier to enforce policies that target emission reductions during specific periods.

AI models also provide insight into the geographic distribution of emissions. Using clustering algorithms, GeoAI can identify pollution hotspots across large regions, linking emissions to specific activities or locations.

Case Study: During the COVID-19 lockdowns, a study led by the European Space Agency (ESA) used satellite imagery to track reductions in emissions across Europe. The AI analysis revealed significant drops in nitrogen dioxide (NO2) levels, especially in urban centers, which was attributed to reduced transportation activities.

16.3 Tracking Pollution Sources with GeoAI

16.3.1 Identifying Major Polluters

Identifying the sources of carbon emissions is key to addressing the root causes of climate change. AI models help pinpoint industrial, agricultural, and residential sources of emissions, which are then monitored through remote sensing data and ground sensors.

In many developing countries, emissions data is limited, and GeoAI helps fill this gap by leveraging freely available satellite imagery combined with machine learning to identify major pollution sources. The use of AI to automatically classify emission types and their locations reduces the need for costly and time-consuming field data collection.

Example: Researchers in India have used GeoAI to track industrial emissions in highly polluted regions like the Indo-Gangetic Plain. By analyzing satellite imagery and pollution data from sensors, they identified key polluting sectors, such as brick kilns and biomass burning, which were contributing significantly to carbon emissions.

16.3.2 GeoAI for Power Plants and Industrial Sites

Power plants, cement factories, and refineries are among the largest industrial sources of carbon emissions. Traditional methods of tracking emissions from these sites are labor-intensive and often unreliable. GeoAI improves emissions monitoring by utilizing satellite thermal data, which can indicate the temperature of smoke stacks or cooling towers, signaling emissions levels.

Example: In the United States, GeoAI models analyze thermal infrared data from satellites to track emissions from power plants and industrial operations. The AI algorithms can estimate the intensity of emissions and identify facilities that are not complying with environmental standards.

16.3.3 Emissions from Agriculture and Deforestation

Agriculture and land-use change are significant contributors to global carbon emissions. Deforestation, particularly in the Amazon, releases vast amounts of carbon dioxide stored in trees, while agricultural practices like rice cultivation emit methane.

GeoAI can track deforestation in real time by analyzing satellite imagery. By monitoring forest cover changes, AI models can calculate how much carbon is being released due to land-use changes. Additionally, AI models can be used to monitor crop emissions by analyzing soil health, water use, and crop types.

Example: In the Amazon rainforest, AI models are used to track illegal logging activities that lead to deforestation. These models use high-resolution satellite imagery to detect changes in forest cover and predict future trends. This information helps NGOs and governmental agencies target enforcement efforts to curb emissions from illegal logging.

16.4 Assessing Carbon Sequestration with GeoAI

16.4.1 Monitoring Forest Carbon Stocks

The Earth's forests play a critical role in sequestering carbon. Through photosynthesis, forests absorb CO_2 from the atmosphere and store it in trees and soil. However, deforestation and forest degradation significantly reduce the carbon sequestration potential of these ecosystems.

GeoAI models help monitor forest carbon stocks by using satellite data to estimate tree biomass, forest density, and health. AI algorithms can be used to predict future carbon stocks, helping to inform forest management decisions.

Example: In Africa, GeoAI systems are used to monitor the carbon storage potential of the Congo Basin's tropical forests. These systems help estimate the amount of carbon stored in the region, providing insights into how deforestation or conservation efforts impact carbon sequestration.

16.4.2 Wetlands, Peatlands, and Other Carbon-Rich Ecosystems

Wetlands and peatlands are among the most efficient carbon sinks on the planet, yet they are often under threat due to agricultural expansion, mining, and drainage. GeoAI tools are used to monitor changes in these ecosystems, assess carbon sequestration rates, and predict the effects of land use change on their carbon storage capacity.

AI-powered monitoring of wetlands and peatlands can detect environmental changes such as drying or land conversion, which can lead to the release of large amounts of stored carbon.

Example: In Southeast Asia, AI-based satellite systems are used to track peatland degradation, which is a significant source of CO_2 emissions. These systems are used to guide conservation efforts and limit land drainage that leads to carbon emissions.

16.4.3 Soil Carbon Dynamics

Soils act as a major reservoir for carbon, but agricultural practices, land degradation, and deforestation can alter the balance, releasing stored carbon into the atmosphere. GeoAI models can be used to monitor soil health and assess the effects of different land management practices on soil carbon storage.

Example: In the United States, AI-based models are used to assess soil carbon content across various agricultural lands. These models analyze satellite data to estimate soil organic matter and provide recommendations for sustainable agricultural practices that enhance carbon sequestration.

16.5 GeoAI for Informing Climate Policies

16.5.2 Policy Development and Carbon Markets

GeoAI provides critical insights that enable governments and organizations to develop policies targeting carbon reduction. One of the key areas where GeoAI supports policy-making is in the development and monitoring of carbon markets. Carbon markets allow countries, corporations, and industries to trade carbon credits, which represent a ton of CO_2 removed from the atmosphere or prevented from being emitted.

GeoAI facilitates the accurate measurement, reporting, and verification (MRV) of emissions reductions, which are essential for ensuring the integrity of carbon trading systems. By automating emissions tracking through satellite data and AI algorithms, GeoAI helps create a transparent and trustworthy foundation for carbon markets.

Example: The European Union Emissions Trading System (EU ETS) incorporates GeoAI technologies to monitor emissions from industrial facilities. These technologies ensure compliance with emissions caps and detect fraudulent reporting, bolstering confidence in the carbon market.

16.5.3 International Collaboration and Climate Agreements

Global climate agreements, such as the Paris Agreement, require member countries to report their greenhouse gas emissions and progress toward reduction targets. GeoAI systems enable standardized and verifiable reporting, fostering transparency and collaboration between nations.

AI models that integrate emissions data from satellites, ground sensors, and inventories provide actionable insights that can be shared with international climate bodies. By offering consistent and reliable data, GeoAI enhances trust among stakeholders and encourages joint action.

Case Study: The Climate TRACE coalition, which uses AI and satellite imagery to track emissions from power plants, industrial facilities, and transportation, provides global emissions data to support the United Nations Framework Convention on Climate Change (UNFCCC). This initiative demonstrates how GeoAI contributes to achieving global climate goals.

16.6 Challenges in GeoAI for Carbon Emissions Tracking

16.6.1 Data Quality and Accessibility

While GeoAI relies on vast amounts of data from satellites and ground-based sensors, ensuring the accuracy, consistency, and accessibility of this data remains a challenge. Factors such as cloud cover, sensor limitations, and data gaps can impact the reliability of emissions estimates.

Moreover, some regions, particularly in the Global South, may lack the infrastructure to collect and share emissions data. Addressing these disparities requires international support and investment in data-sharing platforms.

16.6.2 Computational and Algorithmic Limitations

Processing the massive datasets required for GeoAI applications demands significant computational resources. Advanced AI algorithms, such as deep learning models, are resource-intensive and may face scalability issues when applied to global emissions tracking.

Additionally, biases in AI algorithms, such as underestimating emissions from smaller sources, can lead to inaccurate results. Continuous refinement of models and the incorporation of diverse datasets are necessary to address these limitations.

16.6.3 Political and Economic Barriers

Implementing GeoAI solutions often requires cooperation between governments, industries, and other stakeholders. Political resistance to emissions reduction policies, economic pressures, and competing priorities can hinder the adoption of GeoAI technologies.

For example, countries with economies heavily reliant on fossil fuels may be reluctant to embrace GeoAI solutions that highlight the environmental impact of these industries.

16.7 Future Directions in GeoAI for Carbon Emissions Reduction

16.7.1 Advancements in Remote Sensing Technology

The next generation of Earth observation satellites, equipped with more advanced sensors and AI capabilities, will provide even higher-resolution data for emissions tracking. Innovations such as hyperspectral imaging and active sensing techniques (e.g., LiDAR) will enhance the detection and monitoring of carbon emissions.

16.7.2 Integration with Emerging Technologies

GeoAI is increasingly being integrated with other emerging technologies, such as blockchain and the Internet of Things (IoT). Blockchain can provide a secure and transparent system for carbon credit trading, while IoT devices, such as smart meters and environmental sensors, can supply real-time data to GeoAI models.

Example: IoT-enabled smart cities can use GeoAI to monitor urban emissions in real time, optimizing traffic management and energy use to reduce carbon footprints.

16.7.3 Community and Citizen Science Engagement

Engaging communities and citizen scientists in carbon emissions tracking can help bridge data gaps and raise public awareness. Mobile applications and open data platforms powered by GeoAI can empower individuals to contribute to monitoring efforts and support local climate action.

Example: The GLOBE Observer app, developed by NASA, allows citizens to upload observations of clouds, land cover, and other environmental factors. These contributions complement GeoAI models and enhance their accuracy.

16.7.4 Scaling GeoAI Solutions Globally

To maximize the impact of GeoAI on carbon emissions reduction, efforts must focus on scaling solutions to reach underserved regions. Partnerships between international organizations, governments, and the private sector can help provide the necessary funding and technical support.

Case Study: The SERVIR initiative, a collaboration between NASA and the United States Agency for International Development (USAID), integrates GeoAI tools to address environmental challenges in developing countries. This program demonstrates how global partnerships can advance GeoAI adoption.

16.8 Conclusion

GeoAI is revolutionizing the way we track and reduce carbon emissions, offering unprecedented accuracy, scalability, and actionable insights. From identifying pollution hotspots to assessing carbon sequestration potential, GeoAI provides a comprehensive toolkit for addressing climate change. By integrating satellite data, AI algorithms, and ground-based sensors, GeoAI enables more effective policy-making, enhances transparency in international climate agreements, and supports innovative approaches to emissions reduction.

However, challenges such as data accessibility, computational limitations, and political barriers must be addressed to fully realize the potential of GeoAI. As technology continues to advance and global collaboration strengthens, GeoAI is poised to play a central role in achieving a sustainable, low-carbon future.

Future research and development in GeoAI should prioritize scalability, equity, and the integration of emerging technologies to ensure that these tools are accessible and impactful worldwide. By leveraging the power of GeoAI, humanity can take significant strides toward mitigating the impacts of climate change and achieving global sustainability goals.

Chapter 17: GeoAI for Forest Monitoring and Conservation

17.1 Introduction to Forest Monitoring and Conservation

17.1.1 Importance of Forests in the Global Ecosystem

Forests are integral to maintaining the balance of Earth's ecosystems, playing a crucial role in regulating the climate, preserving biodiversity, and providing resources for human livelihoods. They cover about 31% of the Earth's land area and are home to over 80% of terrestrial species. Forests absorb carbon dioxide, acting as a significant carbon sink, mitigating climate change. Additionally, forests provide vital ecosystem services such as water regulation, soil stabilization, and nutrient cycling.

However, forests face numerous threats due to human activity, including deforestation, illegal logging, and land-use changes. Deforestation contributes significantly to the global carbon emissions, exacerbating climate change. As global forest loss continues, understanding how to monitor, conserve, and restore forests becomes more critical for planetary health.

17.1.2 Overview of GeoAI in Forest Monitoring

GeoAI, the integration of geospatial data with artificial intelligence (AI), represents a transformative tool in monitoring forest ecosystems. By leveraging vast amounts of data from satellites, drones, sensors, and other remote sensing technologies, GeoAI helps track deforestation, monitor forest health, assess biodiversity, and support reforestation efforts. AI algorithms such as machine learning, deep learning, and neural networks allow researchers to process and analyze large datasets efficiently, often in real-time, to detect changes in forest cover, health, and biodiversity.

GeoAI aids in automating tasks that were previously time-consuming or manual, such as mapping forest areas, identifying species, and predicting environmental changes. Moreover, GeoAI helps bridge the gap between data collection and actionable insights, enabling policymakers, conservationists, and local communities to make informed decisions about forest management.

17.2 Remote Sensing for Forest Monitoring

17.2.1 Evolution of Remote Sensing in Forest Monitoring

The field of forest monitoring has evolved dramatically since the advent of remote sensing technologies. Early forest studies relied on aerial photographs, but advances in satellite technology have enabled global-scale forest monitoring. Spaceborne sensors such as the Landsat satellites, launched in the early 1970s, provided the first systematic global observations of Earth's surface. More recently, Sentinel-1 and Sentinel-2 satellites have provided high-resolution imagery that enhances the ability to detect and monitor forests in even remote and cloud-covered areas.

Today, remote sensing data provides invaluable insights into forest dynamics, from detecting deforestation to assessing vegetation health and biodiversity. These data allow scientists to track forest change over time, identify areas of concern, and monitor the effectiveness of conservation measures.

17.2.2 Types of Remote Sensing Data for Forest Monitoring

- **Multispectral and Hyperspectral Imaging**

Multispectral and hyperspectral imaging are key to monitoring forests. These imaging systems capture data across various wavelengths, from visible light to infrared, allowing researchers to identify forest cover, classify vegetation types, and detect environmental stress. The Normalized Difference Vegetation Index (NDVI) is one of the most commonly used vegetation indices derived from satellite imagery, providing a proxy for plant health by measuring the difference between near-infrared and red light reflectance.

● **Synthetic Aperture Radar (SAR)**

SAR technology uses radar to capture detailed information about forest structure, especially in cloudy regions or dense forests where optical imagery might be limited. SAR sensors can measure forest biomass, detect tree height, and identify disturbances such as logging or forest fires. Sentinel-1, for example, uses SAR to provide regular, high-resolution radar images, enabling real-time monitoring of forests, even in areas with persistent cloud cover.

17.2.3 Challenges in Remote Sensing for Forest Monitoring

While remote sensing offers unparalleled opportunities for forest monitoring, several challenges persist:

● **Data Resolution**: High-resolution data are often required to detect small-scale forest disturbances, but this data can be expensive or difficult to obtain.

● **Cloud Cover**: Optical sensors often struggle to penetrate cloud cover, limiting their effectiveness in tropical or rainy regions. Radar-based systems such as SAR help address this issue but come with their own set of limitations.

● **Data Volume and Processing**: The vast amounts of data generated by modern satellites can overwhelm traditional data processing systems. AI-based algorithms, however, are helping automate and speed up the analysis, making it easier to extract meaningful insights from large datasets.

17.3 Forest Cover Mapping with GeoAI

17.3.1 Automated Forest Cover Mapping Techniques

The use of GeoAI in forest cover mapping has been revolutionary, offering more accurate and efficient ways to map forests on a global scale. Traditional methods, which often involved labor-intensive manual mapping, have been supplemented and, in many cases, replaced by AI-driven approaches.

- **Supervised and Unsupervised Learning Approaches**

Supervised learning involves training AI models using labeled datasets to classify forest types, vegetation health, or land cover. Unsupervised learning, on the other hand, identifies patterns or clusters in the data without predefined labels. These methods can analyze large, complex datasets from satellite imagery and produce high-accuracy maps of forest cover, enabling timely responses to deforestation threats.

- **Convolutional Neural Networks (CNNs)**

CNNs, a class of deep learning algorithms, have been particularly successful in automating image classification tasks. CNNs can learn hierarchical features from satellite images, making them ideal for detecting fine-grained patterns such as individual trees, forest types, or small-scale deforestation. Their ability to analyze both spatial and spectral data makes them suitable for complex forest mapping challenges.

17.3.2 Detecting Forest Loss and Degradation

GeoAI is increasingly being used to detect forest loss and degradation, helping to identify deforestation hotspots in near real-time. By analyzing satellite data over time, AI models can track changes in forest cover and pinpoint areas where deforestation is occurring. These models are also capable of detecting illegal logging activities and the impacts of natural disasters such as wildfires.

- **Global Forest Watch (GFW)**

One of the most prominent initiatives in forest monitoring is Global Forest Watch, a platform that uses satellite data to provide real-time information on deforestation. GFW uses AI-driven algorithms to process satellite imagery from sources like Landsat and MODIS, delivering insights on global forest changes to policymakers, NGOs, and local communities. The platform has helped raise awareness about deforestation in critical regions such as the Amazon and Southeast Asia.

17.3.3 Case Studies in Forest Cover Mapping

- **Amazon Rainforest:**

The Amazon rainforest, often referred to as the "lungs of the Earth," has experienced significant deforestation over the past few decades. GeoAI has been instrumental in monitoring this deforestation, with satellite data being used to track the extent of forest loss and identify causes such as agricultural expansion and illegal logging.

- **Southeast Asia:**

In Southeast Asia, GeoAI is being used to monitor deforestation caused by palm oil plantations and other agricultural practices. AI models can distinguish between natural forests and human-modified landscapes, offering insights into how specific land-use practices contribute to deforestation.

17.4 Monitoring Forest Health with GeoAI

17.4.1 Assessing Forest Health Indicators

Forest health is a critical component of global biodiversity and climate regulation. GeoAI can help monitor forest health by analyzing indicators such as vegetation cover, canopy density, and tree vitality. By using remote sensing data, AI algorithms can detect subtle changes in vegetation health that might not be immediately visible to the naked eye.

- **Vegetation Indices**

  NDVI and Enhanced Vegetation Index (EVI) are two key indices used to assess forest health. These indices help identify stressors such as drought, disease, or pests that might be affecting the forest. Healthy vegetation reflects more infrared light, while stressed vegetation reflects more red light, making it distinguishable in satellite images.

17.4.2 AI Models for Predicting Forest Health Trends

Machine learning models, including decision trees, random forests, and deep learning networks, are increasingly being used to predict forest health trends. By analyzing historical data and environmental factors, AI can forecast potential threats to forest ecosystems, such as pest outbreaks, wildfires, and disease spread.

- **Wildfire Prediction**

  AI models are being used to predict wildfire risk by analyzing weather data, historical fire patterns, and vegetation conditions. These models can predict areas most vulnerable to fire, enabling early interventions to protect forests and reduce damage.

17.4.3 Case Studies in Forest Health Monitoring

- **Bark Beetle Infestation in North America:**

In North America, the spread of bark beetles has led to significant tree mortality, especially in pine forests. GeoAI models are being used to monitor these infestations by analyzing satellite imagery and identifying areas where trees are being attacked. The data helps forest managers target pest control efforts more efficiently.

- **Forest Dieback in Europe:**

In parts of Europe, forest dieback has been linked to climate change and pollution. AI-driven analysis of forest health has enabled scientists to track changes in tree canopy density, which is a key indicator of overall forest health. By identifying affected areas early, conservationists can implement measures to mitigate the effects.

17.5 Reforestation and Afforestation Efforts

17.5.1 Planning Reforestation Projects with GeoAI

GeoAI is playing a crucial role in planning and executing reforestation and afforestation projects by analyzing a variety of environmental data to identify the best areas for new forest growth. Traditional methods of selecting reforestation sites often involved a limited set of environmental factors and were slow, making it difficult to prioritize areas of critical importance. However, GeoAI can integrate a broader spectrum of data — from climate conditions to soil health to topography — to provide actionable insights for planting efforts.

AI-driven models process large datasets, such as remote sensing images, climate projections, and historical land-use patterns, to predict how different forest species will thrive in specific locations. These models can also suggest strategies to maximize biodiversity and resilience by recommending diverse species mixes for reforestation efforts, helping to restore ecosystem functions and ensure long-term sustainability.

- **Satellite Data Integration**

Satellite imagery is frequently used to map out areas of land that are suitable for afforestation or reforestation. The integration of satellite data with AI-based models allows for real-time tracking of land conditions, such as soil moisture, temperature, and vegetation cover, which are vital factors in deciding where to plant. Remote sensing technologies, including multispectral and hyperspectral sensors, are capable of detecting different types of vegetation and soil properties, which can assist in site selection.

- **Climate and Environmental Compatibility**

AI models can process climate models to predict future environmental conditions. This helps foresters plan for long-term changes, such as temperature shifts and precipitation patterns, that could affect the success of forest restoration projects. By using machine learning techniques, AI can identify areas that are likely to remain stable or improve under future climate scenarios, thus helping make reforestation efforts more resilient to climate change.

17.5.2 AI Models for Monitoring Reforestation Progress

Once reforestation projects are underway, GeoAI models can be used to monitor the progress and health of newly planted forests. AI algorithms can detect changes in vegetation growth, canopy cover, and forest density over time. These models can compare current forest conditions with historical data to assess whether the restoration efforts are successful and if the trees are thriving as expected.

- **Monitoring Growth Patterns with Machine Learning**

Machine learning algorithms, particularly those based on supervised learning, are used to track forest growth patterns. By training AI models on satellite data, these systems can automatically detect changes in the canopy, allowing forest managers to identify areas where trees may not be growing as expected. This enables early intervention to address issues like drought stress, pest infestations, or soil degradation that may impede tree growth.

● Detecting Changes in Forest Health

In addition to tracking growth, AI models can also assess forest health by measuring indicators such as chlorophyll content, tree vitality, and vegetation indices like NDVI. These metrics help detect early signs of stress in newly planted forests, such as poor soil conditions or inadequate water availability. AI models can also identify disturbances like illegal logging, wildfires, or pest outbreaks that might threaten reforestation progress.

17.5.3 Case Studies in Reforestation

● China's Green Wall Project

China's "Great Green Wall" initiative is one of the largest reforestation efforts in the world, aiming to combat desertification and restore degraded land. GeoAI has been a critical tool in monitoring the project's progress by providing high-resolution satellite imagery to track forest cover and vegetation growth. The AI-driven analysis of remote sensing data has enabled more effective monitoring of the area's health, identifying regions that require additional planting or intervention.

● India's Green India Mission

India's Green India Mission seeks to increase forest cover, restore degraded ecosystems, and enhance carbon sequestration efforts. By integrating GeoAI tools, such as machine learning algorithms for land cover classification and vegetation health monitoring, the program has made significant strides in identifying suitable land for reforestation. AI models are used to track the condition of the newly planted areas, ensuring the sustainability of the restoration efforts.

17.6 Integrating GeoAI with Forest Conservation Policy and Management

17.6.1 AI's Role in Conservation Decision-Making

The integration of GeoAI into forest conservation efforts provides governments, conservationists, and other stakeholders with actionable data to make informed decisions about forest management. By tracking real-time forest conditions and identifying threats such as illegal logging, poaching, or habitat fragmentation, AI-driven systems can inform policy interventions and on-the-ground actions. This data-centric approach allows for evidence-based policy creation that aligns with the global agenda for sustainable forest management.

- **Supporting Policy Development with Data Insights**

AI models can provide data-driven insights for policy development by identifying trends in deforestation, forest degradation, and land-use changes. This helps policymakers allocate resources effectively and enforce laws that protect valuable ecosystems. GeoAI can also help predict the long-term impacts of policies, such as the effect of land-use regulations or conservation efforts on forest health.

- **Assessing Ecosystem Services and Trade-offs**

AI is increasingly used to assess the trade-offs between various land management strategies, such as forest conservation and agricultural expansion. By modeling ecosystem services, including carbon sequestration, biodiversity preservation, and water regulation, GeoAI helps determine the best course of action for balancing conservation and economic development. AI-driven simulations enable policymakers to forecast outcomes of different interventions and select the most sustainable approaches.

17.6.2 Case Studies in GeoAI for Policy Development

• Brazil's Amazon Monitoring Initiative

Brazil has long struggled with illegal deforestation in the Amazon rainforest. GeoAI is being used in initiatives to monitor forest loss in near real-time. AI models analyze satellite imagery from Landsat and other sources to detect deforestation hotspots, enabling the Brazilian government to take swift action against illegal activities. Additionally, these tools are integrated into policymaking, where AI insights contribute to law enforcement and conservation policy decisions.

• African Forest Conservation

In Africa, countries like the Democratic Republic of Congo and Gabon are using GeoAI to protect vital tropical forests. By combining satellite data, AI algorithms, and on-the-ground reports, these countries are developing more effective conservation strategies. AI tools are used to identify areas of high biodiversity that require immediate protection, as well as to monitor human activities such as logging and mining that threaten forest health.

17.7 Future Directions and Challenges in GeoAI for Forest Conservation

17.7.1 Challenges in Scaling Up GeoAI for Forest Monitoring

While GeoAI has shown significant promise in forest monitoring and conservation, there are still challenges to scaling up its use on a global level. The most notable challenge is the cost of acquiring high-resolution satellite data, which can be prohibitive for low-resource countries or small-scale conservation organizations. Additionally, data quality and consistency vary across different regions, making it difficult to implement uniform AI models everywhere.

- **Access to Data and Collaboration**

To overcome data access issues, collaboration between governments, private organizations, and international agencies is essential. Open-source platforms and data-sharing agreements can help provide broader access to the remote sensing data required for AI-based analysis.

- **Improving AI Model Accuracy and Adaptability**

GeoAI models need to be continuously improved to ensure their accuracy and adaptability across various forest ecosystems. This requires ongoing research into AI techniques that can handle the complex dynamics of forest ecosystems, as well as developing new methods for validating the results of AI models in diverse environments.

17.7.2 Looking Ahead: The Role of GeoAI in Global Forest Restoration Goals

Looking to the future, GeoAI is expected to play an increasingly important role in global forest restoration and conservation efforts. As the world faces climate change and biodiversity loss, the need for advanced monitoring and management systems will only grow. GeoAI offers the potential for real-time tracking of forest health, automated detection of threats, and better decision-making in conservation policy.

Future research could focus on integrating more sophisticated AI techniques, such as reinforcement learning, into forest monitoring systems to improve predictive capabilities and automate interventions. Furthermore, the combination of GeoAI with emerging technologies like blockchain could provide enhanced transparency in forest conservation efforts, ensuring that the benefits of restoration are equitably distributed.

17.8 Conclusion

GeoAI is revolutionizing forest monitoring and conservation by providing new tools to track deforestation, assess forest health, and support restoration efforts. Through the integration of satellite imagery, machine learning models, and real-time data analytics, GeoAI has the potential to transform how we manage and conserve the world's forests.

As global pressures on forests continue to rise, GeoAI's role will become increasingly crucial in supporting sustainable forest management, addressing biodiversity loss, and contributing to climate change mitigation. By improving data accessibility, enhancing model accuracy, and fostering international collaboration, GeoAI can continue to play a vital role in forest conservation and the achievement of global sustainability goals.

Chapter 18: The Role of GeoAI in Habitat and Ecosystem Restoration

---

Introduction

Ecosystem restoration has become a cornerstone of global environmental efforts, as humanity faces the dual threats of biodiversity loss and climate change. The restoration of ecosystems aims not only to heal the planet's damaged natural resources but also to restore the critical services that ecosystems provide. These services include clean air, water, climate regulation, and food production, all essential for life on Earth. However, ecosystem restoration is an intricate and challenging process that requires innovative tools to monitor, model, and evaluate restoration efforts effectively. This is where GeoAI, a combination of geospatial data and artificial intelligence (AI), has proven to be transformative.

GeoAI merges vast amounts of remote sensing data, geographic information systems (GIS), and machine learning techniques to analyze, predict, and optimize ecosystem restoration processes. The potential of GeoAI to provide real-time, data-driven insights into habitat recovery is revolutionizing how we restore ecosystems such as forests, wetlands, grasslands, and coastal areas. This chapter explores the critical role of GeoAI in habitat and ecosystem restoration, examining its applications in monitoring soil health, forest restoration, wetland rehabilitation, and the development of predictive models that support informed restoration strategies.

18.1 Understanding Ecosystem Restoration

What is Ecosystem Restoration?

Ecosystem restoration refers to the process of reversing damage to ecosystems by reestablishing their structure, function, and diversity. The primary goals of ecosystem restoration are to restore biodiversity, enhance the quality of ecosystem services, and promote resilience against environmental stressors such as climate change. This can be achieved through interventions such as reforestation, wetland restoration, soil remediation, and the rehabilitation of degraded lands.

There are several types of ecosystems that are targeted for restoration, including:

- **Forests:** Forest ecosystems are critical for carbon sequestration, biodiversity, and the regulation of the water cycle. Restoration efforts focus on reforestation, combating deforestation, and preventing forest degradation.

- **Wetlands:** Wetlands play an essential role in water purification, flood control, and carbon storage. Restoration aims to restore hydrological functions and improve biodiversity.

- **Grasslands and Savannas:** Restoration here focuses on combating desertification, improving soil health, and supporting native plant and animal species.

- **Coastal and Marine Ecosystems:** Coastal ecosystems, such as mangroves and coral reefs, are restored to mitigate coastal erosion, protect biodiversity, and sequester carbon.

Challenges in Ecosystem Restoration

Restoring ecosystems is not without challenges. These include:

- **Data Scarcity:** Reliable data on degraded ecosystems is often limited, making it difficult to identify priorities for restoration.

- **Complexity of Ecosystem Dynamics:** Ecosystems are intricate and respond to multiple variables, making them difficult to restore with precision.

- **Financial and Political Barriers:** Large-scale restoration projects require substantial funding and political will, which can be a barrier in regions with competing development goals.

18.2 The Role of GeoAI in Ecosystem Restoration

Introduction to GeoAI

GeoAI combines spatial data derived from remote sensing technologies (such as satellites, drones, and sensors) with machine learning algorithms to enable informed decision-making and predictive modeling. This convergence allows for large-scale environmental monitoring, providing real-time data that can drive ecosystem restoration strategies. GeoAI is valuable because it can:

- Process vast amounts of spatial data from diverse sources.

- Detect and analyze environmental changes over time.

- Predict restoration outcomes, such as changes in vegetation, soil health, and biodiversity.

GeoAI systems work by integrating geospatial data with machine learning algorithms. For example, satellite imagery can reveal changes in vegetation cover, while AI can identify trends or patterns indicative of ecosystem health. This enables scientists, conservationists, and policymakers to evaluate restoration efforts, predict future changes, and adjust strategies accordingly.

How GeoAI Supports Restoration

GeoAI supports restoration by providing:

- **Real-Time Monitoring:** The integration of satellite imagery, drone data, and ground sensors allows for continuous monitoring of ecosystems, enabling prompt identification of degradation or recovery.

- **Predictive Analytics:** AI-driven models can predict the likely success of restoration efforts by analyzing historical data and projecting future trends, helping prioritize interventions.

- **Optimization of Restoration Interventions:** GeoAI helps to identify the most effective areas for intervention, ensuring that limited resources are allocated to regions with the highest potential for success.

18.3 Predictive Modeling in Ecosystem Restoration

Predictive Modeling Overview

Predictive modeling involves using data to forecast future conditions. In the context of ecosystem restoration, predictive models are used to simulate the potential impacts of restoration efforts and forecast the health and stability of ecosystems over time. These models use a variety of inputs, including environmental variables such as soil type, climate, vegetation cover, and species data.

GeoAI for Restoration Decision-Making

AI plays a pivotal role in restoration decision-making by generating actionable insights based on predictive models. GeoAI models allow restoration practitioners to:

- **Identify Priority Areas:** By analyzing environmental data, AI can pinpoint areas that require urgent attention, such as regions most affected by deforestation or soil degradation.

- **Forecast Ecosystem Recovery:** AI models can simulate how ecosystems will evolve after restoration interventions, predicting how long it will take for ecosystems to recover fully and the types of biodiversity that will be restored.

- **Evaluate the Likelihood of Success:** Predictive modeling can assess the probability of success for different restoration strategies, helping stakeholders make data-driven decisions.

Case Studies

- **Case Study 1: Forest Restoration in the Amazon:** Predictive models using satellite data have been employed to assess the viability of reforestation projects in the Amazon. GeoAI models analyze soil conditions, vegetation types, and climate data to determine the best strategies for replanting native tree species.

- **Case Study 2: Wetland Restoration in the Everglades:** GeoAI-based models have been used to predict the success of wetland restoration in the Florida Everglades. Satellite imagery and hydrological data are integrated into predictive models to simulate the restoration of water flow and the revival of plant and animal species.

18.4 Soil Health and Restoration

Importance of Soil Health in Ecosystem Restoration

Soil health is fundamental to ecosystem function. Healthy soils support plant growth, regulate water cycles, and store carbon. Degraded soils, often caused by erosion, contamination, and unsustainable agricultural practices, are a barrier to successful ecosystem restoration. Soil restoration efforts aim to rebuild soil organic matter, improve fertility, and reduce erosion.

GeoAI Techniques for Soil Monitoring

GeoAI plays a critical role in monitoring soil health and guiding restoration efforts:

- **Soil Mapping:** AI algorithms process satellite imagery and remote sensing data to create detailed soil maps, identifying areas that are nutrient-deprived or at risk of erosion.

- **Soil Classification:** Machine learning models classify soils based on their texture, structure, and nutrient content, providing insights into the specific needs for restoration.

- **Real-Time Soil Monitoring:** Sensors and remote sensing technologies can track changes in soil moisture, temperature, and nutrient levels, providing immediate feedback on restoration progress.

Soil Health and Predictive Modeling

AI models can predict how soil health will evolve after restoration interventions. For instance, AI can forecast the impact of different soil amendments or erosion control techniques, helping restoration practitioners select the most effective strategies for improving soil quality over time.

18.5 Forest Restoration and GeoAI

The Role of Forests in Ecosystem Restoration

Forests play a critical role in regulating the global climate, supporting biodiversity, and maintaining the water cycle. Forest restoration involves replanting native species, managing invasive species, and protecting existing forest ecosystems from further degradation.

GeoAI Applications in Forest Restoration

GeoAI is used extensively to monitor and restore forest ecosystems:

- **Forest Cover Mapping:** Satellite imagery processed by AI algorithms can track changes in forest cover, detect illegal logging, and map areas for reforestation.

- **Species Diversity Monitoring:** AI models can track species composition and help identify areas where biodiversity is at risk.

- **Forest Health Monitoring:** GeoAI is used to detect signs of forest degradation, such as pest infestations, disease outbreaks, or drought-induced stress.

Case Studies in Forest Restoration Using GeoAI

- **Case Study 1: The Great Green Wall:** In Africa, GeoAI is used to monitor and support the restoration of the Sahel region through the Great Green Wall initiative, which aims to combat desertification and promote sustainable land management.

- **Case Study 2: Forest Monitoring in the Amazon:** AI models are employed to monitor the deforestation rates in the Amazon, providing real-time data that informs enforcement efforts and supports reforestation projects.

18.6 Wetland Rehabilitation and GeoAI

Wetlands as Crucial Ecosystems

Wetlands provide essential ecosystem services, including water purification, flood control, and habitat for wildlife. Restoration efforts focus on restoring the hydrological functions of wetlands, controlling pollution, and improving biodiversity.

Using GeoAI to Monitor and Restore Wetlands

GeoAI tools enable the monitoring of wetland health through:

● **Mapping Wetland Extent:** Remote sensing and AI algorithms are used to map wetland boundaries and monitor changes in water levels, vegetation cover, and soil conditions.

● **Water Quality Monitoring:** AI models are used to analyze satellite and sensor data to monitor pollution levels, nutrient concentrations, and the overall health of wetland ecosystems.

● **Biodiversity Tracking:** AI helps track the presence of endangered species, monitor habitat quality, and predict future trends in wetland biodiversity.

Case Studies in Wetland Restoration with GeoAI

● **Case Study 1: The Everglades Restoration Project:** GeoAI is employed in the ongoing restoration of the Everglades in Florida, where AI models help manage water flow and track wildlife recovery.

● **Case Study 2: Coastal Wetland Restoration in Europe:** AI systems are used to monitor salt marshes and other coastal wetlands, tracking changes in water salinity and species health as part of large-scale restoration efforts.

18.7 Integrating GeoAI with Ecosystem Services Evaluation

Understanding Ecosystem Services

Ecosystem services are the benefits provided by ecosystems that support human life, including clean water, air, food, and climate regulation. Evaluating these services is critical to understanding the success of restoration projects.

GeoAI for Ecosystem Services Assessment

GeoAI can quantify changes in ecosystem services during restoration by:

- **Modeling Carbon Sequestration:** AI models predict how forest restoration contributes to carbon storage, providing data essential for climate mitigation.

- **Water Regulation and Purification:** GeoAI tracks changes in water quality and availability as wetlands or forests are restored, ensuring that ecosystem services are improved.

- **Biodiversity Support:** AI helps assess changes in species richness and population stability as ecosystems recover.

18.8 Ensuring Long-Term Sustainability in Ecosystem Restoration

GeoAI for Long-Term Monitoring and Sustainability

Long-term sustainability of restored ecosystems requires continuous monitoring. GeoAI supports this by providing real-time data and predictive insights that help track ecosystem health over time. Monitoring is essential to ensure that restoration efforts continue to provide benefits, such as biodiversity conservation and carbon sequestration, in the long run.

Challenges in Ensuring Sustainability

Despite technological advancements, challenges remain in ensuring the long-term success of ecosystem restoration, including:

- **Human Encroachment:** Illegal logging, mining, and urbanization continue to threaten restored ecosystems.

- **Climate Change:** The changing climate can alter restoration trajectories, making some ecosystems more vulnerable to future degradation.

- **Political and Financial Constraints:** Large-scale restoration efforts require continuous investment and policy support.

Future Directions for GeoAI in Sustainable Restoration

GeoAI has the potential to drive the next generation of restoration efforts by providing adaptive management tools. Future advancements in AI could further optimize restoration strategies, ensuring that ecosystems are resilient to both human and environmental pressures.

18.9 Conclusion

GeoAI is playing an increasingly vital role in supporting habitat and ecosystem restoration efforts around the globe. By leveraging the power of artificial intelligence and geospatial data, GeoAI enables real-time monitoring, predictive modeling, and decision-making to optimize restoration strategies. From forest restoration to wetland rehabilitation, the application of GeoAI is helping ensure the success and sustainability of these critical environmental projects.

The future of GeoAI in ecosystem restoration is promising. As technology continues to advance, we can expect even more sophisticated tools to monitor, predict, and optimize restoration efforts, contributing to the long-term health of our planet's ecosystems.

Chapter 19: GeoAI for Monitoring Extreme Weather Events

19.1 Introduction to Extreme Weather Events and Their Impact

Overview of Extreme Weather Events

Extreme weather events refer to unusual, severe, or unseasonal weather conditions that can cause significant disruption to human and environmental systems. They include hurricanes, cyclones, heatwaves, floods, tornadoes, and wildfires. These events have grown in frequency and intensity, driven largely by climate change. According to the Intergovernmental Panel on Climate Change (IPCC), extreme weather events are expected to become more prevalent in the coming decades, with profound effects on ecosystems, human health, and economies.

The economic costs of extreme weather events are staggering. For example, hurricanes like Hurricane Katrina (2005) and Hurricane Maria (2017) caused billions of dollars in damages. Similarly, heatwaves across Europe, Asia, and the United States have led to thousands of deaths and significant agricultural losses. Extreme flooding, particularly in South Asia and the Americas, has displaced millions of people, while wildfires in the Mediterranean, Australia, and California have become more intense and frequent. These events also exacerbate existing vulnerabilities, such as poverty, and put additional strain on public health and infrastructure systems.

GeoAI (Geospatial Artificial Intelligence) has become a critical tool in understanding, predicting, and responding to these extreme weather events. By harnessing the power of satellite data, remote sensing, and AI algorithms,

"

GeoAI provides timely and actionable insights to help mitigate the impact of these events on communities and ecosystems.

The Role of GeoAI in Addressing the Challenges of Extreme Weather

GeoAI plays a crucial role in improving the predictability and management of extreme weather. Traditional meteorological forecasting methods have made significant strides, but integrating AI and machine learning with geospatial data has added a new dimension to weather forecasting, disaster response, and recovery strategies. GeoAI can process vast amounts of data from multiple sources—such as weather stations, satellites, sensors, and historical records—enabling real-time analysis and predictions.

For example, during the lead-up to an extreme event like a hurricane or flood, GeoAI can be used to predict the event's path, intensity, and impact areas. By analyzing real-time satellite imagery, AI models can improve the accuracy of weather forecasts, providing earlier warnings that allow for timely evacuations, resource distribution, and disaster management. Additionally, after an event has occurred, GeoAI enables the quick assessment of damage and the mobilization of resources for recovery efforts.

19.2 Understanding the Components of GeoAI for Weather Monitoring

What is GeoAI?

GeoAI is an interdisciplinary field that combines machine learning, artificial intelligence, and geospatial data to solve complex environmental, societal, and industrial problems. The integration of geospatial data with AI enables automated processes for data extraction, analysis, and decision-making, which is especially useful in the realm of weather monitoring and extreme event prediction. GeoAI models leverage satellite imagery, weather station data, remote sensing, and even crowdsourced information to generate comprehensive weather forecasts, impact predictions, and disaster response strategies.

Machine learning, a core component of GeoAI, enables the automation of these processes. By training on vast datasets, machine learning algorithms can detect patterns, anomalies, and trends that might be missed by traditional methods. In weather monitoring, these models are trained on historical weather data, satellite imagery, and sensor readings to recognize the early signs of an extreme weather event and predict its behavior.

Key Data Sources in GeoAI for Extreme Weather

To monitor and predict extreme weather, GeoAI relies on several data sources:

1. **Satellite Imagery:** Satellite imagery is a primary data source for weather monitoring and forecasting. Satellites capture high-resolution images of Earth's surface and atmosphere, providing crucial information on cloud cover, temperature, humidity, wind patterns, and sea surface conditions. These images can be processed by AI algorithms to track the development and movement of extreme weather events, such as hurricanes or storms, and to assess environmental changes over time.
   For example, the European Space Agency's Copernicus program provides satellite data that is instrumental in monitoring global weather conditions, including the detection of wildfires, floods, and storms.

2. **Weather Station Data:** Ground-based weather stations provide real-time data on temperature, humidity, wind speed, and atmospheric pressure. This data is critical for the calibration of AI models and for improving the accuracy of weather predictions. By integrating this data with satellite and sensor-based data, GeoAI can provide more reliable forecasts.

3. **Remote Sensing Technologies:** In addition to satellite data, GeoAI utilizes remote sensing technologies, such as drones and unmanned aerial vehicles (UAVs), to gather localized weather data. These tools are especially useful in disaster-stricken areas where ground-based infrastructure may be compromised.

4. **Crowdsourced Data:** In some cases, crowdsourced data from individuals or local authorities, such as reports of flooding, temperature anomalies, or storm damage, can be integrated into GeoAI systems. This additional data enhances the model's ability to make real-time predictions and assessments.

19.3 Predicting Extreme Weather Events with GeoAI

Early Warning Systems and Predictive Modeling

One of the most impactful applications of GeoAI in extreme weather monitoring is its contribution to early warning systems. By processing vast amounts of data in real-time, GeoAI models can predict extreme weather events several days or even weeks before they occur, providing valuable lead time for governments, organizations, and communities to take preventive measures.

For example, the integration of machine learning algorithms with satellite data can help track the development of tropical storms, predicting their path, intensity, and potential for strengthening into hurricanes. AI models can identify the precise conditions that lead to these storms, such as changes in sea surface temperatures and atmospheric pressure, enabling more accurate predictions.

AI-powered early warning systems have already been implemented in several regions, significantly improving preparedness. For example, the Caribbean Meteorological Organization uses AI algorithms to predict the formation of hurricanes in the Atlantic, providing crucial warnings to the region's governments and populations. By analyzing historical data, AI models can learn to recognize the atmospheric and oceanic patterns that precede these dangerous events.

Hurricanes and Cyclones

GeoAI has revolutionized the way we predict hurricanes and cyclones. Traditionally, meteorologists used a combination of satellite data, radar systems, and weather stations to track and predict the path of these storms. However, this method has limitations in terms of accuracy and speed. AI enhances the forecasting process by analyzing historical data and satellite imagery, identifying storm patterns, and predicting the intensity and trajectory of cyclones with greater precision.

For example, the National Hurricane Center (NHC) uses AI and machine learning models to enhance their hurricane forecasting models. The integration of machine learning techniques such as deep learning neural networks allows the NHC to predict cyclone intensity and landfall location with improved accuracy, reducing the margin of error in their predictions.

Heatwaves and Droughts

Heatwaves and droughts are becoming increasingly common as climate change accelerates. GeoAI can predict these extreme events by analyzing temperature anomalies, soil moisture levels, and other atmospheric variables. AI models can forecast the onset of heatwaves by identifying patterns in global temperature trends and atmospheric conditions.

GeoAI's ability to predict droughts also lies in its capacity to analyze long-term weather patterns, satellite images, and rainfall data. Machine learning algorithms can process data from various sources to create drought indices that identify vulnerable regions. For example, the U.S. Drought Monitor uses a GeoAI-based system to track and predict drought conditions across the country.

Flood and Storm Surge Prediction

Flood prediction and storm surge forecasting are essential components of disaster management. By analyzing satellite imagery and combining it with weather data, GeoAI can predict areas at risk of flooding due to heavy rainfall, rising sea levels, or storm surges.

AI models can assess terrain elevation, river levels, and ocean currents to predict which regions will be impacted by floods. For instance, AI-powered flood forecasting systems in the Netherlands integrate high-resolution satellite imagery with weather forecasts to predict flood events and support real-time emergency response.

19.4 Impact Assessment of Extreme Weather Using GeoAI

Real-Time Impact Assessment

After an extreme weather event occurs, GeoAI plays a crucial role in assessing its immediate impact. Satellite imagery, drone data, and sensor readings can be processed by AI models to quickly determine the extent of damage to infrastructure, agriculture, and the environment. This real-time data is essential for making rapid decisions regarding evacuation, resource allocation, and disaster response.

For example, after Hurricane Harvey in 2017, GeoAI was used to assess the flooding damage in Houston, Texas. AI algorithms analyzed satellite images to map the extent of floodwaters, identifying the most severely impacted areas and helping authorities prioritize rescue and recovery efforts.

Damage and Loss Estimation

GeoAI can also be used to estimate the economic and environmental damage caused by extreme weather. By combining satellite images, weather data, and historical trends, AI models can estimate the cost of damage to infrastructure, homes, agriculture, and the environment. These predictions can help guide recovery efforts and inform insurance claims.

For instance, the World Bank used GeoAI to assess the damage caused by Typhoon Haiyan in the Philippines. AI-based damage assessments helped to quickly allocate resources for reconstruction and recovery, ensuring that the most affected areas received timely aid.

Post-Event Monitoring

GeoAI doesn't stop after the event has ended; it also helps monitor the recovery process. Using satellite imagery and AI-based damage assessment tools, authorities can track the rebuilding efforts and monitor changes in the environment, such as

soil erosion, land degradation, or changes in forest cover. These tools ensure that recovery efforts are sustainable and that ecosystems are being restored effectively.

19.5 GeoAI for Real-Time Disaster Response and Recovery

Leveraging GeoAI for Emergency Response

In the aftermath of extreme weather events, rapid response is crucial to saving lives, protecting property, and minimizing long-term damage. GeoAI plays an essential role in the emergency response phase by providing actionable insights for decision-makers. The ability to process and analyze geospatial data in real-time allows authorities to allocate resources, coordinate evacuations, and direct aid to the most affected areas.

For example, during the 2015 Nepal earthquake, GeoAI tools were used to analyze satellite images and assess infrastructure damage. This helped humanitarian organizations identify regions with the most severe damage and determine where to direct emergency medical supplies and personnel. By combining satellite data with local reports and social media feeds, GeoAI created a comprehensive damage assessment model that enhanced the efficiency of rescue operations.

GeoAI also plays a critical role in monitoring populations during evacuations. During hurricanes or floods, AI-powered systems can track population movements and provide authorities with information on where people are going, which routes are being taken, and whether any areas are being left behind. This data can be used to adjust evacuation plans in real-time and ensure that no one is left behind.

The Role of Drones and UAVs in Post-Event Analysis

Drones and unmanned aerial vehicles (UAVs) are increasingly being used for real-time damage assessment after extreme weather events. These devices can be equipped with high-resolution cameras, thermal sensors, and LiDAR to capture detailed images of the affected areas. Combined with AI models, drones can quickly assess damage to infrastructure, estimate the extent of flooding, and even evaluate environmental impacts such as deforestation or habitat destruction.

A notable example is the use of drones in the aftermath of Typhoon Haiyan in 2013. After the typhoon devastated parts of the Philippines, drones were deployed to capture aerial images of the damage. AI algorithms processed these images to assess the destruction of buildings, roads, and power lines. This enabled more efficient allocation of resources and helped identify areas that needed immediate attention.

Additionally, drones equipped with sensors can monitor environmental changes in the aftermath of a disaster. For example, in the case of forest fires, drones can track changes in vegetation cover, soil moisture levels, and air quality, helping authorities to understand the full extent of the damage and plan restoration efforts.

19.6 Future Directions and Innovations in GeoAI for Weather Monitoring

The Role of Artificial Intelligence in Climate Adaptation

As extreme weather events continue to increase in frequency and intensity, AI will play an even more critical role in climate adaptation strategies. Beyond disaster response and recovery, GeoAI can be used to build resilience in vulnerable communities. AI models can identify regions that are most at risk of extreme weather, enabling policymakers to implement mitigation strategies before disasters strike.

GeoAI can also contribute to developing climate-resilient infrastructure, such as buildings and roads that can withstand higher temperatures, stronger winds, and heavier rainfall. Predictive models powered by machine learning can inform urban planning decisions, ensuring that cities and rural areas are better equipped to handle future extreme weather events.

One innovative example of GeoAI in climate adaptation is the use of AI-powered flood modeling systems in Bangladesh. By combining historical weather data, satellite imagery, and real-time flood data, GeoAI can predict potential flood events months in advance. This allows farmers to adjust planting schedules, governments to prepare evacuation plans, and communities to implement flood mitigation measures such as levees or flood-resistant infrastructure.

Advancing Machine Learning Algorithms for More Accurate Forecasting

As weather patterns become increasingly complex due to climate change, more sophisticated machine learning algorithms will be required to improve weather prediction accuracy. Current AI models use data from satellites, weather stations, and remote sensors to predict the path and intensity of storms. However, there is still much room for improvement, particularly when it comes to predicting local weather patterns and identifying rare or extreme events.

Deep learning algorithms, particularly convolutional neural networks (CNNs), are being explored to improve image recognition in satellite data. This can enhance the ability to detect early signs of extreme weather, such as storm formation or changes in atmospheric pressure. Additionally, AI techniques like reinforcement learning may be applied to continuously improve forecasting models as more data is collected.

Another area for innovation is the development of AI models that can predict compound extreme weather events. For instance, simultaneous heatwaves and wildfires or cyclones and flooding can have compounded impacts, and current models often focus on individual events. By combining data streams and improving algorithms, GeoAI can better predict these complex, overlapping events and provide early warnings to help communities prepare for a range of scenarios.

Integration of GeoAI with Climate Change Models

GeoAI is increasingly being integrated with climate change models to simulate long-term environmental changes and predict how extreme weather events will evolve over time. By processing historical data on climate patterns, AI can predict the impact of climate change on the frequency, intensity, and distribution of extreme weather events.

For example, AI models can integrate projections of global temperature rise, changes in atmospheric circulation, and other climate variables to predict how specific regions will be affected by extreme weather. This data can be used to inform climate policies, disaster planning, and infrastructure development that will help mitigate the effects of climate change in the future.

One such model is the use of GeoAI in studying the impacts of sea-level rise on coastal communities. As temperatures rise and glaciers melt, GeoAI can predict the areas at highest risk of flooding due to storm surges or rising sea levels. This enables policymakers to make more informed decisions about coastal development and flood protection strategies.

19.7 Conclusion: The Role of GeoAI in Enhancing Resilience to Extreme Weather Events

GeoAI is revolutionizing the way we understand, predict, and respond to extreme weather events. By integrating geospatial data with advanced machine learning algorithms, GeoAI enables real-time monitoring, early warning systems, and precise damage assessments that help mitigate the impact of these disasters on people and ecosystems. From hurricanes and heatwaves to floods and wildfires, GeoAI's ability to analyze vast amounts of data and deliver actionable insights has proven invaluable in disaster management and recovery efforts.

As we look to the future, the role of GeoAI in enhancing climate resilience and developing sustainable adaptation strategies will only grow more critical. By improving the accuracy of weather forecasts, enabling more efficient disaster response, and informing long-term climate adaptation planning, GeoAI will be at the forefront of global efforts to combat the growing threat of extreme weather and climate change.

Furthermore, continuous advancements in machine learning, satellite technology, and geospatial data analysis will only enhance the potential of GeoAI in disaster risk reduction. The integration of AI with climate models, predictive weather forecasting, and real-time data collection will play a central role in safeguarding communities, protecting ecosystems, and building resilience against the unpredictable nature of extreme weather events.

Chapter 20: GeoAI in Environmental Policy and Governance

20.1 Introduction to GeoAI in Environmental Policy

Environmental policy is at the forefront of addressing challenges like climate change, biodiversity loss, and pollution. However, effective policymaking and enforcement require robust tools to gather, analyze, and interpret data. GeoAI, the integration of geographic information systems (GIS) with artificial intelligence (AI), has emerged as a transformative solution for enhancing decision-making in environmental governance. By combining spatial data analysis with AI-driven insights, GeoAI enables policymakers to track environmental changes, enforce regulations, and evaluate policy outcomes with unprecedented precision.

For instance, satellite imagery coupled with machine learning algorithms can detect illegal deforestation in real-time, allowing immediate enforcement actions. Similarly, GeoAI tools assist in monitoring air and water quality, ensuring compliance with environmental standards. The potential of GeoAI extends beyond monitoring; it informs sustainable policy frameworks by predicting future scenarios based on historical and real-time data.

This chapter explores how GeoAI contributes to environmental governance, focusing on monitoring, enforcement, and the alignment of policies with global environmental agreements.

20.2 GeoAI for Environmental Monitoring and Regulation Enforcement

20.2.1 Monitoring Compliance with Environmental Laws

GeoAI provides tools to ensure adherence to environmental regulations by offering actionable insights derived from vast datasets. For example, high-resolution satellite imagery combined with AI algorithms can detect unauthorized mining activities or industrial pollution discharges. Organizations like Global Forest Watch employ GeoAI to monitor deforestation and inform governments about illegal logging operations.

Case Study: In Indonesia, GeoAI tools have been used to monitor illegal palm oil plantations, enabling authorities to identify and shut down operations that violate conservation laws. Machine learning models analyzed satellite imagery to detect land clearing patterns characteristic of plantation development.

20.2.2 Tracking Pollution and Emissions

Air, water, and soil pollution monitoring have significantly benefited from GeoAI. Real-time data from satellite sensors, such as Sentinel-5P, combined with AI models, track pollutants like nitrogen dioxide and particulate matter. This integration aids in pinpointing pollution hotspots and enforcing emission limits.

Example: In Beijing, China, AI-powered platforms analyze satellite data to identify sources of air pollution, such as industrial plants and vehicular emissions. This information has guided regulatory actions, reducing harmful emissions in urban areas.

20.2.3 Land Use Monitoring for Regulatory Compliance

GeoAI's capabilities in detecting unauthorized land use changes have revolutionized zoning regulation enforcement. For instance, deep learning models trained on satellite imagery can identify illegal urban expansion or encroachments into protected areas.

Application: Brazil has leveraged GeoAI to monitor deforestation in the Amazon. Algorithms detect land cover changes, such as forest loss due to agricultural encroachment, and alert authorities for swift action.

20.3 GeoAI in Supporting International Environmental Agreements

20.3.1 GeoAI for Carbon Accounting under Climate Agreements

Under agreements like the Paris Accord, countries are required to report their carbon emissions and mitigation efforts. GeoAI facilitates accurate carbon accounting by integrating remote sensing data with AI models to estimate emissions and track sequestration efforts.

Example: Projects like "REDD+ (Reducing Emissions from Deforestation and Forest Degradation)" use GeoAI to quantify carbon stocks in forests, ensuring transparent reporting of emission reductions.

20.3.2 Monitoring Biodiversity Commitments

The Convention on Biological Diversity (CBD) emphasizes the need for monitoring species and habitats. GeoAI tools analyze satellite and drone imagery to map habitats, track wildlife populations, and assess ecosystem health.

Case Study: In Kenya, AI-powered drones monitor wildlife in protected areas, ensuring compliance with biodiversity conservation targets. These tools also help detect poaching activities by analyzing patterns in movement and disturbances.

20.3.3 GeoAI and Ocean Governance

GeoAI plays a critical role in enforcing marine conservation laws under the United Nations Convention on the Law of the Sea (UNCLOS). Tools like machine learning-based ocean monitoring systems track illegal fishing activities and marine pollution.

Example: The European Space Agency's "Copernicus Marine Service" uses AI to monitor oil spills and ensure compliance with maritime pollution regulations.

20.4 Case Studies of GeoAI in Environmental Governance

20.4.1 Deforestation Monitoring in the Amazon

The Amazon rainforest is a critical global carbon sink, yet it faces threats from deforestation. GeoAI has been instrumental in monitoring and mitigating these activities. Satellite imagery analyzed through convolutional neural networks (CNNs) detects deforestation patterns and alerts authorities.

20.4.2 Air Quality Management in Urban Areas

Cities like New Delhi and Los Angeles use GeoAI to track air pollution levels. Predictive models integrate weather data with pollution sources, enabling city planners to implement targeted interventions, such as traffic regulation during high-pollution periods.

20.4.3 Water Resource Governance in Arid Regions

In water-scarce regions like the Middle East, GeoAI informs policies on water allocation and conservation. AI models predict water availability by analyzing hydrological data from satellites, aiding sustainable resource management.

20.5 Challenges and Limitations in Integrating GeoAI into Governance

20.5.1 Data Privacy and Ethical Concerns

While GeoAI offers significant benefits, its use raises concerns about data privacy. For example, monitoring illegal activities could inadvertently expose sensitive personal or corporate data, necessitating robust privacy safeguards.

20.5.2 Accessibility and Capacity Building

Low-resource countries face challenges in adopting GeoAI due to limited access to technology and expertise. Bridging this gap requires investments in capacity building and affordable GeoAI solutions.

20.5.3 Technical and Financial Barriers

Deploying and maintaining GeoAI systems can be costly. Additionally, the quality and availability of geospatial data vary globally, impacting the effectiveness of GeoAI applications.

20.6 Future Directions for GeoAI in Policy and Governance

20.6.1 Integration with Global Policy Frameworks

GeoAI can enhance collaboration among nations by providing standardized tools for environmental monitoring. These tools could support unified reporting for international agreements like the SDGs.

20.6.2 Advancing AI Models for Policy Support

Machine learning models capable of simulating policy outcomes offer potential for proactive governance. Policymakers can test scenarios, such as emission reduction targets, before implementing them.

20.6.3 Leveraging Citizen Science and Crowdsourced Data

GeoAI platforms integrating citizen-reported data can enhance monitoring efforts. For instance, mobile apps allowing users to report pollution incidents contribute to comprehensive environmental databases.

20.7 Conclusion

GeoAI is revolutionizing environmental policy and governance by offering innovative solutions for monitoring, enforcement, and decision-making. Its applications in tracking deforestation, air and water pollution, and biodiversity conservation illustrate its transformative potential. However, challenges like data privacy, accessibility, and financial constraints must be addressed to fully realize GeoAI's capabilities.

As technology evolves, GeoAI will play an increasingly vital role in shaping sustainable policies, fostering international collaboration, and ensuring accountability. By integrating GeoAI into governance frameworks, we can advance toward a more equitable and environmentally resilient future.

Chapter 21: GeoAI for Disaster Preparedness and Recovery

21.1 Introduction to GeoAI in Disaster Preparedness and Recovery

Disasters—both natural and human-induced—pose severe risks to human lives, economies, and ecosystems. From tsunamis and earthquakes to wildfires and hurricanes, these events often strike without warning, leaving devastation in their wake. The complexity of managing such crises has necessitated advanced tools for prediction, response, and recovery. GeoAI, an integration of Geographic Information Systems (GIS) and Artificial Intelligence (AI), is emerging as a transformative technology in this domain. By combining spatial analytics with machine learning, GeoAI enables comprehensive disaster management strategies that are timely, efficient, and effective.

GeoAI is capable of processing massive datasets from diverse sources such as satellites, ground sensors, drones, and social media. It can predict disaster scenarios, optimize resource allocation during emergencies, and provide actionable insights for long-term recovery planning. This chapter explores the role of GeoAI in disaster preparedness and recovery, focusing on its applications, challenges, and future potential.

21.2 Predicting and Modeling Disaster Scenarios

21.2.1 Early Warning Systems with GeoAI

Early warning systems are critical in mitigating the impact of disasters. GeoAI leverages real-time data from seismic sensors, weather stations, ocean buoys, and satellite imagery to generate accurate alerts for events like tsunamis, cyclones, and earthquakes. For instance, the Pacific Tsunami

Warning Center (PTWC) uses AI algorithms to analyze oceanic wave patterns, predicting tsunami propagation with high precision.

In Japan, GeoAI tools analyze seismic activity patterns to predict earthquakes and issue timely alerts, enabling communities to evacuate or secure critical infrastructure. Similarly, AI-driven meteorological models, such as IBM's Deep Thunder, enhance weather forecasting by processing historical and live weather data to predict cyclonic paths and intensities.

21.2.2 Scenario Modeling and Risk Assessment

GeoAI's capacity to model disaster scenarios is invaluable for risk assessment and planning. Advanced simulation tools integrate spatial data with machine learning to identify high-risk areas for earthquakes, floods, and landslides. For example, FEMA's Risk MAP program in the United States uses AI-enhanced flood risk mapping to guide urban planning and flood insurance policies.

These models incorporate variables such as topography, climate data, and land use to simulate various disaster scenarios. Predictive analytics enable policymakers to prioritize investments in disaster mitigation infrastructure, such as flood barriers and earthquake-resistant buildings.

21.2.3 Data-Driven Disaster Preparedness Plans

GeoAI aids in the development of data-driven disaster preparedness plans by analyzing historical trends and real-time data. Planners use these insights to design evacuation routes, allocate resources, and establish emergency protocols tailored to specific risks in a region. For example, in India, the National Disaster Management Authority integrates GeoAI tools to prepare for annual monsoon floods, safeguarding millions of lives and properties.

21.3 Real-Time Monitoring and Disaster Response

21.3.1 Monitoring Disasters in Progress

During a disaster, real-time monitoring is critical for situational awareness. GeoAI systems process live feeds from satellites, drones, and IoT devices to provide an up-to-date picture of affected areas. For instance, during Cyclone Idai in Mozambique, GeoAI tools were deployed to track the cyclone's movement and assess the extent of flooding. This information enabled targeted rescue and relief operations.

GeoAI-powered platforms like Sentinel Hub allow responders to access processed satellite imagery in near real-time. This capability is particularly useful for tracking wildfires, as GeoAI algorithms can detect heat signatures and smoke plumes, guiding firefighting efforts.

21.3.2 Coordination of Relief and Rescue Operations

Efficient disaster response requires the coordination of resources and personnel. GeoAI optimizes this process by mapping affected areas, prioritizing high-need zones, and identifying accessible routes for relief delivery. During the 2010 Haiti earthquake, GeoAI tools were instrumental in assessing damage and directing international aid efforts.

Social media and crowdsourced data are increasingly integrated into GeoAI systems for disaster response. Platforms like Ushahidi use AI to analyze tweets, posts, and reports, providing real-time insights into the needs and locations of affected populations.

21.4 Post-Disaster Damage Assessment

21.4.1 Rapid Assessment of Infrastructure Damage

GeoAI accelerates post-disaster damage assessment by processing high-resolution satellite images to identify destroyed or damaged infrastructure. AI models trained on pre-disaster and post-disaster imagery can detect changes with high accuracy. For instance, after Hurricane Katrina, GeoAI systems analyzed satellite data to assess road and bridge damage, enabling quicker restoration efforts.

21.4.2 Evaluating Environmental and Economic Impacts

The environmental impacts of disasters, such as oil spills, forest destruction, and water contamination, are often assessed using GeoAI. Machine learning algorithms analyze spectral satellite imagery to detect anomalies and quantify damage. Similarly, GeoAI tools integrate economic and census data to assess the broader socioeconomic impacts, such as job losses and displacement.

21.4.3 Community Recovery Planning

GeoAI supports long-term recovery planning by simulating various reconstruction scenarios. By analyzing spatial data on land use, population density, and environmental risks, GeoAI helps design resilient communities. After the 2011 Tohoku earthquake and tsunami in Japan, GeoAI-guided planning focused on creating disaster-resistant infrastructure while minimizing environmental impact.

21.5 GeoAI for Long-Term Risk Reduction

21.5.1 Hazard Mapping and Zoning

GeoAI's ability to create detailed hazard maps is essential for long-term risk reduction. By analyzing geological, hydrological, and climatic data, GeoAI identifies zones prone to disasters such as landslides or floods. These maps inform urban zoning regulations, ensuring safer land use practices.

21.5.2 Predictive Maintenance of Critical Infrastructure

GeoAI tools monitor the structural integrity of critical infrastructure, such as dams and bridges, using data from sensors and remote imaging. Predictive analytics identify potential failure points, enabling proactive maintenance and reducing disaster risks.

21.6 Challenges and Limitations of GeoAI in Disaster Management

21.6.1 Data Accessibility and Quality

The effectiveness of GeoAI depends on the availability of high-quality, up-to-date spatial data. In many regions, data is fragmented or inaccessible, limiting GeoAI's potential. Collaborative initiatives like the Group on Earth Observations (GEO) are working to address these challenges by promoting open data sharing.

21.6.2 Ethical and Privacy Concerns

Using GeoAI for disaster management raises ethical questions, particularly regarding surveillance and data privacy. Transparent governance and ethical guidelines are essential to balance the benefits of GeoAI with individual rights.

21.6.3 Technical Barriers and Resource Constraints

Deploying GeoAI in resource-limited regions often faces challenges such as inadequate infrastructure, limited internet connectivity, and lack of technical expertise. Investments in capacity-building and technology transfer are critical to overcoming these barriers.

21.7 Future Directions in GeoAI for Disaster Preparedness and Recovery

21.7.1 Enhanced Integration with IoT and Big Data

Future advancements in GeoAI will likely involve deeper integration with IoT devices, enabling hyper-localized monitoring and response. Smart flood sensors and AI-powered weather stations could provide granular insights into disaster dynamics.

21.7.2 Leveraging Cloud Computing for Scalability

Cloud-based GeoAI platforms offer scalable solutions for disaster management. These platforms facilitate the processing of massive datasets, enabling global collaboration in disaster response efforts.

21.7.3 Community-Centric GeoAI Solutions

The future of GeoAI lies in developing community-centric tools that empower local populations to participate in disaster management. Crowdsourced data and participatory mapping initiatives will play a pivotal role in this evolution.

21.8 Conclusion

GeoAI has revolutionized disaster preparedness and recovery by offering predictive, real-time, and post-event analytical capabilities. From reducing disaster impacts to facilitating resilient reconstruction, GeoAI serves as an indispensable tool in global disaster management efforts. However, addressing challenges like data accessibility, ethical concerns, and resource constraints is crucial for maximizing GeoAI's impact. As technology advances and global collaborations strengthen, GeoAI will continue to play a transformative role in safeguarding communities and fostering resilience against disasters.

Chapter 22: GeoAI in Environmental Impact Assessment (EIA)

22.1 Introduction to Environmental Impact Assessment (EIA) and GeoAI

Environmental Impact Assessment (EIA) is a systematic process designed to evaluate the potential environmental consequences of proposed projects before they are implemented. It plays a critical role in decision-making, helping stakeholders balance developmental aspirations with ecological sustainability. With advancements in technology, the integration of GeoAI—geospatial artificial intelligence—has transformed the traditional EIA process into a more precise, predictive, and dynamic framework.

22.1.1 Overview of Environmental Impact Assessment (EIA)

The concept of EIA originated in the 1970s, following the enactment of the U.S. National Environmental Policy Act (NEPA). It mandates that any significant development project undergoes environmental scrutiny to prevent irreversible damage. Over the decades, EIA has become a global practice, influencing projects ranging from infrastructure development and industrial expansion to resource extraction.

22.1.2 Introduction to GeoAI in EIA

GeoAI merges geospatial data with artificial intelligence to extract insights, make predictions, and assist in decision-making. This technology enhances the EIA process by enabling real-time monitoring, analyzing large datasets, and automating complex assessments. GeoAI can uncover hidden patterns, predict environmental impacts, and visualize scenarios, offering decision-makers a comprehensive understanding of potential outcomes.

22.1.3 Why GeoAI is Essential for EIA

The integration of GeoAI into EIA is vital in addressing the challenges of contemporary environmental management. Traditional EIAs are often limited by static assessments, delays, and data gaps. GeoAI overcomes these limitations by offering dynamic, data-rich, and scalable solutions. For example, when assessing the environmental impact of urban development, GeoAI can combine satellite imagery, traffic patterns, and air quality indices to deliver actionable insights.

22.2 Data Integration in GeoAI for EIA

Effective EIA relies on diverse datasets that capture environmental, social, and economic dimensions. GeoAI's ability to integrate and analyze such datasets enhances the depth and accuracy of impact assessments.

22.2.1 Types of Data Used in EIA with GeoAI

Data used in GeoAI-driven EIA can be categorized into:

- **Geospatial Data:** Satellite imagery, GIS maps, and aerial photography provide spatial context.

- **Environmental Data:** Data on air quality, water quality, and biodiversity inform ecosystem health.

- **Socioeconomic Data:** Demographic statistics, land use patterns, and economic activities reveal human-environment interactions.

22.2.2 Data Sources and Acquisition Methods

Key data sources include open platforms like NASA's Earth Observing System Data and Information System (EOSDIS), Sentinel Hub, and commercial providers like Planet Labs. On-the-ground IoT sensors and crowdsourced data further enrich datasets, allowing localized insights into environmental variables.

22.2.3 Challenges in Data Integration

Despite its potential, data integration in GeoAI faces hurdles:

- **Inconsistencies in Data Formats:** Data from varied sources often require preprocessing.

- **Data Accessibility:** Restricted access to proprietary or high-resolution datasets.

- **Scalability Issues:** Handling large datasets demands significant computational resources.

GeoAI technologies like Google Earth Engine mitigate these challenges by providing cloud-based solutions for data analysis.

22.3 Predicting Environmental Impacts Using GeoAI

GeoAI models are revolutionizing the prediction of environmental impacts, allowing proactive interventions.

22.3.1 GeoAI Models for Environmental Predictions

AI techniques such as supervised learning, unsupervised clustering, and neural networks enable accurate environmental modeling. For example, convolutional neural networks (CNNs) have been employed to detect deforestation patterns from satellite imagery.

22.3.2 Case Studies in Predictive Environmental Modeling

- **Deforestation in the Amazon:** GeoAI models have mapped deforestation risks by analyzing historical trends and socioeconomic drivers.

- **Urban Heat Islands in Asia:** GeoAI has predicted the impact of urban expansion on microclimates, enabling urban planners to incorporate green infrastructure.

22.3.3 Tools and Techniques in Predictive Modeling

Popular tools include TensorFlow and PyTorch for building AI models and QGIS for spatial analysis. These platforms integrate seamlessly with satellite data providers, allowing researchers to generate predictive models.

22.4 Risk Assessment with GeoAI

Risk assessment is a cornerstone of EIA, and GeoAI enhances its precision and reliability.

22.4.1 Identifying and Quantifying Environmental Risks

GeoAI systems analyze geospatial patterns to identify risks like erosion, flooding, and biodiversity loss. For instance, AI algorithms can assess soil erosion potential in agricultural projects by combining topographic and climatic data.

22.4.2 Vulnerability Mapping and Hotspot Detection

GeoAI-powered mapping tools identify regions at heightened risk. For example, during a hydropower project assessment, GeoAI can pinpoint areas prone to flooding and sedimentation.

22.4.3 Stakeholder Engagement in Risk Assessment

Visual tools like interactive maps enable stakeholders to comprehend complex data. Such tools promote transparency, ensuring that communities understand the implications of proposed developments.

22.5 Supporting Sustainable Development Practices with

GeoAI

GeoAI aligns with sustainable development goals (SDGs) by facilitating informed decision-making and ensuring environmental compliance.

22.5.1 Monitoring Compliance with Environmental Standards

GeoAI aids in monitoring real-time compliance with regulatory standards. For example, mining companies use drones equipped with AI algorithms to track reclamation activities.

22.5.2 Enhancing Decision-Making for Sustainable Outcomes

AI-driven decision support systems optimize trade-offs between economic growth and ecological preservation. A notable example is the use of GeoAI in siting renewable energy projects to minimize habitat disruption.

22.5.3 Promoting Circular Economy Practices

GeoAI identifies waste management inefficiencies, supporting recycling initiatives. For instance, spatial analyses have mapped e-waste recycling networks in urban areas.

22.6 Applications of GeoAI in Different Sectors of EIA

22.6.1 Infrastructure Development

GeoAI helps assess the environmental footprint of large-scale infrastructure projects. For example, road construction projects benefit from erosion risk modeling.

22.6.2 Mining and Resource Extraction

AI models monitor deforestation and water contamination around mining sites, ensuring responsible resource extraction.

22.6.3 Agricultural Expansion

GeoAI evaluates land-use changes, such as shifts from forests to farmland, and their impact on soil health and biodiversity.

22.6.4 Renewable Energy Projects

Wind and solar farms leverage GeoAI to identify low-impact installation sites, preserving sensitive ecosystems.

22.7 Challenges and Limitations of GeoAI in EIA

22.7.1 Technical Barriers

AI models can struggle with ecological complexity, requiring domain expertise for fine-tuning.

22.7.2 Ethical and Legal Considerations

The use of geospatial data raises privacy concerns, necessitating robust data governance frameworks.

22.7.3 Institutional and Regulatory Challenges

Slow adoption of AI technologies in traditional regulatory frameworks remains a significant bottleneck.

22.8 Future Directions in GeoAI for EIA

22.8.1 Emerging Technologies in GeoAI for EIA

Quantum computing and immersive technologies like VR offer untapped potential for environmental modeling.

22.8.2 Strengthening Collaboration Across Sectors

GeoAI's future depends on public-private partnerships and open-source innovation.

22.8.3 Towards Real-Time Environmental Assessments

Developing adaptive GeoAI systems will enable dynamic responses to environmental challenges.

22.9 Conclusion

GeoAI has redefined the Environmental Impact Assessment landscape, offering unprecedented accuracy and predictive capabilities. While challenges persist, innovations in technology and policy hold promise for a more sustainable future. By fostering collaboration and addressing ethical concerns, GeoAI can pave the way for balanced development and ecological stewardship.

Chapter 23: GeoAI for Climate Resilience and Adaptation Strategies

23.1 Introduction to Climate Resilience and Adaptation

23.1.1 Defining Climate Resilience and Adaptation

Climate resilience refers to the capacity of a system—be it an ecosystem, community, or infrastructure—to absorb disturbances caused by climate-related events, adapt to these changes, and recover efficiently. Adaptation, in the context of climate change, focuses on the deliberate adjustments or strategies implemented to minimize vulnerability to the adverse effects of changing climatic conditions, while taking into account future risks.

In the face of increasing climate variability, GeoAI (Geospatial Artificial Intelligence) has emerged as an indispensable tool in both assessing and enhancing climate resilience. By combining geographic data with artificial intelligence techniques like machine learning, GeoAI facilitates climate adaptation by providing insights that can guide decision-making at local, regional, and global levels.

23.1.2 The Role of GeoAI in Climate Resilience

GeoAI integrates spatial data, satellite imagery, remote sensing data, environmental models, and machine learning to create powerful tools that support climate adaptation strategies. These technologies enable predictive analytics, spatial planning, vulnerability assessments, and dynamic climate scenario modeling, thereby helping communities and governments anticipate and mitigate the impacts of climate change. GeoAI can also play a significant role in real-time monitoring, allowing for proactive responses to climate-induced stresses.

Key to GeoAI's utility is its ability to process vast amounts of environmental data, from historical weather patterns to land-use changes, to project future climate risks. For example, satellite imagery combined with AI can help model how rising sea levels will affect coastal zones, or how shifting rainfall patterns will impact agricultural regions.

23.1.3 Importance of Climate Adaptation Strategies

Climate change is causing significant alterations in weather patterns, sea-level rise, and increasing frequency and intensity of extreme weather events. The UN Climate Change Adaptation Framework calls for urgent action to safeguard vulnerable populations and ensure long-term sustainability. Climate adaptation strategies are necessary not just to address the immediate consequences of climate change but also to anticipate and prepare for future risks. As such, GeoAI provides a critical toolset for informed, data-driven climate adaptation decision-making.

Adaptation strategies are diverse and sector-specific. For instance, in agriculture, adaptive strategies may include crop diversification and water-efficient irrigation practices, whereas in urban areas, climate-resilient infrastructure may be prioritized. GeoAI helps in tailoring these strategies according to local environmental, economic, and social contexts.

23.2 GeoAI-Driven Climate Risk Assessment

23.2.1 Identifying Vulnerable Areas and Populations

GeoAI's integration of spatial data with demographic information allows for detailed vulnerability assessments. By using AI algorithms to analyze geographical regions in the context of socio-economic variables, it is possible to identify communities that are particularly at risk from specific climate impacts.

For example, AI models can determine the likelihood of flooding based on proximity to water bodies, elevation, and historical rainfall patterns. Vulnerable populations, such as those living in floodplains or informal settlements with inadequate infrastructure, can be identified as being particularly at risk. This insight helps governments prioritize resources and interventions.

Case Example: In the Philippines, GeoAI tools have been used to map the flood vulnerability of different regions, enabling targeted evacuation plans and improved resilience planning for communities living in flood-prone zones.

23.2.2 Modeling Climate-Driven Hazards

GeoAI excels in climate hazard modeling, using historical data and real-time environmental inputs to predict future climate extremes, such as hurricanes, heatwaves, droughts, and heavy rainfall. By applying machine learning techniques to vast datasets, GeoAI can simulate the occurrence and impact of these events.

For instance, a combination of satellite data, ocean temperature readings, and atmospheric pressure patterns can help predict the formation of cyclones. By analyzing these data through AI models, authorities can generate accurate early warnings, allowing for timely evacuations and preparedness measures.

Case Example: In the U.S., NOAA (National Oceanic and Atmospheric Administration) employs GeoAI to predict the intensity and path of hurricanes. In 2017, this helped improve the accuracy of forecasts for Hurricane Irma, potentially saving countless lives by allowing timely evacuations.

23.2.3 Case Studies in GeoAI-Based Risk Assessment

A case study from Africa showcases how GeoAI has been used to predict and assess drought risks. Using AI models trained on satellite data (such as rainfall patterns, soil moisture levels, and temperature), local authorities in Ethiopia can now predict droughts up to several months in advance. These predictions enable farmers to prepare for water shortages by switching to drought-resistant crops or by adjusting irrigation schedules, ultimately saving crops and lives.

Another example from Southeast Asia demonstrates how GeoAI models track urban heat island effects. In cities like Jakarta, where rapid urbanization has led to the loss of green spaces, GeoAI analyzes land surface temperatures and urban density to map heat islands. These maps help urban planners implement cooling strategies, such as creating green roofs or expanding green spaces to combat heat stress.

23.3 Adaptive Strategies for Agriculture

23.3.1 GeoAI for Drought-Resilient Crops

Climate change has made agricultural productivity increasingly unpredictable, with shifts in rainfall patterns and more frequent droughts. GeoAI helps by assessing soil moisture, weather patterns, and crop suitability, enabling farmers to select drought-resistant crops. AI can also optimize irrigation by analyzing soil and crop water requirements in real-time, improving water-use efficiency.

For instance, AI-powered platforms can collect data from sensors embedded in fields, then process this data to provide real-time recommendations for irrigation management, crop rotation, and pest control.

Case Example: In India, the Indian Council of Agricultural Research (ICAR) has been utilizing GeoAI to identify areas most susceptible to droughts. This information guides the choice of crops, with drought-resistant crops like millet being recommended for dry regions, ensuring food security even under changing climate conditions.

23.3.2 Precision Agriculture for Climate Adaptation

Precision agriculture harnesses GeoAI to optimize the use of inputs like water, fertilizers, and pesticides. Using satellite imagery and sensors, AI can analyze data on crop health, soil properties, and weather conditions. Based on this information, it generates recommendations on when and where to irrigate, apply fertilizers, or manage pests, all while minimizing resource waste and maximizing crop yield.

Case Example: In Australia, GeoAI has been applied to manage irrigation in vineyards. Sensors placed in the fields track moisture levels, and AI algorithms provide real-time recommendations on irrigation schedules. This has allowed farmers to reduce water usage by up to 30%, while maintaining crop yields even during drought years.

23.3.3 Case Study: Agriculture in Arid Regions

In Rajasthan, India, GeoAI tools have been instrumental in transforming the agricultural landscape. The region, often plagued by droughts, has adopted AI-driven systems to predict water availability and optimize irrigation. Additionally, AI has helped local farmers identify climate-resilient crop varieties such as sorghum and millet, which are better suited to the changing weather patterns. This adaptation has led to more stable yields and higher food security in the region.

23.4 Coastal Management and GeoAI Applications

23.4.1 Mapping and Monitoring Coastal Vulnerabilities

GeoAI uses satellite data and remote sensing technology to monitor coastal areas, identifying vulnerable regions prone to flooding, erosion, and sea-level rise. These models can predict the impacts of storms and tidal surges on coastal infrastructure, helping cities prepare for and mitigate these events.

For example, GeoAI models can simulate the impact of rising sea levels on coastal communities by analyzing elevation data, historical storm data, and land-use patterns. This predictive modeling can inform disaster preparedness strategies and help in planning adaptive infrastructure like seawalls or tidal barriers.

Case Example: In the Caribbean, GeoAI is used to track coastal erosion rates. This helps governments identify areas at risk of losing vital infrastructure, such as roads and tourist resorts, due to rising sea levels.

23.4.2 GeoAI for Sustainable Coastal Planning

In coastal zones, GeoAI supports sustainable development by balancing human activities with ecosystem protection. AI algorithms analyze the environmental impact of proposed infrastructure projects, such as the construction of harbors or resorts. The technology helps determine the potential effects on marine ecosystems, including coral reefs and mangroves, and recommends mitigation strategies.

Case Example: In the Maldives, GeoAI has been used to assess the long-term viability of coastal development projects. By integrating satellite data, GIS mapping, and AI, the Maldives' government has been able to ensure that new developments do not harm sensitive ecosystems such as coral reefs or breeding grounds for marine life.

23.5 Urban Planning and Infrastructure Adaptation

23.5.1 Designing Climate-Resilient Cities

Urban areas are particularly vulnerable to the effects of climate change, from heatwaves to flooding. GeoAI supports city planning by analyzing data on population density, infrastructure, weather patterns, and land-use. This enables urban planners to create adaptive designs, such as expanding green spaces to reduce heat island effects, improving stormwater drainage to prevent flooding, and ensuring energy efficiency in buildings.

AI-driven urban models simulate the impact of different planning strategies, helping decision-makers choose the most effective solutions for climate resilience.

23.5.2 Real-Time Monitoring of Urban Climate Impacts

Real-time monitoring is essential for responding to immediate climate threats, such as heatwaves or heavy rainfall. GeoAI sensors, placed throughout urban environments, can track temperature, humidity, and precipitation levels, providing critical data that helps cities manage emergency responses. GeoAI can also predict urban risks based on historical data and environmental changes, facilitating early intervention.

23.5.3 Case Study: Smart Cities for Climate Resilience

Singapore is an exemplary case where GeoAI has been integral to urban climate adaptation. The city-state has developed an advanced system that integrates AI, satellite data, and sensors to optimize resource use and enhance climate resilience. These tools are used to monitor air quality, energy consumption, and water usage, while also managing urban heat islands through green infrastructure and the promotion of sustainable building designs.

23.6 Infrastructure Planning for Resilience

23.6.1 GeoAI for Infrastructure Risk Analysis

GeoAI analyzes risks to infrastructure, such as transportation networks, energy grids, and water systems, by considering climate projections like extreme temperatures, storm events, or flooding. For example, AI can assess the risk of roads washing away during heavy rainfall or power lines being knocked down during high winds, helping planners design more resilient infrastructure.

23.6.2 Climate-Proofing Infrastructure Development

GeoAI supports the climate-proofing of infrastructure by simulating the effects of climate change on buildings, roads, bridges, and other critical infrastructure. AI-based models evaluate the durability of materials under varying climate scenarios, recommending construction methods and materials that offer greater resilience to climate impacts.

23.7 Policy and Governance for GeoAI-Based Adaptation

23.7.1 Developing GeoAI-Informed Climate Policies

Governments worldwide are integrating GeoAI into their policy frameworks to design evidence-based climate adaptation strategies. By using GeoAI insights, policymakers can identify vulnerable regions, predict the impacts of proposed interventions, and prioritize resources effectively.

23.7.2 Supporting Community-Led Adaptation Efforts

GeoAI is also being used to empower local communities, enabling them to design adaptation strategies based on local climate data and needs. By using simple, accessible platforms, communities can monitor their environments and take actions based on real-time data.

23.7.3 International Collaboration and GeoAI

Global organizations such as the United Nations and the World Bank use GeoAI to support cross-border climate adaptation efforts. GeoAI models can help harmonize adaptation policies and create coordinated responses to transnational climate challenges, such as cross-border water management and disaster response.

23.8 Challenges and Limitations in GeoAI for Climate Adaptation

23.8.1 Data Gaps and Accessibility

Despite the advancements in GeoAI, data gaps and accessibility issues remain significant barriers, especially in developing countries. Limited access to high-quality, high-resolution data can hinder the effectiveness of climate modeling and adaptation planning.

23.8.2 Technical and Computational Challenges

The computational complexity of GeoAI models poses challenges, particularly when dealing with massive datasets and real-time processing. While advances in cloud computing and AI techniques have mitigated some of these challenges, they remain significant concerns for widespread adoption.

23.8.3 Ethical and Equity Considerations

GeoAI solutions must be implemented with sensitivity to ethical concerns. Unequal access to technology or biased AI algorithms can exacerbate inequalities in climate adaptation efforts. Ensuring that adaptation strategies do not disadvantage marginalized communities is a central issue in the equitable deployment of GeoAI.

23.9 Future Directions for GeoAI in Climate Resilience

23.9.1 Innovations in Predictive Modeling

As AI technologies continue to evolve, GeoAI's predictive modeling capabilities are expected to improve. New AI algorithms, such as deep learning models and reinforcement learning, promise even higher accuracy in climate predictions and adaptation scenarios.

23.9.2 Enhancing Community Engagement

Future GeoAI tools should focus on user-friendly interfaces that empower local stakeholders and communities to actively engage in climate adaptation efforts. By integrating participatory approaches, GeoAI can ensure that adaptation strategies are tailored to the specific needs of vulnerable populations.

23.9.3 Towards Global Climate Adaptation Frameworks

To maximize the impact of GeoAI, it will be essential to integrate these technologies into broader global climate adaptation frameworks. Coordination across nations, sectors, and communities is crucial for implementing effective, large-scale adaptation measures.

23.10 Conclusion

GeoAI is revolutionizing climate resilience and adaptation by providing data-driven, scalable, and precise solutions for addressing the impacts of climate change. From agriculture to urban planning, GeoAI facilitates more informed decision-making, helping communities and industries adapt to climate risks. While there are challenges in terms of data access and ethical considerations, the future of GeoAI holds immense potential for driving sustainable adaptation strategies and building a climate-resilient world. The continued evolution of AI models and data technologies promises even greater capabilities, offering hope for managing climate risks in an increasingly uncertain future.

Chapter 24: GeoAI for Urban Heat Island Mapping and Mitigation

24.1 Introduction to Urban Heat Islands (UHI) and Their Impact

24.1.1 Defining Urban Heat Islands

Urban Heat Islands (UHIs) are urban areas that experience significantly higher temperatures than their surrounding rural areas due to human activities and the physical characteristics of the built environment. These localized temperature increases are mainly caused by the modification of land surfaces and the generation of heat from human activities. Urban heat islands can lead to various problems, ranging from heat stress to increased energy consumption.

UHIs are primarily attributed to:

- **Reduced Vegetation**: Urban environments often lack the vegetation cover that naturally cools the environment. As forests, fields, and grasslands are replaced by buildings, roads, and other impervious surfaces, the landscape's ability to absorb heat diminishes.

- **Concentration of Heat Sources**: Activities such as transportation, industrial operations, and energy consumption all contribute to waste heat in urban environments. This additional heat exacerbates the UHI effect, especially during hot weather.

- **Building Materials**: Materials like concrete, asphalt, and metal absorb and retain heat, contributing to higher temperatures.

These materials have a high thermal mass and are more effective at trapping heat compared to natural landscapes.

The UHI effect is not a transient phenomenon. In fact, it amplifies during the night when urban areas continue to release stored heat, while rural areas cool down rapidly.

24.1.2 The Impact of Urban Heat Islands on Human Health and the Environment

The consequences of UHI are multifaceted and go beyond simply uncomfortable temperatures. The increased urban temperatures can affect health, the economy, and the environment in various significant ways.

- **Human Health:**

  o Increased air pollution: The elevated temperatures from UHI intensify the formation of ground-level ozone, leading to poor air quality, which can exacerbate respiratory and cardiovascular diseases.

  o Heat-related health risks: Prolonged exposure to high temperatures, especially during heatwaves, increases the risk of heat-related illnesses, such as heat stroke, dehydration, and heat exhaustion. This is especially dangerous for vulnerable populations such as the elderly, children, and those with chronic health conditions.

  o Mortality and morbidity: In extreme cases, the UHI effect contributes to premature deaths, particularly in cities where there is insufficient green space or where buildings lack proper cooling systems.

- **Energy Consumption:**

  o Urban heat islands significantly increase energy demand, particularly during the summer months. The higher temperatures result in greater reliance on air conditioning systems, leading to higher electricity usage. This not only strains the power grid but also results in higher energy costs for residents.

○ Energy consumption for cooling can also exacerbate greenhouse gas emissions if the energy is sourced from non-renewable sources, further contributing to climate change.

● **Environmental Impact**:

○ Altered ecosystems: The UHI effect disrupts the natural microclimates of urban areas, affecting local ecosystems, biodiversity, and soil health. Higher temperatures can also change precipitation patterns, leading to water shortages or flood risks.

○ Increased greenhouse gases: As cities become hotter, the UHI effect enhances the emission of pollutants like CO_2 and particulate matter, worsening the city's carbon footprint and contributing to global climate change.

● **Social and Economic Burdens**:

○ Increased healthcare costs: With the rise in heat-related illnesses and deaths, cities face significant healthcare costs related to treating the victims of heatwaves and respiratory problems.

○ Decreased productivity: Heat stress also affects productivity in workspaces, reducing work efficiency, especially in outdoor labor sectors.

24.1.3 The Role of GeoAI in Mapping and Mitigating UHIs

GeoAI plays an essential role in mitigating the effects of UHI by helping urban planners and policymakers better understand heat patterns and implement solutions. GeoAI integrates geospatial data, satellite imagery, and machine learning algorithms to analyze UHI, predict its effects, and offer mitigation strategies.

GeoAI offers:

- **Data-Driven Insights**: Satellite imagery, remote sensing, and AI algorithms process vast quantities of data to pinpoint urban heat hotspots, predict their growth, and assess mitigation opportunities.

- **Predictive Modeling**: AI models can predict how UHIs will evolve in the future, allowing cities to plan ahead. These predictions help urban planners anticipate the impacts of future urbanization and develop strategies to manage UHI before they worsen.

- **Real-Time Monitoring**: GeoAI systems can continuously monitor UHI in real-time using a combination of satellite sensors, weather data, and IoT-enabled temperature sensors. This real-time data allows for quicker interventions and adaptive strategies during extreme heat events.

24.2 Identifying Urban Heat Islands Using Satellite Imagery and GeoAI

24.2.1 Satellite Imaging Technologies for UHI Mapping

Satellite imagery is invaluable for the mapping of UHI. These technologies provide insights into urban temperature variations over time, enabling comprehensive monitoring of UHI dynamics. Advanced satellite platforms equipped with thermal infrared imaging, multispectral, and hyperspectral sensors are particularly useful for assessing UHI.

Key satellite technologies include:

- **Landsat Satellites**: The Landsat series, managed by NASA and the U.S. Geological Survey (USGS), has been collecting multispectral data for over four decades. With the availability of thermal infrared bands, Landsat satellites can provide valuable insights into temperature patterns over time. The long-term data archive is essential for tracking how UHI intensifies over decades.

- **MODIS (Moderate Resolution Imaging Spectroradiometer)**: MODIS, aboard NASA's Terra and Aqua satellites, provides near-real-time data on surface temperatures and land cover at various spatial resolutions. MODIS is often used for monitoring UHI globally because of its daily coverage and its ability to provide temperature information across large urban areas.

- **Sentinel-2 Satellites**: Managed by the European Space Agency (ESA), the Sentinel-2 satellites are part of the Copernicus program and provide high-resolution optical and infrared imagery. These satellites are ideal for high-precision mapping of urban heat islands, with temporal data that can track seasonal and diurnal changes in urban heat.

Satellite data collected from these systems is processed to produce **thermal maps** that highlight heat distribution across urban areas, identifying specific locations that are susceptible to the UHI effect.

24.2.2 Role of AI in UHI Detection

GeoAI algorithms, especially machine learning techniques, significantly enhance the accuracy and scalability of UHI detection. AI models can analyze large volumes of satellite data to identify heat hotspots, model temperature variations, and predict future trends.

Key AI techniques for UHI detection:

- **Supervised Learning**: Algorithms like Random Forest and Support Vector Machines (SVM) are used to classify areas based on thermal properties. These models are trained using labeled data from known UHI locations, enabling the AI to identify and map heat islands in uncharted territories.

- **Clustering**: AI techniques such as k-means clustering allow GeoAI systems to identify groups of pixels with similar temperature characteristics. This is crucial for identifying heat hotspots and understanding the spatial distribution of UHI in urban areas.

- **Deep Learning (CNNs)**: Convolutional Neural Networks (CNNs) are used to extract complex spatial patterns from high-resolution satellite imagery. These deep learning models are ideal for detecting UHI effects in high-density urban areas and identifying subtle temperature variations that traditional methods might miss.

GeoAI systems process these datasets to generate actionable heat maps, highlighting areas that require urgent attention and possible mitigation strategies.

24.2.3 Case Study: UHI Mapping in Major Cities

A key case study of UHI mapping using GeoAI is the **New York City Urban Heat Island Initiative**. Using Landsat imagery and machine learning algorithms, researchers were able to map the city's heat islands with high spatial resolution. This work revealed temperature differences of up to 7°C between the hottest urban areas and cooler green spaces. The data informed heat vulnerability maps, which are crucial for identifying communities most at risk during heatwaves and targeting interventions such as cooling centers and green infrastructure installations.

Similarly, **Los Angeles** used GeoAI in partnership with NASA's Earth Science Division to assess the city's UHI. By integrating satellite data and

AI-driven models, the city was able to design a heat mitigation strategy that included the installation of cool roofs and the creation of urban parks in the hottest areas. The project has resulted in a noticeable reduction in urban heat, particularly in historically underserved neighborhoods.

24.3 Understanding Heat Patterns and Urbanization's Role

24.3.1 Analyzing Heat Patterns with GeoAI

GeoAI enhances the understanding of how heat spreads through cities and how urbanization influences UHI. By combining geospatial data, such as surface temperatures, land-use information, and demographic data, GeoAI systems offer deep insights into the spatial distribution of heat in urban environments.

Time-series Analysis: GeoAI enables cities to analyze seasonal and long-term temperature changes. By processing satellite data over multiple years, AI models identify whether urban heat is becoming more concentrated or if it is expanding into previously cooler areas. This information is key to understanding how future development may exacerbate the UHI effect and informs the design of adaptive interventions.

Spatial Analysis: AI-driven spatial models can also help urban planners understand **heat islands' geographic features**, such as proximity to major transportation routes or large commercial hubs. This type of analysis can pinpoint which areas of a city would benefit the most from cooling measures such as tree planting, green roofs, or the creation of reflective surfaces.

24.3.2 The Influence of Urbanization on UHI Formation

Urbanization amplifies the UHI effect by replacing natural vegetation with impervious surfaces that absorb and retain heat. Dense urban areas tend to experience more pronounced heat island effects because of the higher concentration of buildings, vehicles, and energy consumption.

GeoAI models allow cities to:

- **Understand the Relationship**: By analyzing both urban growth patterns and heat intensity, AI can identify how specific urbanization processes—such as the construction of roads, shopping centers, or industrial parks—contribute to temperature increases.

- **Anticipate Future Growth**: As cities continue to expand, GeoAI systems can predict how new development projects might affect heat levels and where urban growth could exacerbate UHI. For example, AI can assess whether expanding urban sprawl in a certain direction will push heat further into residential areas and impact the quality of life.

These insights are used to inform **sustainable development policies**, ensuring that new urban development accounts for UHI mitigation, reducing the negative impacts of urban growth on climate resilience.

24.4 Mitigating Urban Heat Islands: GeoAI-Driven Strategies

24.4.1 Implementing Cool Roofs and Reflective Surfaces

One of the most cost-effective and immediate ways to address UHI is the widespread implementation of **cool roofs**. These are roofing materials that reflect more sunlight and absorb less heat compared to traditional roofing materials, thus lowering surrounding temperatures.

GeoAI models can:

- **Simulate Cool Roof Effects**: AI-driven simulations predict how the introduction of cool roofs in certain districts would lower temperatures across neighborhoods. These models also forecast how cool roofs reduce energy consumption in buildings, making the mitigation strategy both environmentally and economically beneficial.

- **Identify High-Impact Areas**: GeoAI identifies which neighborhoods would benefit most from the installation of cool roofs based on factors like solar exposure, current temperature, and building types. These predictive models are crucial in prioritizing areas with the greatest potential for heat reduction.

In **Chicago**, the city's cool roof program used GeoAI models to map temperature gradients and identify which roofs would have the greatest cooling impact. The city expanded its cool roof program after AI predictions demonstrated a substantial reduction in ambient temperatures.

24.4.2 Green Infrastructure and Green Roofs

The introduction of green infrastructure—particularly urban greening and the installation of green roofs—is another effective way to mitigate the UHI effect. **Green roofs**, which are partially or fully covered with vegetation, absorb sunlight, provide shade, and facilitate evaporative cooling.

GeoAI helps:

- **Model Cooling Potential**: By assessing land-use data and available space, GeoAI can predict the cooling effects of green roofs, parks, and tree canopy coverage. This allows city planners to understand which green infrastructure interventions would be most effective.

- **Assess Cost-Benefit Analysis**: In some cases, green infrastructure can be expensive. GeoAI models allow cities to analyze the financial and environmental trade-offs of various greening strategies, helping prioritize projects that offer the greatest return on investment in terms of cooling and sustainability.

A notable case of **green roofs** is **Toronto**, where GeoAI modeling played a significant role in identifying areas with the highest potential for green roof installation. The city's successful green roof program helped significantly reduce heat in residential areas and encouraged other municipalities to adopt similar strategies.

24.5 Role of GeoAI in Heatwave Prediction and Real-Time Monitoring

24.5.1 Predicting Heatwaves and Future UHI Trends

One of the significant challenges with Urban Heat Islands (UHI) is their unpredictability, especially when combined with extreme weather events like heatwaves. GeoAI plays an essential role in predicting heatwaves and their potential impact on urban areas by integrating historical temperature data, weather forecasts, and real-time environmental monitoring.

AI-based predictive models are capable of:

- **Forecasting Heatwave Events**: Machine learning algorithms, such as **ensemble models** or **deep learning networks**, can be trained on large datasets of historical weather data, satellite imagery, and climate models. These algorithms can predict when and where a heatwave is likely to occur, especially in cities known to experience intense UHI effects.

- **Understanding Seasonal Trends**: GeoAI helps cities model **seasonal variations** in UHI intensity, helping urban planners prepare for the specific challenges of summer months. By analyzing long-term data, AI can identify patterns in temperature rise that correlate with human activities or geographical factors, helping to predict areas most at risk for heatwaves.

For example, **Los Angeles**, which faces heatwaves regularly, uses GeoAI to predict heat events, analyze temperature spikes, and take preemptive actions such as issuing heat advisories, setting up cooling centers, or optimizing emergency services.

24.5.2 Real-Time UHI Monitoring with IoT and Satellite Data

Real-time monitoring of UHI is crucial for effective response strategies during heatwaves. While satellites provide broad coverage of temperature patterns, combining **IoT (Internet of Things)** sensors with GeoAI provides highly localized, real-time data.

IoT-enabled temperature sensors placed in different parts of the city send data back to a central system where AI models process this information to generate immediate feedback on UHI intensities. These sensors can be placed on streetlights, buildings, or utility poles, providing temperature data that is updated every few minutes. When combined with satellite imagery, this system allows for a more comprehensive and immediate assessment of urban heat distribution.

- **Heat Vulnerability Assessment**: AI models can analyze real-time temperature data to assess vulnerable populations. For instance, during heatwaves, GeoAI models help cities target interventions in areas where the elderly, children, or low-income populations live, who are at higher risk of heat-related illnesses.

- **Urban Heat Mitigation Decisions**: In places where real-time monitoring indicates a spike in urban temperatures, AI systems can provide instant mitigation recommendations, such as the activation of cooling centers or the provision of water through public systems in areas where UHI is at its most intense.

The **City of Paris** used IoT and AI to implement a **"Heat Wave Alert System"**, where temperature sensors integrated with satellite data and weather models provided real-time monitoring of heat islands. This allowed the city to issue warnings and mobilize emergency services during heatwaves, improving resilience in vulnerable communities.

24.6 Implementing Mitigation Measures Using GeoAI Insights

24.6.1 Green Spaces and Urban Cooling Strategies

One of the most effective ways to reduce the impact of Urban Heat Islands is the expansion of **green spaces** such as urban parks, forests, and community gardens. Green infrastructure has a cooling effect due to the evapotranspiration process, where plants release water vapor that cools the surrounding air.

GeoAI assists in:

- **Identifying Optimal Locations for Green Spaces**: AI-powered land-use classification systems can analyze satellite images and other geospatial data to identify where new green spaces or parks could be created. GeoAI can assess the local temperature and air quality to select areas where greening will have the highest cooling effect.

- **Modeling Vegetation Impact**: Machine learning models can simulate how the introduction of trees, plants, and parks would influence surrounding temperature and airflow. This helps urban planners decide how much vegetation is needed to combat the UHI effect and what types of plants would be most effective for specific climates.

For instance, **Singapore**, renowned for its "City in a Garden" initiative, uses GeoAI to plan the installation of parks and green roofs. AI models analyze temperature hotspots, wind patterns, and land availability to design the most effective green spaces to combat UHI.

24.6.2 Cool Roofs and Reflective Surfaces

Cool roofs are another widely adopted strategy to mitigate UHI. These roofs are designed with materials that reflect more sunlight and absorb less heat compared to traditional roofs. GeoAI helps in the strategic placement of cool roofs by evaluating the thermal properties of individual buildings and their surrounding environments.

GeoAI can:

- **Assess the Impact of Cool Roofs**: Using machine learning models and thermal imagery, GeoAI evaluates how cool roofs would affect temperature reduction at a neighborhood scale. These models also take into account factors like **roof orientation**, **building height**, and **surrounding shade** to optimize roof material selection and placement.

- **Prioritize Areas for Cool Roof Installation**: AI models predict the most effective areas to install cool roofs based on urban heat hotspots. In areas where temperatures are known to rise sharply, cool roofs can be prioritized for both public and private buildings.

Cities like **New York City** and **Los Angeles** have successfully implemented cool roof programs. Through GeoAI models, New York has been able to measure the reduction in building temperatures and track energy savings due to cool roof installations. In **Los Angeles**, the city has targeted its cool roof strategy to lower peak temperatures in disadvantaged communities, where UHI effects are most pronounced.

24.6.3 Urban Forestry and Tree Canopy Expansion

Expanding urban forests and increasing tree canopy cover is another effective strategy for mitigating UHI. Trees and shrubs provide shade, cool the environment through evapotranspiration, and improve air quality by absorbing pollutants.

GeoAI contributes by:

- **Scalability and Cost**: Implementing GeoAI solutions on a city-wide scale requires significant investment in infrastructure, training, and technology. Therefore, it is essential for policymakers to ensure that the benefits of UHI mitigation reach all communities, particularly those most vulnerable.

In the future, **AI advancements**—including the integration of **edge computing**, **cloud-based AI models**, and **enhanced satellite technology**—will likely expand the scope and capabilities of GeoAI systems. These innovations will continue to refine UHI mitigation efforts and help cities build resilience against the growing challenges of climate change.

GeoAI's potential to mitigate the effects of urban heat islands offers hope for cities worldwide, contributing to the creation of more sustainable, healthy, and climate-resilient urban environments.

Chapter 25: GeoAI and Smart Agriculture for Sustainable Food Systems

25.1 Introduction to GeoAI in Agriculture

In recent years, the agricultural sector has undergone a technological revolution, shifting from traditional practices to more data-driven, efficient methods. **GeoAI**, a combination of **geospatial data** and **artificial intelligence (AI)**, plays a pivotal role in this transformation. With the ability to integrate vast amounts of data from remote sensing, satellite imagery, and in-field sensors, GeoAI enables farmers to make more informed decisions, optimize their resource use, and improve the sustainability of their farming practices.

Precision agriculture—a modern farming approach that uses advanced technologies to monitor and manage agricultural processes—relies heavily on GeoAI for managing resources such as water, fertilizers, and land. Through precise data collection and analysis, farmers can not only maximize crop production but also minimize their environmental footprint, thus contributing to a sustainable food system.

GeoAI's main promise lies in its capacity to merge spatial and temporal data with AI algorithms, providing insights that were previously unattainable with traditional farming practices. This results in **increased productivity**, **resource conservation**, and **reduced environmental impact**—all vital for ensuring global food security and sustainability in the face of challenges such as population growth, climate change, and limited natural resources.

25.2 Integration of GeoAI with IoT in Smart Agriculture

The integration of **GeoAI** with **Internet of Things (IoT)** technology forms the backbone of smart agriculture, transforming how data is collected, analyzed, and acted upon in real-time. IoT devices, such as **sensors, drones,** and **connected machinery**, are deployed in agricultural environments to monitor everything from soil moisture to air quality. The data collected by these devices provides the foundation for AI-powered insights that help farmers manage their land and resources more efficiently.

The Role of IoT in Agriculture

IoT technology facilitates the collection of real-time data from across the farm. Sensors placed in the soil can measure moisture levels, temperature, and nutrient content, while drones and satellites capture aerial imagery to monitor crop health. These data sources can be processed using AI models to detect patterns and identify areas that need attention. For instance, soil moisture sensors can inform irrigation decisions, allowing farmers to water only where needed, thereby reducing water waste.

IoT sensors can also track **weather conditions**, **pests**, **disease outbreaks**, and **soil degradation**, enabling predictive models that anticipate issues before they become significant problems. This not only saves time and resources but also contributes to **long-term sustainability** by preventing overuse or mismanagement of inputs.

How GeoAI Processes IoT Data

The combination of **GeoAI** and **IoT** offers a powerful synergy. While IoT collects real-time, localized data, GeoAI brings in the ability to analyze spatial data and run complex algorithms to interpret the large datasets generated by these devices. Machine learning algorithms help process information by finding hidden patterns in the data and making accurate predictions.

For example, an AI algorithm can identify underperforming areas of a farm based on IoT-supplied data such as soil moisture levels, temperature, and crop health. This allows for targeted interventions such as adjusting irrigation systems or applying fertilizer only where necessary, thus improving both **crop yield** and **resource efficiency**.

Case Study: Precision Irrigation

A notable application of GeoAI and IoT integration is in **precision irrigation**. In regions where water scarcity is a pressing issue, smart irrigation systems that leverage **soil moisture sensors** and **weather forecasts** are crucial. GeoAI can predict weather patterns and adjust irrigation schedules accordingly, ensuring water is only used when necessary. This approach conserves water, reduces costs, and ensures that crops are adequately nourished.

In Israel, for example, **Netafim**, a company specializing in precision irrigation, uses IoT sensors in combination with AI-powered systems to monitor soil moisture levels and automate irrigation. The system ensures crops receive optimal water without wastage, contributing to water conservation in arid regions and significantly increasing crop yields.

25.3 Optimizing Crop Production with GeoAI

GeoAI plays a crucial role in **crop production optimization**, helping farmers to increase efficiency and maximize yields. Through satellite imagery, drone data, and field sensors, GeoAI helps farmers monitor crop health and productivity on a continuous basis. AI-powered systems can process this data to identify patterns and predict outcomes, making crop production more predictable and less reliant on trial and error.

Crop Yield Prediction

Predicting crop yields with high accuracy is a challenge, particularly in the face of changing weather patterns and unpredictable environmental conditions. By analyzing historical data, weather forecasts, and real-time inputs like soil moisture levels, GeoAI models are capable of providing farmers with predictions about expected yields before harvest time. These insights help farmers make critical decisions on when to harvest and whether additional interventions (like irrigation or pest control) are required.

For instance, machine learning algorithms can predict the yield of wheat, corn, or rice crops based on data from weather stations and remote sensing. These predictions allow farmers to plan for harvest and distribution in advance, reducing food waste and optimizing supply chains.

Real-Time Crop Monitoring

GeoAI enables **real-time crop monitoring** through the use of drones, satellites, and IoT devices. By collecting high-resolution images of crop fields, AI models can analyze the images to detect signs of diseases, pests, or nutrient deficiencies. Early detection allows farmers to take prompt action, minimizing losses and optimizing crop health.

For example, drones equipped with **NDVI (Normalized Difference Vegetation Index)** sensors can provide high-resolution images that help monitor plant health. AI algorithms can then process this imagery to detect anomalies, such as wilting, yellowing, or pest infestations. The AI model can then provide recommendations for timely intervention, whether it's adjusting irrigation schedules or applying specific pesticides.

Case Study: Yield Prediction in Wheat Farming

In India, a **GeoAI-based platform** was implemented to predict the yield of wheat crops. The system uses satellite imagery, weather data, and field sensor data to predict yield outcomes with high accuracy. This system was able to significantly improve decision-making, reducing uncertainty around crop output and enabling farmers to better manage their supply chains.

The system not only predicted yields but also provided insights into **optimal harvesting times**, which prevented the over-ripening of crops and allowed for better timing of distribution. This application contributed to increased farmer incomes and reduced losses from food spoilage.

25.4 Soil Health and Fertility Management with GeoAI

Maintaining soil health and fertility is essential for long-term agricultural productivity. GeoAI helps optimize soil management practices by providing detailed insights into soil quality, nutrient levels, and moisture content. This allows farmers to take a more **scientific** approach to fertilization, irrigation, and crop rotation.

Soil Monitoring Using GeoAI

Soil health is a critical factor that influences crop yield and sustainability. GeoAI-enabled soil monitoring systems can measure key indicators such as **soil pH**, **organic matter**, and **nutrient levels**. This data is essential for creating soil-specific fertility management plans that ensure the long-term viability of farmland.

In precision agriculture, GeoAI models can track soil conditions over time, identifying trends such as nutrient depletion or compaction, which may require specific interventions such as soil aeration, organic fertilization, or crop rotation.

Precision Fertilization

Traditional fertilizer application often leads to overuse, resulting in environmental pollution, nutrient runoff, and soil degradation. GeoAI provides a solution through **precision fertilization**. By using **satellite imagery**, **soil sensors**, and AI models, GeoAI can guide farmers on the exact amount of fertilizer required for each area of the field. This targeted approach maximizes crop growth while minimizing fertilizer waste and environmental impact.

A study in Brazil demonstrated that GeoAI-based precision fertilization led to **20% lower fertilizer use** and **15% higher crop yields**, significantly reducing input costs and environmental harm.

Case Study: Precision Fertilization in Rice Farming

In Southeast Asia, **GeoAI models** have been used to optimize rice farming practices. Through satellite imagery, sensors, and AI-powered algorithms, farmers can determine the precise amount of fertilizer and water needed for each part of the rice field. This approach not only boosts rice yields but also conserves valuable resources such as water and fertilizers, contributing to both economic and environmental sustainability.

25.5 Pest and Disease Detection Using GeoAI

Pests and diseases pose a significant threat to crops worldwide, often resulting in severe losses and requiring costly interventions. GeoAI allows for early detection of pests and diseases, enabling farmers to act swiftly and minimize damage.

AI for Early Pest and Disease Detection

GeoAI's ability to analyze **satellite imagery** and **drone-captured imagery** allows farmers to identify pest and disease outbreaks early. Using **machine learning algorithms**, AI can detect subtle changes in crop health that are indicative of pest infestations or diseases. For instance, AI systems can detect changes in crop leaf color or texture, which might signal a fungal infection or pest damage.

By identifying issues early, farmers can apply **pesticides** or **biological controls** only in the affected areas, reducing pesticide use and minimizing environmental harm.

Case Study: GeoAI for Pest Control in Cotton Farming

In the cotton farming industry, GeoAI has been used to detect **bollworm infestations** early in the growing season. By analyzing drone imagery, AI algorithms can detect subtle symptoms of pest damage, prompting timely intervention. This early intervention helped cotton farmers reduce pesticide application by **30%**, which led to both cost savings and a reduction in chemical use.

25.6 Resource Management and Sustainability in Agriculture

GeoAI supports **resource management** in agriculture, helping farmers use water, fertilizers, and pesticides more efficiently. By analyzing spatial and temporal data, GeoAI models optimize **resource allocation** to ensure that inputs are applied only where needed, reducing waste and promoting sustainability.

Water Resource Management

One of the most pressing challenges in agriculture is water scarcity. GeoAI models, combined with IoT-based soil moisture sensors and weather data, help farmers optimize their irrigation systems. By predicting rainfall and moisture content in the soil, AI-powered irrigation systems can deliver water only when needed, ensuring water is conserved while maintaining crop health.

Energy Efficiency

GeoAI can also optimize energy use in agricultural operations, particularly in energy-intensive areas like **greenhouses** and **livestock management**. AI models can predict energy needs for temperature control and ventilation in greenhouses, adjusting systems in real-time to minimize energy consumption while maintaining optimal growing conditions.

Waste Reduction

GeoAI models can track resource usage across the farm, helping farmers identify inefficiencies and reduce waste. By accurately predicting resource needs and ensuring they are applied only where necessary, GeoAI promotes **sustainability** and reduces the environmental footprint of agriculture.

25.7 GeoAI and Climate Resilience in Agriculture

The impacts of **climate change** on agriculture are already evident, with shifts in weather patterns, rising temperatures, and changing precipitation levels. GeoAI helps farmers develop adaptive strategies for **climate resilience**, ensuring that agricultural practices can withstand and thrive despite unpredictable climate conditions.

Climate Change Impacts on Agriculture

GeoAI provides detailed insights into how climate change affects agricultural systems. AI models can predict changes in temperature, rainfall, and other climate factors, allowing farmers to adjust their practices accordingly. This proactive approach helps mitigate risks associated with climate change and ensures consistent crop yields.

Adaptive Strategies for Resilient Agriculture

GeoAI helps farmers adopt **climate-resilient crops**, adjust **planting schedules**, and select locations that are better suited to the changing climate. Additionally, **data-driven decisions** can help farmers select crops that are more likely to thrive under future climate conditions, increasing resilience to droughts and floods.

Case Study: Climate Resilience in Maize Farming

In sub-Saharan Africa, farmers are adopting **climate-resilient maize varieties** using GeoAI models. These models use climate projections, soil data, and other environmental variables to recommend maize varieties that are likely to perform well in future climate scenarios. This adaptive strategy helps farmers cope with uncertain climate conditions and ensures food security.

25.8 GeoAI for Food Security and Supply Chain Optimization

GeoAI can significantly enhance **food security** by improving food distribution and reducing **supply chain inefficiencies**. By predicting food shortages, optimizing logistics, and improving **crop management**, GeoAI contributes to ensuring that food reaches those who need it most.

Predicting Food Shortages

GeoAI models predict food shortages based on crop performance data, weather patterns, and historical production trends. This information helps governments and organizations prepare for potential food crises, allowing them to take preemptive measures to ensure food availability.

Optimizing Food Distribution

By analyzing data on crop yields, supply chain logistics, and demand patterns, GeoAI can optimize the distribution of food. This reduces waste by ensuring that food is transported to where it is needed most and at the right time.

Case Study: Food Security in Sub-Saharan Africa

GeoAI-driven platforms have been used to predict crop failures and optimize food aid distribution in regions such as **Sub-Saharan Africa**, where food security is often at risk due to unpredictable weather patterns. These systems allow organizations to identify at-risk areas and ensure timely food delivery, reducing famine risks.

25.9 Policy and Governance in Smart Agriculture

GeoAI also plays an important role in shaping **agricultural policies**. By providing governments with data-driven insights into agricultural practices, sustainability, and resource management, GeoAI can guide **policy**

formulation that promotes smart agriculture and **environmental protection**.

GeoAI in Agricultural Policy

Governments can use GeoAI models to assess the impacts of different agricultural practices, formulate regulations to encourage sustainability, and provide farmers with guidelines for **smart farming techniques**.

Regulating Agricultural Inputs

GeoAI helps regulators track the use of **fertilizers**, **pesticides**, and **water** in agriculture. AI-powered systems can monitor whether farms are adhering to sustainability guidelines, reducing the overuse of harmful chemicals and promoting eco-friendly farming.

Case Study: Smart Farming Policies in India

India's use of GeoAI to implement **smart farming policies** showcases the power of AI in agriculture. Government initiatives focused on precision agriculture, supported by AI-powered tools, have improved productivity and sustainability, particularly in areas where smallholder farmers dominate.

25.10 Challenges and Future Directions in GeoAI for Agriculture

While GeoAI offers immense potential, there are several **challenges** that need to be addressed to fully realize its benefits. These include **data accuracy**, **technological accessibility**, and **integration with traditional farming practices**.

Challenges in Data Availability and Accuracy

Accurate data is crucial for GeoAI models, but in many rural areas, access to high-quality data or advanced technologies is limited. Overcoming these barriers is necessary to ensure that GeoAI can reach all farmers, especially in **developing countries**.

AI Integration with Traditional Farming Practices

For GeoAI to be successful, it must be integrated with traditional farming methods, many of which are based on local knowledge. This requires a balance between high-tech systems and local agricultural practices to create **inclusive** solutions.

Future Trends

As technology advances, **autonomous systems** such as AI-driven tractors, drones, and robots will play a more significant role in agriculture. GeoAI will continue to evolve, providing farmers with even more precise and actionable insights, contributing to more resilient and sustainable agricultural systems.

25.11 Conclusion

GeoAI has the potential to revolutionize agriculture, improving productivity, sustainability, and food security. Through the integration of IoT, machine learning, and geospatial data, farmers can optimize crop production, manage resources more efficiently, and adapt to the challenges posed by climate change. While there are challenges in data accessibility and integration, the future of GeoAI in agriculture holds great promise, ensuring that the agricultural sector is prepared for a more sustainable and secure food system.

Chapter 26: GeoAI for Coastal and Marine Resource Management

26.1 Introduction to GeoAI in Coastal and Marine Resource Management

Overview of Coastal and Marine Ecosystem Importance

Coastal and marine ecosystems are among the most vital yet vulnerable ecosystems on Earth. They provide crucial resources for food, biodiversity, and carbon sequestration, and they also protect coastal communities from storms and erosion. From mangrove forests and coral reefs to seagrass meadows and coastal wetlands, these ecosystems serve as the lifeblood of both local and global economies. The **fisheries industry**, which supports millions of livelihoods worldwide, relies heavily on the health of marine ecosystems. Coastal regions, home to over 40% of the world's population, are facing increasing pressures due to urbanization, pollution, overfishing, and climate change. However, these ecosystems are also remarkably resilient, and modern technologies like **GeoAI** are playing a transformative role in their monitoring and management.

GeoAI (Geospatial Artificial Intelligence) represents the integration of geospatial technologies, such as **remote sensing** and **satellite imagery**, with artificial intelligence (AI) models to process and analyze spatial data. By combining these technologies, GeoAI enables unprecedented monitoring, prediction, and management of marine and coastal resources, providing essential insights for sustainable development, conservation efforts, and policy-making.

Challenges in Marine Resource Management

Despite their importance, coastal and marine ecosystems are under constant threat. Issues such as **pollution**, **overfishing**, **coastal erosion**, and the **degradation of marine habitats** continue to escalate. The impacts of climate change, including **rising sea levels**, **ocean acidification**, and the **warming of oceans**, have further stressed these ecosystems. Traditional methods of monitoring, such as physical surveys and limited sampling, are increasingly inadequate for managing vast and dynamic marine environments.

GeoAI offers a solution by enabling large-scale, real-time data collection, processing, and analysis, allowing resource managers and policymakers to monitor marine and coastal environments more efficiently and effectively. GeoAI models are capable of detecting environmental changes, tracking pollution, identifying areas in need of conservation, and predicting future trends based on current data.

Role of GeoAI

GeoAI plays a crucial role in enabling sustainable management of coastal and marine ecosystems by providing real-time, actionable insights. From **coral reef monitoring** to **fisheries management** and **marine pollution control**, GeoAI combines **satellite imagery**, **sensor data**, and **AI algorithms** to analyze vast amounts of data, offering deeper insights than traditional methods. By leveraging machine learning models, GeoAI can detect anomalies, forecast environmental impacts, and provide precise recommendations for policy and management strategies. Furthermore, it can help streamline decision-making by offering visualizations and predictive models that highlight areas of concern and suggest corrective actions.

26.2 Satellite Data and Remote Sensing for Coastal and Marine Monitoring

Role of Satellite Imagery in Coastal Monitoring

Satellite imagery has revolutionized the monitoring of coastal ecosystems. Historically, the challenge in monitoring vast and inaccessible marine areas was the lack of consistent data. However, advancements in **remote sensing technologies** have allowed the collection of high-resolution imagery of coastal and marine environments from space, offering insights into previously unreachable areas.

Satellites equipped with specialized sensors can measure a wide range of environmental factors, such as **sea surface temperature**, **chlorophyll concentration**, **salinity levels**, and **coastal land cover changes**. These measurements are essential for monitoring the health of marine ecosystems, such as **coral reefs**, **seagrasses**, and **mangrove forests**, which are highly sensitive to environmental changes. For example, **Sentinel-2 satellites**, part of the European Space Agency's **Copernicus program**, provide high-resolution imagery (10–60 meters) that can be used to detect changes in vegetation, coastal erosion, and pollution levels.

Types of Data Collected

Several types of data can be collected through satellite imagery and remote sensing techniques, all crucial for monitoring coastal and marine environments:

1. **Water Quality**: Data such as **turbidity, chlorophyll-a concentration**, and **nutrient levels** can be used to assess pollution levels and algal bloom risks.
2. **Vegetation Cover**: Satellites can track changes in coastal vegetation, such as mangroves, salt marshes, and seagrass beds, which are essential for coastal protection and biodiversity.
3. **Sea Surface Temperature (SST)**: SST data helps track the

warming of ocean waters, which can affect marine biodiversity and lead to coral bleaching.

4. **Coastal Erosion**: Remote sensing data is instrumental in monitoring coastal erosion and land loss, helping inform decisions about coastal protection and restoration.

GeoAI for Image Processing

Processing satellite imagery and transforming it into usable data is a complex task that requires advanced techniques in image analysis. GeoAI technologies, including machine learning and deep learning models, are used to automate and enhance this process.

For instance, **convolutional neural networks (CNNs)** can be applied to satellite images to detect specific features in coastal regions, such as **mangrove deforestation** or **coral bleaching**. By training AI algorithms on large datasets, these models can detect patterns in the images that might otherwise go unnoticed. **Anomaly detection** techniques can identify unusual events like **oil spills** or **illegal fishing activities** in real-time, helping resource managers and authorities respond quickly.

AI-powered image processing is not limited to analysis but extends to providing meaningful interpretations and predictions. For example, AI can forecast **habitat loss** or **fish population shifts** based on current environmental conditions and historical data.

Benefits of Satellite Data

The advantages of using satellite data for coastal monitoring are numerous:

- **Cost-effectiveness**: Satellite data is often less expensive and less labor-intensive than traditional field-based data collection methods.

- **Global Coverage**: Satellites can monitor vast areas of the ocean and coastal regions, including remote and hard-to-reach areas.

- **Real-time Monitoring**: Satellites can provide near-real-time data, enabling quick responses to environmental changes and pollution events.

- **Long-term Data Collection**: Satellites allow for continuous data collection over long periods, enabling the tracking of environmental trends and the identification of changes over time.

26.3 Monitoring Marine Pollution Using GeoAI

Types of Marine Pollution

Marine pollution is a growing global problem, with harmful substances such as plastics, oil, chemicals, and untreated sewage being discharged into the oceans at alarming rates. These pollutants pose serious threats to marine life and coastal communities. In addition, marine pollution is a significant contributor to the degradation of ecosystems like coral reefs, mangroves, and coastal wetlands.

1. **Plastic Pollution**: The accumulation of plastics in marine environments is one of the most visible and widespread forms of pollution. Plastics can be found in nearly every corner of the world's oceans, affecting marine animals and ecosystems.
2. **Oil Spills**: Accidental oil spills, whether from shipping accidents or offshore drilling, can have devastating effects on marine life, particularly in sensitive coastal and estuarine habitats.
3. **Chemical Pollution**: Agricultural runoff, industrial waste, and sewage discharge contribute to the contamination of oceans with toxic chemicals, heavy metals, and excess nutrients.
4. **Noise Pollution**: Increased human activity in oceans, such as shipping and industrial activities, also leads to noise pollution, which affects marine species like whales and dolphins.

Role of GeoAI in Pollution Detection

GeoAI plays a pivotal role in monitoring and mitigating marine pollution by providing real-time data and predictive models to assess and address pollution events. Some of the most important applications of GeoAI in marine pollution detection include:

1. **Oil Spill Detection**: Satellites equipped with **synthetic aperture radar (SAR)** can detect oil spills on the ocean's surface. These radar systems can penetrate clouds and darkness, allowing for continuous monitoring even in adverse weather conditions. GeoAI models can automatically process and analyze the SAR data to identify oil spill locations and estimate their size. For example, during the **Deepwater Horizon oil spill**, satellite and SAR data were used, along with AI algorithms, to track the spill's spread in real-time.
2. **Plastic Waste Monitoring**: AI-powered image recognition tools are increasingly being used to detect plastic waste floating on the ocean's surface. GeoAI algorithms can classify objects in satellite imagery, helping to identify areas with high concentrations of debris, which can then be targeted for cleanup efforts.
3. **Water Quality Monitoring**: GeoAI systems process satellite data to monitor **chlorophyll-a** concentrations, which can indicate harmful algal blooms (HABs). These blooms are often caused by nutrient pollution and can have deadly effects on marine ecosystems and fisheries.

Case Study: Oil Spill Monitoring in the Gulf of Mexico

In 2010, the **Deepwater Horizon oil spill** released millions of barrels of oil into the Gulf of Mexico, causing devastating environmental damage. GeoAI technologies, particularly satellite-based SAR, were instrumental in tracking the spread of the oil slick in real time. AI algorithms were used to process the satellite data, enabling faster decision-making and targeted clean-up operations. The success of this effort demonstrated the potential of GeoAI in managing pollution and minimizing the environmental and economic impacts of oil spills.

Applications in Policy and Enforcement

GeoAI can help enforce international regulations related to marine pollution. For example, the **International Maritime Organization (IMO)** sets regulations for shipping companies to minimize oil discharges into the oceans. By using satellite data and AI algorithms to track vessels and monitor their compliance with these regulations, GeoAI technologies enable authorities to take swift action against violators. Additionally,

GeoAI helps countries monitor pollution levels in their exclusive economic zones (EEZs) and maintain compliance with international environmental agreements, such as the **Convention for the Protection of the Mediterranean Sea Against Pollution** (Barcelona Convention).

26.4 Coral Reef Health Monitoring with GeoAI

Importance of Coral Reefs

Coral reefs are critical to marine biodiversity, supporting approximately 25% of all marine species. They also provide essential ecosystem services, such as coastal protection from storms and erosion, and they support local economies through tourism and fisheries. However, coral reefs are highly sensitive to changes in temperature, water quality, and other environmental stressors, and they are increasingly threatened by **ocean acidification**, **coral bleaching**, **pollution**, and **overfishing**.

Role of GeoAI in Coral Reef Monitoring

GeoAI technologies are essential in monitoring the health of coral reefs, which often suffer from **bleaching** due to rising sea temperatures. By combining satellite imagery with AI algorithms, GeoAI can provide real-time assessments of coral reef conditions, enabling early detection of threats and guiding conservation efforts.

1. **Coral Bleaching Detection**: Using **thermal imagery** and **sea surface temperature** data from satellites, GeoAI algorithms can detect **anomalies** in water temperature that trigger coral bleaching. Machine learning models can also be trained to identify signs of bleaching from high-resolution satellite images.
2. **Coral Coverage Mapping**: AI models can automatically classify coral reef habitats from satellite imagery, helping to map the extent of coral coverage and detect areas at risk of degradation.
3. **Ecosystem Health Assessment**: GeoAI can assess the health of coral reef ecosystems by tracking changes in **fish populations**, **seaweed coverage**, and **sedimentation rates**—all of which can impact coral reef survival.

26.5 The Role of AI in Fisheries Management

Challenges in Fisheries Management

Fisheries around the world face significant challenges related to overfishing, illegal, unreported, and unregulated (IUU) fishing, and the depletion of fish stocks. Traditional methods of monitoring fish populations and fishing activities have often been ineffective due to limited resources and the vastness of marine environments. Overfishing, if not controlled, can lead to the collapse of fisheries, endangering the livelihoods of millions of people, particularly in coastal communities dependent on fish as their primary source of protein and income.

The introduction of **GeoAI** in fisheries management provides a more sustainable, data-driven approach to tracking fish populations, regulating fishing practices, and ensuring sustainable yields. By integrating satellite data, real-time monitoring systems, and AI-powered predictive models, GeoAI helps optimize the management of fisheries, minimizing the risk of depletion and promoting responsible fishing practices.

GeoAI in Fish Stock Assessment

AI models can play a vital role in assessing fish stocks by analyzing large datasets obtained from various sources, such as satellite imagery, sonar data, and marine sensors. For example, GeoAI can predict **fish population trends** based on environmental variables like water temperature, salinity, and currents. Machine learning algorithms can be used to detect fish aggregations by processing sonar data and satellite imagery to estimate fish density in a given area. These AI models can also be trained on historical data to predict the future abundance of different fish species, assisting resource managers in determining sustainable harvest limits.

In addition, AI models can assess the impact of environmental changes, such as shifts in water temperature due to climate change, on fish migration patterns. By understanding these dynamics, managers can develop strategies to prevent overfishing in vulnerable regions or seasons, ensuring the long-term health of fish populations.

Monitoring and Combating Illegal Fishing

IUU fishing remains a significant threat to global marine resources. Illegal fishers often exploit weak enforcement mechanisms and operate in remote or unmonitored areas, making it difficult for authorities to detect and respond to illegal activities in real-time. GeoAI technologies have the potential to revolutionize the monitoring of fishing activities by using satellite data to track vessels' locations, behaviors, and fishing patterns.

By analyzing **Automatic Identification System (AIS)** data, **vessel monitoring system (VMS)** data, and satellite-based imagery, AI models can detect suspicious vessel movements and fishing behaviors indicative of IUU activities. These models can identify patterns in ship trajectories, such as those that suggest fishing in restricted areas or during closed seasons, and send alerts to relevant authorities for prompt intervention.

One notable example of this technology in action is the collaboration between the **Global Fishing Watch (GFW)**, **Google Earth Engine**, and

SkyTruth. Using satellite data and AI algorithms, GFW monitors global fishing activities, helping governments and NGOs identify illegal fishing practices and hold offenders accountable.

Case Study: AI in Fisheries Management in the Pacific Ocean

In the Pacific Ocean, an AI-driven project called **Fishery Analysis and Management (FAM)** uses machine learning to predict fish stock health and optimize management practices. The system combines satellite data, marine forecasts, and onboard sensor data from fishing vessels to monitor fish populations in real time. By predicting fish stock health, this system allows fisheries managers to adjust fishing quotas dynamically and reduce overfishing. Additionally, AI helps detect and flag IUU fishing activities, enabling timely enforcement action.

This approach has been particularly effective in regions like the **Western and Central Pacific Fisheries Commission (WCPFC)**, where AI models have helped mitigate overfishing of species like tuna and billfish. By combining AI with satellite data, this program ensures that fishing practices remain within sustainable limits and that marine biodiversity is preserved.

26.6 Marine Protected Areas (MPAs) and Conservation Efforts

Role of GeoAI in Marine Conservation

Marine Protected Areas (MPAs) are designated regions of the ocean where human activity is restricted to safeguard marine biodiversity. MPAs have been shown to be effective in promoting the recovery of depleted fish stocks, protecting endangered species, and preserving critical ecosystems like coral reefs and mangrove forests. However, enforcing MPA boundaries and ensuring their success can be challenging, especially in large, remote, or high-risk areas.

GeoAI helps overcome these challenges by providing tools for **monitoring MPA effectiveness**, ensuring compliance with protection measures, and assessing the ecological health of these areas. GeoAI technologies support the identification of optimal MPA locations, track changes in biodiversity, and evaluate the effectiveness of protection efforts.

Satellite Imagery for MPA Monitoring

Satellites provide an invaluable tool for monitoring the health of MPAs. GeoAI models can process satellite data to assess the status of ecosystems within protected areas, such as coral reef health, mangrove coverage, and fish populations. These models can automatically detect habitat degradation or violations of MPA boundaries, helping authorities take swift action to protect these critical areas.

One of the key benefits of using satellite data for MPA monitoring is that it provides high spatial and temporal resolution, allowing for regular assessments of ecosystem health. For example, GeoAI algorithms can analyze **high-resolution imagery** to detect shifts in coral reef coverage, indicating coral bleaching or damage from human activities. By identifying these threats early, conservation efforts can be redirected or intensified in areas at risk.

Predictive Modeling for MPA Effectiveness

GeoAI can also be used to **predict the long-term effectiveness** of MPAs by modeling the potential outcomes of various management strategies. AI-powered predictive models take into account a wide range of variables, including environmental conditions, fishing pressures, and climate change, to forecast how different protection strategies will affect biodiversity and ecosystem health. These models can be used to simulate various scenarios and determine the optimal management approach for each MPA, improving conservation outcomes.

For example, AI models can predict how an MPA will recover from overfishing or coral bleaching based on current environmental trends and restoration efforts. This enables conservationists to adjust management practices and resources more effectively, ensuring that MPAs are resilient to future challenges.

26.7 Enhancing Sustainable Resource Management with GeoAI

Sustainable Fisheries Management and GeoAI

Sustainability in marine resource management relies on balancing the needs of human populations with the capacity of ecosystems to regenerate. GeoAI provides valuable insights for improving sustainability by monitoring **fishing practices**, ensuring **resource conservation**, and assessing the long-term impacts of human activity on marine ecosystems.

GeoAI can be used to optimize **fisheries management** by providing data on fish stock health, migratory patterns, and the distribution of fishing vessels. By integrating this data with real-time environmental monitoring, managers can adjust fishing quotas and timing to avoid overfishing and prevent the depletion of important species. AI models also help identify areas that are **ecologically sensitive**, ensuring that conservation efforts are focused on regions that are most vulnerable to degradation.

Sustainable Aquaculture

GeoAI is also playing a role in **aquaculture**, which is an increasingly important source of global seafood production. Aquaculture, particularly fish farming, can have significant environmental impacts, including water pollution, habitat destruction, and the spread of disease. However, GeoAI can optimize the sustainability of aquaculture operations by analyzing environmental data to improve water quality management, fish health, and farm operations.

AI models can predict changes in water temperature, oxygen levels, and salinity that could affect the health of farmed fish, allowing aquaculture operators to adjust environmental conditions proactively. Additionally, GeoAI can help optimize feed management and monitor disease outbreaks, reducing the environmental footprint of aquaculture practices.

Case Study: GeoAI in Sustainable Fisheries in the Mediterranean Sea

In the Mediterranean, a project called **SMARTFISH** is using **machine learning** and **AI-powered predictive models** to improve fisheries management in the region. The project integrates satellite imagery, fish stock data, and environmental variables to predict fish populations and optimize harvest strategies. By predicting fish stock trends, the system enables authorities to establish more accurate quotas, prevent overfishing, and promote sustainable fishing practices.

26.8 The Future of GeoAI in Coastal and Marine Resource Management

Emerging Technologies

As the field of GeoAI continues to evolve, new technologies will enhance the ability to monitor and manage coastal and marine ecosystems. **Edge computing**, for instance, could enable real-time processing of data collected from remote sensors and drones deployed in coastal regions. Additionally, the integration of **5G technology** could facilitate faster communication between monitoring devices, allowing for quicker responses to environmental threats like oil spills or illegal fishing activities.

Deep learning models are expected to improve in accuracy and speed, providing more detailed insights into marine ecosystems and supporting more complex predictions about climate change impacts, biodiversity loss, and habitat degradation. Furthermore, the rise of **quantum computing** holds the potential to revolutionize GeoAI's processing capabilities, enabling faster and more efficient analysis of large datasets.

Ethical Considerations and Data Privacy

As with any AI-driven technology, the use of GeoAI in coastal and marine resource management raises important ethical considerations. Data privacy concerns, especially when it comes to the collection and sharing of vessel location data or sensitive environmental information, must be addressed. Transparent data policies and international collaborations will be essential to ensuring that GeoAI is used responsibly and ethically.

26.9 Conclusion

GeoAI is rapidly becoming a cornerstone of coastal and marine resource management. By harnessing the power of satellite imagery, machine learning algorithms, and predictive models, GeoAI is transforming how we monitor and conserve marine ecosystems. From fisheries management to coral reef conservation, GeoAI enables better decision-making, more efficient resource management, and a deeper understanding of the complex dynamics within coastal and marine environments.

As technology continues to advance, the role of GeoAI in ensuring the sustainability of our oceans will only grow. Collaborative efforts across nations, industries, and research institutions will be key to addressing the challenges facing our oceans and ensuring their long-term health and resilience.

This chapter has explored how GeoAI is transforming coastal and marine resource management by providing real-time data, predictive models, and actionable insights. The integration of satellite imagery, machine learning, and IoT sensors has enabled more effective monitoring of marine pollution, fish stocks, coral reefs, and marine protected areas. Case studies demonstrate the practical applications of GeoAI in addressing real-world challenges like illegal fishing, overfishing, and coral bleaching. Moving forward, the continued development of AI technologies and international cooperation will be crucial in ensuring the sustainability of marine resources and achieving global conservation goals.

Chapter 27: GeoAI for Wildlife Conservation and Habitat Protection

Introduction

Wildlife conservation and habitat protection have become pressing global concerns in the face of rapid environmental degradation, biodiversity loss, and human encroachment. With an estimated one million species facing extinction in the coming decades due to habitat loss, poaching, and climate change, the need for effective conservation strategies has never been more urgent. In recent years, the integration of GeoAI (Geospatial Artificial Intelligence) technologies has emerged as a powerful tool in revolutionizing conservation efforts. GeoAI brings together geographic information systems (GIS), remote sensing data, satellite imagery, and machine learning algorithms to provide real-time insights into wildlife populations, ecosystems, and the ever-changing conditions of the planet's most vulnerable habitats.

This chapter delves into how GeoAI is transforming wildlife conservation and habitat protection. By utilizing data from satellite imagery, IoT devices, drones, and predictive AI models, GeoAI enables more precise tracking of animal migrations, identification of critical habitats, assessment of biodiversity health, and mitigation of illegal poaching activities. Additionally, the chapter explores how AI-based models support species protection, habitat restoration, and provide early warning systems for emerging threats, offering hope for long-term sustainability in wildlife conservation.

GeoAI serves as a bridge between cutting-edge technology and traditional conservation methods, enabling global collaboration and smarter decision-making that ultimately supports biodiversity conservation efforts. By leveraging these technological advancements, conservationists, policymakers, and organizations are now empowered with tools to tackle the complex challenges of protecting wildlife and their habitats in a rapidly changing world.

27.1 GeoAI in Tracking Animal Migration Patterns

Introduction to Animal Migration

Animal migration is an essential biological phenomenon that supports ecological balance, biodiversity, and species survival. From the annual migration of monarch butterflies across North America to the seasonal movements of elephants in Africa, migration patterns help maintain the health of ecosystems and ensure that species have access to the resources they need for breeding, feeding, and shelter. However, tracking these migrations has traditionally been a challenging task due to the vast distances animals travel and the often inaccessible terrains they cross.

In this context, GeoAI has emerged as a game-changer in wildlife tracking. By combining satellite data, GPS technology, IoT sensors, and AI-driven algorithms, GeoAI can track the movements of animals across entire continents, providing real-time insights into their migration behaviors, challenges, and environmental changes that may affect their journey.

Satellite and Sensor Integration in Migration Tracking

GeoAI leverages satellite data to monitor large-scale migration patterns, providing a broader scope and granularity of information than previously possible. Through the use of remote sensing, conservationists can analyze temperature fluctuations, vegetation health, and seasonal weather conditions that affect migratory species. Additionally, by integrating GPS-enabled tags or collars worn by animals, researchers can pinpoint exact migration routes, stopover points, and the timing of migration events.

For example, elephants in Africa, which migrate over vast areas, are often tagged with GPS collars that relay their positions to researchers. This data is then analyzed using AI algorithms that interpret the animal's movement patterns, identify migration hotspots, and predict future routes. The integration of satellite imagery enhances this by providing landscape context, helping researchers understand the environment through which these migrations occur. The AI algorithms can process thousands of data points in real-time, producing actionable insights for managing wildlife corridors and preventing human-wildlife conflicts.

AI Algorithms for Migration Prediction

Machine learning algorithms play a vital role in predicting migration patterns. These algorithms use historical data, environmental variables, and real-time satellite and sensor information to create predictive models of animal movements. By training these models with years of migration data, GeoAI can forecast future migration events with remarkable accuracy.

For instance, researchers studying the migration of sea turtles use AI models to predict the timing and routes of turtle nesting events based on ocean currents, temperature, and environmental conditions. This allows for better protection strategies and improved conservation efforts in areas where turtles nest, ultimately increasing the survival rate of hatchlings.

Case Study: Elephants in Africa

One notable application of GeoAI is the tracking of African elephants, whose migration patterns are influenced by factors such as water availability, food sources, and human activities. In a groundbreaking project in Botswana, researchers have used GPS collars and GeoAI algorithms to track the movements of elephant herds across the Kalahari Desert. The collected data has revealed that elephants frequently travel through areas marked by human settlements, which often leads to human-wildlife conflict.

Using AI models, researchers are now able to predict areas where elephant migrations overlap with human populations, allowing for more effective wildlife management and the development of wildlife corridors that minimize conflicts. The AI-powered system has also proven invaluable in understanding the impact of climate change on elephant migration, particularly how shifting rainfall patterns influence the animals' movement.

Impact of Climate Change on Migration Patterns

Climate change poses a significant threat to animal migration patterns. Rising temperatures, changing precipitation patterns, and more frequent extreme weather events are altering the ecosystems animals rely on for their migrations. For example, migratory birds may encounter altered breeding and feeding conditions, while marine species like fish and whales may face shifts in the availability of prey due to ocean temperature changes.

GeoAI's predictive models are crucial in assessing how climate change will affect these migration patterns. By analyzing historical climate data, current environmental conditions, and species-specific migration patterns, GeoAI can provide insights into how ecosystems and species might adapt, migrate, or struggle to survive in the face of climate shifts.

27.2 Identifying Critical Habitats for Wildlife Protection

Habitat Mapping with GeoAI

Critical habitats are those areas essential for the survival of species, particularly endangered ones. These habitats may include breeding grounds, feeding areas, or places where animals seek refuge during seasonal changes. Identifying and mapping these habitats is one of the most important steps in wildlife conservation. Traditional methods of habitat identification often involve field surveys, which can be labor-intensive and limited in scope. However, GeoAI has revolutionized habitat mapping by leveraging remote sensing data and satellite imagery.

GeoAI systems analyze satellite imagery to assess land cover, vegetation types, and environmental features that are crucial for species' survival. By using AI-powered algorithms to interpret this data, conservationists can pinpoint areas where species are most likely to be found and determine the health of their habitats.

AI-Based Analysis of Habitat Suitability

GeoAI also plays a key role in assessing the quality of habitats and determining whether they can support specific species. Habitat suitability models powered by machine learning algorithms analyze factors such as soil quality, water availability, temperature, and vegetation to predict the likelihood that a given area can sustain certain wildlife populations.

These models are especially valuable for predicting the potential effects of human activities like urbanization, deforestation, and agriculture, which often disrupt ecosystems. By combining data on habitat conditions and species needs, GeoAI can help prioritize conservation efforts, targeting the most critical habitats that need immediate attention.

Restoration of Degraded Habitats

As many habitats worldwide are being degraded by deforestation, pollution, and climate change, GeoAI helps identify areas that need restoration and predict the best methods for rehabilitation. AI algorithms analyze past land use, soil composition, and climate conditions to determine the best species for restoration and the most effective restoration techniques, such as reforestation, wetland rehabilitation, or erosion control.

Case Study: Amazon Rainforest

The Amazon rainforest, often referred to as the "lungs of the Earth," is a critical habitat for countless species. Unfortunately, deforestation and illegal logging have been severely impacting this region. GeoAI has been used extensively to monitor deforestation and degradation in the Amazon, helping to identify hotspots of illegal activity and deforestation trends in real-time.

Through satellite imagery analysis and AI algorithms, researchers can now detect even the smallest signs of illegal logging and deforestation. The AI models also predict which areas are most at risk of degradation and prioritize them for conservation and restoration efforts. This technology has empowered governments, NGOs, and international organizations to take faster action in preserving the Amazon's biodiversity.

27.3 Species Protection and Monitoring Using GeoAI

Introduction to Species Protection

The protection of endangered species is at the heart of conservation efforts worldwide. Whether it's the iconic Bengal tiger, the critically endangered Amur leopard, or the elusive vaquita porpoise, species face numerous threats from habitat loss, human encroachment, poaching, and climate change. Traditional conservation methods often relied on human observation and field studies, but these can be labor-intensive, time-consuming, and difficult to implement in remote or challenging environments. GeoAI, with its combination of satellite imagery, machine learning, and real-time monitoring tools, has revolutionized species protection by providing more efficient and data-driven approaches to conservation.

GeoAI for Species Tracking and Population Monitoring

GeoAI utilizes a wide range of technologies, including GPS collars, camera traps, and acoustic sensors, to track the movements and populations of various species. These tracking systems generate massive datasets, which GeoAI algorithms analyze to identify patterns in animal behavior, population trends, and habitat use. Through satellite data, researchers can also monitor migration routes and seasonal movements of species in real-time, facilitating more effective protection measures.

For example, researchers studying polar bears in the Arctic use GPS collars to track the animals' movements across vast, remote regions. By integrating this data with satellite imagery, scientists can gain insight into how melting sea ice due to climate change is impacting polar bear habitats. GeoAI models can predict future habitat loss and suggest intervention strategies to protect critical regions for breeding and feeding.

AI-Driven Population Health Assessments

GeoAI also plays an essential role in monitoring the health of species populations. Using machine learning, AI can process large amounts of ecological data to assess population health, detect signs of disease, and predict potential threats to biodiversity. This is especially valuable for monitoring elusive or difficult-to-access species, such as big cats, amphibians, and marine life.

For instance, AI-powered algorithms have been used to analyze camera trap footage of endangered tigers in India. By automating the analysis of thousands of images, AI can identify individual animals, track their movements, and assess population density, all without the need for human intervention. This approach helps researchers estimate population sizes, monitor the effects of poaching, and detect changes in reproductive success over time.

Case Study: Amur Leopard Conservation in Russia

The Amur leopard, a critically endangered species native to the Russian Far East, is one of the rarest big cats in the world, with fewer than 100 individuals left in the wild. In recent years, GeoAI has been instrumental in the protection of the Amur leopard through an innovative conservation project that combines camera traps, satellite imagery, and machine learning models to track the leopards' movements and assess the condition of their habitats.

By utilizing AI algorithms, researchers can identify individual leopards from camera trap images and track their movements across vast, rugged landscapes. Satellite imagery provides real-time insights into habitat quality, deforestation, and human encroachment. This combination of technologies allows for targeted conservation interventions, such as identifying critical corridors for the leopards to move freely between protected areas and preventing human-wildlife conflict.

Impact of Climate Change on Species Protection

The impact of climate change on species and ecosystems cannot be underestimated. Rising temperatures, changing precipitation patterns, and extreme weather events affect species' survival and reproductive cycles. GeoAI models help predict how climate change might affect species distributions, seasonal behavior, and the overall health of ecosystems.

AI models that incorporate climate projections and environmental data can predict shifts in species' ranges and highlight areas of increasing vulnerability. For instance, GeoAI can help predict that certain species of amphibians may shift their habitats to higher elevations as temperatures rise, providing data to guide the creation of wildlife corridors to allow for such migrations.

27.4 Habitat Restoration and Ecological Rehabilitation with GeoAI

Introduction to Habitat Restoration

Habitat restoration is a critical aspect of conservation. Many ecosystems have been degraded by human activities, such as deforestation, mining, agriculture, and urban expansion. Restoring these ecosystems is essential to ensure the survival of species that rely on them. However, successful habitat restoration requires detailed knowledge of the land, including its ecological history, soil quality, vegetation, and climate conditions. GeoAI combines these data sources to design and implement more effective restoration strategies.

GeoAI-Driven Restoration Strategies

GeoAI can be used to develop predictive models that determine the best approaches to habitat restoration. By analyzing satellite imagery and historical land use data, AI algorithms can identify the most suitable areas for restoration, predict the success of various restoration methods (such as reforestation or wetland restoration), and monitor the ongoing health of restored ecosystems.

AI can also assist in selecting appropriate plant species for reforestation projects, as some species may be better suited to changing environmental conditions. For example, AI models can analyze soil types, rainfall patterns, and temperature fluctuations to recommend species that are most likely to thrive in a given area.

Restoring Coral Reefs Using GeoAI

GeoAI is also making strides in marine conservation, particularly in the restoration of coral reefs, which are highly vulnerable to ocean acidification, warming temperatures, and pollution. Satellite imagery and AI models can assess the health of coral reefs by identifying bleaching events, mapping coral cover, and monitoring ocean temperature changes. By integrating this data with real-time monitoring of water quality and human activities (such as fishing and coastal development), GeoAI can help prioritize areas for restoration.

For example, a GeoAI-powered initiative in the Philippines has been used to map and assess coral reef health and to predict the effectiveness of restoration efforts. AI-based models help determine which regions are most likely to recover naturally and which require active intervention, such as coral transplantation or the removal of invasive species.

AI in Wetland Rehabilitation

Wetlands are some of the most productive and ecologically valuable ecosystems, providing important services like water filtration, carbon sequestration, and habitat for wildlife. However, wetlands around the world are being drained or polluted at an alarming rate. GeoAI has been utilized to track changes in wetland ecosystems, assess their health, and inform rehabilitation efforts. AI models can predict the outcomes of wetland restoration, such as reintroducing native vegetation or restoring hydrological cycles.

27.5 Preventing Illegal Poaching Activities with GeoAI

Introduction to Poaching and its Impact on Wildlife

Illegal poaching remains one of the greatest threats to wildlife around the world. Poaching is driven by the illegal trade in animal parts, such as ivory, rhino horns, tiger pelts, and exotic pets. Poaching not only threatens endangered species but also destabilizes ecosystems and deprives local communities of resources. GeoAI is playing an increasingly important role in combating poaching by providing real-time surveillance, predictive models, and actionable intelligence to law enforcement and conservation groups.

GeoAI for Poaching Detection and Prevention

GeoAI uses a combination of satellite imagery, drones, camera traps, and AI-powered analytics to monitor protected areas for signs of illegal activity. By analyzing data from various sources, AI models can detect unusual patterns, such as the presence of vehicles or human activity in restricted areas. These models can then trigger alerts to park rangers and law enforcement agencies, enabling rapid response to poaching threats.

For example, in Africa, the use of drones equipped with cameras and AI software has revolutionized anti-poaching efforts in national parks. Drones can cover vast areas of terrain and capture high-resolution images of wildlife populations, which AI algorithms analyze to detect the presence of illegal activities, such as the poaching of elephants or rhinos. AI models can also predict the likelihood of poaching in certain areas based on historical trends and environmental factors, allowing for targeted patrols and proactive measures.

AI for Real-Time Monitoring of Protected Areas

GeoAI facilitates continuous, real-time monitoring of protected areas using various sensors, such as infrared cameras, acoustic sensors, and GPS trackers. These technologies, when combined with AI, allow for the rapid detection of poaching events, even in remote or difficult-to-reach locations. This ability to provide near-instantaneous alerts is crucial for preventing wildlife crime and protecting species in their habitats.

For instance, in India's Kaziranga National Park, home to the world's largest population of one-horned rhinos, GeoAI has been used to monitor the park's boundaries using AI-powered camera traps. These traps capture images of animals and potential poachers, and the AI system can differentiate between animals and humans, sending real-time alerts to park rangers if unauthorized activity is detected.

27.6 Conclusion and Future Directions

The integration of GeoAI into wildlife conservation and habitat protection is transforming the way we monitor and manage biodiversity. By enabling real-time tracking of species, predicting migration patterns, and identifying critical habitats, GeoAI provides valuable insights that guide conservation efforts. In addition, it enhances our ability to combat poaching, restore degraded ecosystems, and ensure the long-term health of the planet's biodiversity.

Looking ahead, the future of GeoAI in wildlife conservation holds immense promise. As AI technologies evolve, we can expect even more sophisticated models that integrate diverse data sources, such as genomic data, environmental DNA, and social media intelligence. The application of deep learning and neural networks could lead to breakthroughs in species identification, predictive modeling, and environmental monitoring.

Moreover, as climate change accelerates, the need for adaptive conservation strategies will grow, making GeoAI's role in habitat restoration and species protection even more critical. Collaborative efforts between governments, conservation organizations, and technology companies will be essential in scaling GeoAI solutions and ensuring their integration into global conservation frameworks.

In the face of ongoing environmental challenges, GeoAI offers a new frontier in wildlife protection—one that is data-driven, adaptive, and scalable, offering hope for a sustainable future for wildlife and their habitats.

Chapter 28: GeoAI for Green Infrastructure Planning

Introduction

The rapid expansion of urban areas, coupled with the challenges posed by climate change, has brought green infrastructure to the forefront of sustainable urban planning. As cities grow, there is an increasing need to address not only the environmental impact of urbanization but also the challenges posed by natural hazards, such as flooding, extreme heat, and loss of biodiversity. Green infrastructure—such as urban parks, green roofs, wetlands, and permeable surfaces—offers cities a cost-effective, multifunctional solution. By integrating natural systems into urban settings, green infrastructure can improve air and water quality, reduce energy consumption, promote biodiversity, and mitigate the impacts of climate change.

GeoAI (Geospatial Artificial Intelligence) is revolutionizing the way cities plan, design, and manage green infrastructure. GeoAI combines geographic data with artificial intelligence (AI) to generate actionable insights that can optimize land use, predict environmental changes, and enhance decision-making processes. This chapter explores the role of GeoAI in planning and implementing green infrastructure in urban environments, focusing on key areas such as land use optimization, green roof design, stormwater management, climate resilience, and the integration of smart technologies.

By leveraging AI, big data, and satellite imagery, GeoAI enables planners and decision-makers to assess environmental conditions, model various scenarios, and make data-driven decisions to create more sustainable, resilient urban environments. Through a series of real-world applications, case studies, and research, this chapter will examine how GeoAI is being used to design urban spaces that are not only green but also more adaptive to the challenges of the 21st century.

28.1 Optimizing Land Use for Green Infrastructure with GeoAI

As urban areas continue to expand, finding space for green infrastructure within densely built environments can be a challenging task. Traditional urban planning approaches often prioritize economic development and infrastructure growth without fully considering the environmental benefits that green spaces provide. GeoAI helps overcome this challenge by offering a systematic approach to land use optimization.

Role of Land Use Optimization: GeoAI is instrumental in identifying areas where green infrastructure can be most beneficial, by evaluating factors such as soil quality, water retention capacity, proximity to residential areas, and the availability of open space. AI-powered algorithms can analyze vast amounts of spatial data—ranging from land cover and topography to socio-economic indicators—and suggest the optimal placement of green infrastructure elements, such as parks, green roofs, and rain gardens.

GeoAI for Land Suitability Analysis: Through advanced spatial analysis, GeoAI can conduct land suitability assessments, considering multiple variables to determine where specific types of green infrastructure are most needed. For example, in areas prone to flooding, GeoAI might suggest the implementation of permeable surfaces or bioswales, while in heat-affected zones, urban parks or green roofs could be prioritized to reduce the urban heat island effect.

Case Study: Urban Parks in Dense Cities: In cities like New York and Tokyo, where space is at a premium, GeoAI has been used to identify underutilized spaces that could be converted into green parks. In New York City, the Department of Environmental Protection (DEP) has utilized AI-driven analysis of vacant land parcels to pinpoint areas that could be transformed into green spaces to improve air quality, reduce stormwater runoff, and enhance residents' quality of life. Similarly, in Tokyo, AI-driven simulations have been used to create green corridors that connect existing parks and improve the urban ecosystem.

Urban Heat Island Effect: Urban heat islands (UHIs) are areas within cities that experience higher temperatures than their rural surroundings due to human activities, infrastructure, and lack of green spaces. This phenomenon exacerbates heatwaves, increases energy consumption, and worsens air pollution. GeoAI allows for the mapping of UHI hotspots using satellite imagery and thermal data. By analyzing this data, AI can identify areas where urban heat islands are most severe and help planners design green infrastructure that reduces heat absorption, such as the strategic placement of trees and reflective surfaces.

28.2 Green Roofs and Vegetation Mapping through GeoAI

What are Green Roofs? Green roofs, also known as living roofs, are an innovative solution to mitigate environmental challenges in urban areas. They consist of vegetation planted on the rooftops of buildings and provide several benefits, including improved energy efficiency, reduced stormwater runoff, and increased biodiversity. Green roofs help regulate building temperatures, thus reducing the need for air conditioning and heating, and they also capture rainwater, which can be filtered and reused.

GeoAI for Roof Suitability Assessment: Determining which buildings are suitable for green roofs requires a detailed analysis of several factors, including roof size, structural integrity, sunlight exposure, and proximity to water sources. GeoAI can process satellite imagery, 3D building models, and other spatial data to identify buildings with the highest potential for green roof installation. AI algorithms assess factors such as roof slope, load-bearing capacity, and access to irrigation systems, creating a comprehensive dataset that guides the planning process.

Vegetation Mapping: AI-powered tools like convolutional neural networks (CNNs) can be used to analyze satellite imagery and automatically classify vegetation types across urban landscapes. By mapping existing vegetation and identifying areas with insufficient greenery, GeoAI provides valuable insights into where green roofs can have the most significant impact. This approach also allows for ongoing monitoring of green roof health, identifying areas where vegetation may be underperforming and require maintenance.

Case Study: Green Roofs in Berlin: Berlin has embraced green roofs as part of its commitment to sustainability. The city's climate strategy focuses on reducing its carbon footprint, improving air quality, and enhancing urban biodiversity. Through GeoAI, Berlin has mapped the city's rooftops and analyzed which buildings would benefit the most from green roof installation. The integration of GeoAI into the planning process has helped the city maximize the environmental benefits of green roofs and streamline their implementation.

28.3 GeoAI for Stormwater Management and Flood Mitigation

Introduction to Stormwater Management: Stormwater runoff is a major concern in urban areas, as impermeable surfaces like roads and buildings prevent rainwater from soaking into the ground, leading to flooding, water pollution, and ecosystem disruption. Green infrastructure plays a critical role in mitigating these issues by promoting the infiltration and management of stormwater. Elements such as permeable pavements, rain gardens, green roofs, and wetlands are effective solutions that can reduce flood risks and improve water quality.

AI for Predictive Modeling of Rainfall and Stormwater Flows: GeoAI allows for the creation of predictive models that forecast rainfall patterns, stormwater flows, and potential flooding risks. By integrating historical weather data, real-time sensor inputs, and hydrological simulations, GeoAI can help urban planners design stormwater management systems that anticipate future environmental conditions and optimize infrastructure placement. For example, AI can predict how a given rainfall event will impact specific areas and suggest the best locations for green infrastructure to capture and manage the runoff.

Designing Green Stormwater Infrastructure: GeoAI also aids in designing green infrastructure solutions such as bioswales, rain gardens, and vegetated stormwater management systems. By analyzing the topography and hydrology of urban landscapes, AI can determine the most efficient and cost-effective configurations for stormwater management. Additionally, AI-driven simulations can help optimize the size and location of stormwater infrastructure to maximize water retention while minimizing the risk of flooding.

Case Study: Sponge City Initiative (China): In response to the increasing frequency of urban flooding, China launched the "Sponge Cities" initiative, which aims to integrate green infrastructure into urban areas to absorb and manage rainwater. Through GeoAI, the Chinese government has been able to predict flood risks, model stormwater flows, and design green infrastructure solutions such as permeable pavements, green roofs, and rainwater harvesting systems. The initiative has been implemented in cities like Wuhan, where AI-driven models guide the placement and effectiveness of green stormwater infrastructure.

28.4 Enhancing Urban Resilience to Climate Change with GeoAI

Urban Resilience and Climate Change: Urban areas are increasingly vulnerable to the impacts of climate change, including rising temperatures, extreme weather events, and sea-level rise. Green infrastructure plays a vital role in enhancing the resilience of cities to these climate challenges. GeoAI enables the assessment of climate risks and the identification of areas most in need of climate adaptation strategies, such as the implementation of green infrastructure.

GeoAI for Climate Impact Assessment: GeoAI can assess the potential impacts of climate change on urban areas by analyzing historical data, environmental factors, and climate projections. By using machine learning algorithms and GIS, urban planners can model different climate scenarios and evaluate the effectiveness of various green infrastructure solutions. This predictive analysis helps prioritize investments in areas that will benefit the most from climate resilience strategies.

Green Infrastructure as Climate Adaptation: Green infrastructure not only mitigates the effects of climate change but also provides valuable ecosystem services that enhance urban resilience. For instance, urban parks can reduce the heat island effect, while wetlands can buffer coastal cities from storm surges. Through GeoAI, cities can identify which types of green infrastructure are most suitable for specific climate risks, helping to create targeted, cost-effective adaptation strategies.

Case Study: Resilient Cities in the US: Cities like Miami, New York, and Los Angeles have adopted green infrastructure as part of their climate resilience strategies. In Miami, for example, GeoAI is used to assess sea-level rise risks and identify areas that require the implementation of coastal wetlands or green flood barriers. In New York, AI models have been used to predict how green roofs and urban parks can reduce the heat island effect, improving the city's resilience to heatwaves.

28.5 Sustainable Urban Mobility and Green Infrastructure Integration

Introduction to Sustainable Mobility: Sustainable urban mobility refers to transportation systems that reduce environmental impact while promoting accessibility, health, and equity. Green infrastructure plays an important role in supporting sustainable mobility by creating green corridors, bike paths, and pedestrian-friendly spaces that reduce reliance on cars and promote healthier, more active lifestyles.

GeoAI in Planning Sustainable Mobility: GeoAI can help plan and design urban mobility systems that integrate green infrastructure, such as bike lanes, pedestrian pathways, and green streets. By analyzing transportation patterns, traffic data, and environmental factors, AI can optimize the placement of these green mobility solutions to maximize their impact on air quality, traffic congestion, and public health.

AI-Powered Smart City Integration: In smart cities, GeoAI can be integrated with IoT (Internet of Things) technologies to create connected urban systems that seamlessly combine transportation, green infrastructure, and energy management. For example, sensors embedded in green streets can monitor air quality, soil moisture, and weather conditions, while AI algorithms can analyze this data to optimize urban mobility routes and green infrastructure maintenance schedules.

Case Study: The Green Infrastructure of Copenhagen: Copenhagen is recognized as one of the world's leading sustainable cities. The city has integrated green infrastructure with its sustainable mobility initiatives, creating green corridors and bike-friendly streets. Through the use of GeoAI, Copenhagen has been able to optimize the design and placement of green spaces to support cycling, walking, and other eco-friendly modes of transportation.

28.6 Monitoring and Maintenance of Green Infrastructure with GeoAI

Challenges in Monitoring and Maintenance: The long-term success of green infrastructure depends on regular monitoring and maintenance. Traditional methods of monitoring, such as visual inspections, can be time-consuming and costly. GeoAI offers a more efficient solution by enabling real-time monitoring of green infrastructure through remote sensing, drones, and satellite imagery.

GeoAI for Remote Sensing and Monitoring: GeoAI allows for the continuous monitoring of green infrastructure elements, such as vegetation health, soil conditions, and water quality. AI-powered image processing tools can analyze satellite or drone images to assess the condition of urban green spaces and identify areas that require attention. By automating the monitoring process, GeoAI reduces the need for manual inspections and enables more efficient resource allocation.

Automation in Maintenance: GeoAI can also automate maintenance processes, such as scheduling irrigation or pruning trees. By analyzing environmental data, AI can predict when specific areas of green infrastructure will require maintenance, ensuring that resources are allocated effectively and reducing costs.

Case Study: Green Infrastructure Monitoring in Singapore: Singapore has implemented a comprehensive system for monitoring its green infrastructure, using satellite imagery, drones, and AI to track the condition of parks, green roofs, and urban forests. The city's AI-powered platform allows urban planners to detect issues such as plant diseases or waterlogging in real time, enabling proactive maintenance and ensuring the long-term success of green infrastructure projects.

28.7 Conclusion

GeoAI is transforming the way cities plan, design, and maintain green infrastructure. From land use optimization and stormwater management to enhancing urban resilience and promoting sustainable mobility, GeoAI provides urban planners with powerful tools to create more sustainable, livable, and resilient cities. The integration of green infrastructure with AI not only addresses the environmental challenges cities face today but also paves the way for a more sustainable future. As technology continues to evolve, the role of GeoAI in green infrastructure planning will only grow, offering new possibilities for smarter, greener urban spaces.

Chapter 29: GeoAI for Environmental Justice and Equity

Introduction

Environmental justice is an imperative principle that calls for equal protection from environmental hazards, the fair treatment of all people regardless of race, color, national origin, or income, and the involvement of all groups in environmental decision-making processes. Unfortunately, marginalized and low-income communities, particularly communities of color, often bear a disproportionate burden of environmental degradation, including air and water pollution, poor waste management, and land degradation. These communities are more likely to live in areas that are vulnerable to environmental hazards, yet less likely to have the resources to mitigate these risks. As climate change exacerbates environmental inequalities, it becomes even more critical to implement strategies that ensure environmental justice.

GeoAI, which integrates Geographic Information Systems (GIS) with Artificial Intelligence (AI), presents a groundbreaking opportunity to address these disparities. By leveraging satellite data, machine learning, and geospatial analytics, GeoAI can identify areas where marginalized communities are disproportionately affected by environmental hazards, map pollution hotspots, and enable policymakers to make data-driven decisions to mitigate risks and promote equity. This chapter delves into the role of GeoAI in advancing environmental justice, exploring how it identifies disparities, maps environmental risks, and helps ensure that vulnerable populations are not overlooked in environmental decision-making.

29.1 Understanding Environmental Justice and Equity in the Context of GeoAI

Definition and Context of Environmental Justice

Environmental justice is founded on the belief that no group of people should bear a disproportionate share of negative environmental impacts. Historically, marginalized communities—those with lower socio-economic status, minority racial groups, indigenous populations, and others—have been more likely to experience high levels of environmental degradation. This includes exposure to toxic pollution, poor air quality, contaminated water, and unsafe housing conditions, all of which significantly impact the health and well-being of these populations.

Environmental justice is often framed around three key principles:

1. **Fair Treatment**: Ensuring that no group suffers a disproportionate share of negative environmental consequences.
2. **Meaningful Involvement**: Engaging all people, especially those affected by environmental hazards, in decision-making processes that affect their environment.
3. **Access to a Healthy Environment**: Ensuring that everyone has access to clean air, water, and green spaces.

These principles can be applied across all stages of environmental policy—from the creation and enforcement of regulations to the development of infrastructure. GeoAI, with its ability to process vast amounts of environmental data, can play a pivotal role in implementing these principles.

GeoAI's Role in Environmental Justice

GeoAI allows for the analysis of geospatial data with AI algorithms to identify areas of environmental concern. AI technologies can process satellite data, aerial imagery, and sensor data to detect pollution, land degradation, deforestation, water contamination, and other environmental stressors. The ability to apply machine learning and data mining techniques to this spatial data provides deeper insights into the scale and scope of environmental hazards.

Through GeoAI, environmental justice initiatives can be empowered with:

- **Precision** in mapping hazardous areas.

- **Predictive analytics** to anticipate future environmental risks.

- **Real-time monitoring** that ensures swift responses to emerging issues.

- **Informed decision-making** that promotes equitable policies.

Key Challenges Addressed by GeoAI in Environmental Justice

GeoAI plays an instrumental role in overcoming several challenges in environmental justice:

- **Environmental Racism**: The historical neglect of marginalized communities often means that they are left exposed to higher environmental risks. GeoAI tools can help uncover these issues by mapping pollution hotspots in low-income neighborhoods or communities of color.

- **Health Impacts**: Environmental degradation often leads to health disparities, particularly in vulnerable populations. GeoAI enables the integration of health data with environmental monitoring to assess the full scope of risks.

- **Access to Resources**: GeoAI can ensure that vulnerable communities are provided access to critical resources like clean air, water, and green spaces by highlighting gaps and directing resources where they are most needed.

29.2 Using Satellite Data to Map Pollution Disparities

Satellite Remote Sensing in Environmental Monitoring

Satellite data plays a central role in GeoAI because it allows for large-scale monitoring of environmental conditions, offering insights that would be difficult or impossible to achieve through ground-based methods alone. Remote sensing technologies, such as Landsat, Sentinel, and MODIS satellites, capture detailed images of the Earth's surface, providing data on air quality, water quality, land use, and vegetation.

- **Air Quality**: Satellites equipped with remote sensing instruments, such as the Ozone Monitoring Instrument (OMI) and the Atmospheric Infrared Sounder (AIRS), provide data on pollutants such as nitrogen dioxide (NO2), sulfur dioxide (SO2), and particulate matter (PM2.5). This data can be analyzed using AI to identify pollution hotspots, especially in urban areas or near industrial zones.

- **Water and Soil Pollution**: Satellites also monitor water bodies, detecting changes in water quality, such as increased turbidity or chemical contamination, and soil erosion or degradation due to deforestation or agriculture.

GeoAI for Identifying Pollution Hotspots

GeoAI algorithms can process satellite imagery to identify pollution hotspots and track the movement of pollutants. For example, AI models can detect high levels of particulate matter in the air and correlate these with socio-economic data, revealing how certain communities—often disadvantaged or marginalized—are disproportionately affected by poor air quality. The use of GeoAI in identifying pollution hotspots is critical in designing effective environmental policies and health interventions.

Example Applications:

1. **Air Pollution in Los Angeles**: By integrating satellite data on air quality and local health data, GeoAI tools have been used to map areas with high levels of air pollution, helping public health agencies target interventions for communities most at risk.

2. **Water Contamination in Flint, Michigan**: GeoAI was used to map the areas affected by lead contamination in Flint's water system, enabling policymakers to pinpoint communities that required urgent intervention.

Assessing Health Risks Using Pollution Data

GeoAI's power extends beyond environmental monitoring—it can also be used to assess the health impacts of environmental hazards. By integrating data on pollution with health data (such as rates of respiratory diseases, cancer, and other health issues), AI models can assess the extent to which vulnerable populations are affected by poor air quality or contaminated water. This data can then inform health policies aimed at reducing these risks in disadvantaged communities.

29.3 GeoAI for Mapping Land Degradation and Resource Access

Land Degradation and Its Impact on Vulnerable Communities

Land degradation, including desertification, deforestation, and soil erosion, disproportionately impacts marginalized communities that depend on agriculture or natural resources for their livelihoods. These communities are often located in areas that are most vulnerable to environmental degradation, making it crucial to monitor and manage land resources carefully.

GeoAI for Land Degradation Monitoring

GeoAI models can monitor land degradation in real-time by analyzing satellite imagery, such as that provided by Landsat or Sentinel-2 satellites. By applying AI techniques like image classification and change detection, these tools can identify areas experiencing significant changes in land cover, such as deforestation or soil erosion. This data is essential for guiding restoration and conservation efforts in regions that are most vulnerable to land degradation.

Case Study: Land Degradation in Sub-Saharan Africa

In regions like Sub-Saharan Africa, where agriculture is the primary livelihood, land degradation due to overgrazing, deforestation, and unsustainable farming practices can have devastating effects. GeoAI has been used to monitor deforestation rates, track soil erosion, and develop restoration strategies for degraded lands.

Access to Environmental Resources

GeoAI can also assess whether marginalized communities have adequate access to vital resources such as clean water, waste management, and green spaces. By combining satellite data on water bodies and green cover with socio-economic data, GeoAI can identify areas that lack essential resources and help direct resources to where they are most needed.

Example: Mapping Food Deserts in Urban Areas

Food deserts, areas where residents lack access to affordable and nutritious food, are often located in low-income, urban areas. GeoAI tools can map these areas by combining satellite data on land use with socio-economic information. This data is valuable for policymakers and urban planners who aim to improve food access and promote sustainability.

29.4 AI for Identifying and Addressing Vulnerability to Environmental Hazards

Social Vulnerability Index (SVI) and GeoAI

The Social Vulnerability Index (SVI) is a tool used to assess the vulnerability of populations to environmental hazards, considering factors such as income, housing quality, age, and access to healthcare. By integrating SVI with satellite data on environmental conditions, GeoAI models can more effectively identify communities that are at risk of harm from natural disasters or environmental degradation.

GeoAI for Disaster Preparedness and Mitigation

GeoAI plays a key role in disaster preparedness by identifying areas most vulnerable to extreme weather events, such as floods, hurricanes, and heatwaves. Using real-time satellite data, AI models can simulate disaster scenarios and predict which areas will be hardest hit, enabling governments and humanitarian organizations to allocate resources and develop mitigation strategies in advance.

Case Study: Flooding in Bangladesh

In Bangladesh, GeoAI has been used to model flood risks, using satellite data to map flood-prone areas and predict the severity of flooding during the monsoon season. This information helps local authorities prepare evacuation plans and direct resources to the most vulnerable areas.

29.5 GeoAI for Ensuring Access to Environmental Services

Mapping Access to Clean Air, Water, and Green Spaces

GeoAI helps identify disparities in access to essential environmental services. By analyzing satellite imagery and combining it with socio-economic data, GeoAI tools can map areas that suffer from inadequate access to clean air, potable water, and green spaces. This data informs the development of policies that aim to ensure all communities have equitable access to these vital resources.

GeoAI for Waste Management and Pollution Control

Waste management is another area where GeoAI can help address environmental inequalities. Using satellite and sensor data, GeoAI models can identify areas with inadequate waste disposal infrastructure or where pollution levels are high due to improper waste management. In urban slums or informal settlements, these insights can be used to develop targeted interventions to improve waste management and reduce health risks.

29.6 GeoAI for Community Engagement and Empowerment

Community-Based Data Collection and Citizen Science

GeoAI empowers marginalized communities by involving them in data collection and decision-making processes. Through citizen science programs and mobile apps, community members can contribute to data collection, helping to fill gaps in environmental monitoring and ensuring that local knowledge is integrated into the decision-making process.

Equitable Policy Development through Data Transparency

GeoAI also plays a role in promoting transparency and accountability in environmental policy development. By making environmental data accessible to the public, GeoAI ensures that community members can participate in discussions about environmental risks and contribute to solutions.

29.7 GeoAI and Future Directions in Environmental Justice

Potential for Scaling GeoAI for Global Equity

GeoAI has the potential to scale environmental justice efforts globally, offering solutions to problems that disproportionately affect marginalized communities worldwide. As satellite and AI technologies become more accessible, the ability to monitor environmental hazards in real-time will become increasingly available to low-income regions, empowering communities globally to demand fair treatment and protection from environmental risks.

AI for Global Advocacy and Policy Influence

By providing data-driven insights, GeoAI can influence policy at local, national, and global levels. Policymakers and environmental organizations can use this data to advocate for stronger environmental justice laws, fair resource distribution, and effective climate change mitigation policies.

29.8 Conclusion

GeoAI is transforming the field of environmental justice by providing powerful tools to identify disparities, map pollution, and monitor land degradation. By combining satellite data with AI technologies, GeoAI enables real-time monitoring, precise mapping, and predictive modeling that can address the needs of marginalized communities. The integration of GeoAI into environmental decision-making processes promises a more equitable and sustainable future for all, ensuring that no community is left behind in the face of environmental challenges.

Chapter 30: Ethical Considerations and Bias in GeoAI Applications

Introduction

The rapid advancement of GeoAI—merging geographic information systems (GIS) with artificial intelligence (AI)—has transformed how we understand and address global environmental challenges. From monitoring deforestation to predicting climate change impacts, GeoAI promises to revolutionize environmental management and sustainability. However, with these advances come significant ethical challenges that need careful consideration.

As GeoAI applications grow in influence, issues such as data privacy, algorithmic bias, and transparency in decision-making are becoming increasingly important. If these concerns are not addressed, there is a risk that GeoAI could perpetuate existing inequities, harm vulnerable communities, or lead to decisions that are difficult to justify or explain.

This chapter explores the ethical considerations surrounding the use of GeoAI, focusing on its role in environmental monitoring, planetary health, and global governance. We will explore the risks of algorithmic bias, issues related to data privacy, and the implications of GeoAI in terms of fairness, accountability, and transparency. Additionally, we will look at real-world examples and case studies, highlighting how these issues manifest in GeoAI applications and the steps being taken to mitigate them.

30.1 Ethical Challenges in GeoAI Applications

Overview of Ethical Concerns

GeoAI's growing use in environmental management brings about a host of ethical challenges. At the heart of these issues is the balance between harnessing the power of AI to address pressing global challenges and ensuring that this technology is used responsibly and equitably. The primary ethical concerns surrounding GeoAI include:

- **Data Privacy and Security**: GeoAI relies on vast amounts of geospatial data, including satellite images, sensor networks, and location data, to monitor environmental changes. These data sources, particularly when they include information about individuals or communities, raise significant privacy concerns. Unauthorized surveillance, misuse of personal data, or data leaks could undermine public trust in GeoAI systems.

- **Algorithmic Bias**: AI models learn from the data they are fed. If that data reflects historical biases or systemic inequalities, these biases can be perpetuated by AI systems. In the context of GeoAI, this might manifest as biased environmental policies or unequal access to resources based on skewed geospatial data.

- **Transparency and Accountability**: As GeoAI systems become more involved in decision-making, especially in areas such as climate policy or disaster response, it becomes essential that these models are transparent and explainable. The lack of understanding of how AI systems make decisions can hinder their effectiveness and fairness. Moreover, the responsibility for outcomes based on AI predictions must be clear.

30.2 Data Privacy in GeoAI: Balancing Accessibility and Security

The Role of Geospatial Data in Environmental Monitoring

GeoAI systems often rely on geospatial data—whether from satellites, drones, or ground sensors—to provide real-time insights into environmental phenomena such as land use changes, pollution, climate shifts, and biodiversity loss. These data sources are pivotal for monitoring the health of ecosystems and tracking the impact of human activities on the environment.

However, this data can also reveal sensitive information about individuals, communities, and even nations. With the increasing sophistication of GeoAI tools, questions about privacy and security have gained urgency. How do we balance the need for broad access to geospatial data with the rights of individuals or communities whose privacy might be compromised by such information?

Privacy Concerns in Satellite and Location-Based Data

In particular, satellite data—although invaluable for large-scale environmental monitoring—can sometimes capture images or signals that are specific enough to identify personal or private spaces. This could include informal settlements, sensitive infrastructures, or even private property. For instance, while monitoring forest loss or urban sprawl, the data could inadvertently identify private residences or activities in rural areas.

- **Surveillance Risk**: The use of satellite imagery to monitor environmental conditions can also be used for surveillance purposes. Governments or corporations may use such information to monitor populations, track movements, or intervene in local affairs without consent.

- **Informed Consent**: Ethical issues arise when geospatial data is collected without clear consent from the people or communities whose data is being captured. In some cases, this might involve tracking environmental hazards, agricultural activities, or resource usage, but without any form of acknowledgment from the affected parties.

Ensuring Privacy and Data Security

To ensure privacy, several steps can be taken:

- **Anonymization**: Anonymizing the data can help avoid linking it to specific individuals or communities, preserving privacy while still allowing for large-scale analysis.

- **Aggregate Data**: Rather than focusing on highly specific or individual data points, aggregating data into broader trends can provide meaningful insights while protecting sensitive information.

- **Data Encryption**: Encrypting sensitive geospatial data ensures that unauthorized parties cannot access or misuse it.

International frameworks, such as the European Union's General Data Protection Regulation (GDPR), have set important precedents for protecting personal information in a digital world. Implementing similar standards in GeoAI applications can help protect individuals' rights while enabling the use of these powerful technologies for global environmental management.

30.3 Algorithmic Bias in GeoAI: Addressing Fairness in Decision-Making

Understanding Algorithmic Bias

Algorithmic bias is a pervasive challenge in AI systems. The concept refers to systematic and unfair discrimination against certain groups, individuals, or outcomes due to the data that AI models are trained on. In GeoAI, this bias can result in inaccurate predictions, unfair environmental policies, or biased resource distribution, particularly when the data reflects historical inequalities.

Bias in Environmental Data

GeoAI applications often rely on historical data for training. However, if the data used for these applications is incomplete or skewed in certain ways, the resulting AI models can perpetuate these biases. Consider the following examples:

- **Land Use and Deforestation Models**: Geospatial data that is used to track deforestation may be limited by historical data that underrepresents certain regions or ecosystems, leading to inaccurate assessments of deforestation hotspots. Furthermore, if Indigenous lands or marginalized communities' territories are overlooked in the data, their environmental needs might be ignored.

- **Climate Change and Vulnerability**: If climate vulnerability models are based on outdated or incomplete data, they may fail to adequately identify communities that are most at risk from climate change. This could exacerbate the environmental inequalities that already exist.

- **Biodiversity and Conservation Models**: Biodiversity conservation models may also be impacted by biases if certain species or ecosystems are underrepresented in the data or if conservation efforts favor more commercially viable or politically prominent species over others.

Impact of Bias on Environmental Justice

GeoAI systems used in environmental management, such as disaster response or climate resilience modeling, can impact marginalized communities if the data does not reflect their realities. If AI models perpetuate biases—such as assuming a certain level of infrastructure or preparedness based on wealthier areas—this can result in inadequate responses or support for more vulnerable populations.

For instance, if AI is used to allocate disaster relief funds based on damage predictions, regions with historical underrepresentation in data might receive fewer resources, even though they may be equally or more vulnerable.

Mitigating Bias in GeoAI

To mitigate algorithmic bias in GeoAI, several approaches can be adopted:

- **Data Diversification**: Ensuring that the training data includes a broad range of environments, communities, and scenarios. This includes prioritizing underrepresented or vulnerable regions in environmental models.

- **Bias Audits**: Regularly auditing AI models for fairness and bias, including checking for discriminatory outcomes, is critical. This can be done by evaluating the performance of GeoAI systems across different populations or regions.

- **Collaborative Decision-Making**: Involving local communities and stakeholders in the development and application of GeoAI tools ensures that the models take into account the needs and realities of those most impacted by environmental issues.

30.4 Transparency and Accountability in GeoAI Systems

Ensuring AI Transparency

Transparency in GeoAI is crucial to ensuring that decisions made using AI systems are understandable, justifiable, and open to scrutiny. This is particularly important when AI is used to inform policy decisions related to environmental protection, climate change mitigation, or disaster management. Without transparency, there is a risk that AI models could be used to justify decisions that are opaque or difficult to contest.

Challenges to Accountability

Determining accountability in GeoAI applications is a complex issue. If an AI system makes a prediction about a natural disaster or environmental degradation that leads to harmful consequences, who is responsible for that decision? The AI system itself, the developers of the system, the policymakers using the system's output, or the organizations providing the data?

Accountability can be particularly complicated in the case of large-scale environmental interventions, such as climate adaptation strategies or land-use planning. If these interventions are based on flawed AI models, the long-term impacts may disproportionately affect certain communities or ecosystems.

Ensuring Accountability

To ensure accountability, it is essential to:

- **Maintain Detailed Documentation**: Document the decision-making process, including the data sources, algorithms, and reasoning used in GeoAI applications.

- **Establish Clear Accountability Frameworks**: Create policies that define who is responsible for the outcomes of GeoAI-driven decisions, and make these policies enforceable.

30.5 Social Implications of GeoAI in Monitoring Planetary Health

The Role of GeoAI in Monitoring Planetary Health

GeoAI plays a key role in monitoring global environmental health, from tracking deforestation and land degradation to assessing climate change impacts and biodiversity loss. These technologies can provide real-time insights into how ecosystems are changing, enabling swift responses and interventions.

However, the social implications of using GeoAI for planetary health monitoring are profound. There are significant risks of exacerbating social inequalities, particularly when it comes to the uneven distribution of technology and resources.

Ensuring Equitable Use of GeoAI

To ensure the ethical use of GeoAI for monitoring

planetary health, it is essential to:

- **Promote Global Access**: Encourage international collaboration and the sharing of GeoAI resources and data, particularly with developing nations that may lack the technical capacity to harness these technologies themselves.

- **Include Local Communities in Decision-Making**: Respect and incorporate the knowledge and needs of local communities, especially Indigenous groups, in the development and application of GeoAI models for environmental monitoring.

30.6 Conclusion: Navigating the Ethical Future of GeoAI

As GeoAI continues to evolve and integrate into environmental management systems, addressing ethical challenges will be critical. By fostering transparency, accountability, and inclusivity, the GeoAI community can mitigate the risks of bias and inequality. Responsible governance and the ethical design of AI systems can ensure that GeoAI contributes to environmental sustainability without exacerbating social inequities.

The future of GeoAI depends on the ability of stakeholders—governments, tech companies, academic institutions, and civil society—to work together to create frameworks that prioritize fairness, equity, and transparency. By doing so, GeoAI can fulfill its potential as a powerful tool for environmental monitoring and planetary health without compromising ethical principles.

Chapter 31: The Role of GeoAI in Policy and Global Climate Negotiations

Introduction

The looming threat of climate change demands a transformative approach to environmental policymaking. With escalating concerns about rising global temperatures, shifting weather patterns, and extreme natural events, the integration of advanced technologies like GeoAI (Geospatial Artificial Intelligence) into the policy and climate negotiation process has become critical. GeoAI, which combines geospatial data with artificial intelligence, offers a revolutionary method for managing and interpreting vast amounts of environmental information. This fusion can provide real-time insights into the state of the planet, help develop more effective climate policies, and foster international cooperation.

GeoAI plays a pivotal role in empowering policymakers and negotiators with data-driven insights that can enhance decision-making, enable long-term climate strategy development, and foster trust in international climate agreements. This chapter explores how GeoAI supports climate policy development, informs global climate negotiations, and shapes national strategies to address the impacts of climate change. Through predictive modeling, scenario analysis, and vulnerability mapping, GeoAI tools can optimize climate strategies and drive a more coordinated global response to environmental challenges.

31.1 The Role of GeoAI in Climate Policy

Integrating GeoAI into Climate Policy Development

Climate policy formulation is a complex and multi-layered process that requires a thorough understanding of both the global and local impacts of climate change. GeoAI technologies enable governments and policymakers to assess potential scenarios, predict future environmental conditions, and evaluate the impact of various mitigation and adaptation strategies.

GeoAI supports climate policy development in several key areas:

1. Predictive Modeling and Scenario Analysis

○ GeoAI's ability to simulate different climate scenarios based on varying levels of greenhouse gas emissions provides policymakers with clear projections of future environmental conditions. For example, by modeling the potential outcomes of a 1.5°C, 2°C, or 3°C temperature increase, policymakers can better understand the risks of each scenario and formulate strategies to mitigate the impacts.

○ An example of GeoAI's impact can be seen in the European Union's **Climate Adaptation Strategy**, where geospatial data models have been used to assess future flood risks and inform urban planning decisions.

○ Another case is **NASA's Earth Science Division**, which uses satellite-based climate data and AI-driven algorithms to forecast the impacts of climate change on ecosystems, agriculture, and human settlements.

2. Risk Assessment and Vulnerability Mapping

○ GeoAI allows for precise vulnerability mapping, identifying areas that are most at risk from the impacts of climate change. This includes mapping the threats of rising sea levels, droughts, wildfires, and extreme weather events.

○ For example, the **Climate Risk and Early Warning Systems (CREWS)** program leverages GeoAI tools to predict climate-related risks, such as floods and cyclones, enabling governments to develop targeted risk-reduction strategies.

○ In the United States, the **Federal Emergency Management Agency (FEMA)** uses GeoAI to develop floodplain maps and assess disaster risks to infrastructure, guiding disaster response and recovery efforts.

3. Policy Impact Evaluation

○ GeoAI can also be used to assess the effectiveness of climate policies over time. By comparing pre- and post-policy environmental data, GeoAI can reveal whether emissions reductions, deforestation controls, or other mitigation strategies are having their intended effects.

○ In **Canada**, the government employs GeoAI to monitor forest health and track carbon sequestration efforts, ensuring that the country is on track to meet its carbon neutrality targets.

GeoAI in Long-term Climate Strategy Formulation

Long-term climate strategies are essential for achieving international climate goals, such as those outlined in the **Paris Agreement**. These strategies focus on reducing emissions, transitioning to renewable energy, and ensuring resilience in the face of inevitable climate impacts. GeoAI assists in long-term strategy formulation by offering real-time insights and predictive models to guide action.

1. Emissions Tracking and Reductions

○ GeoAI can help track global emissions in real-time, offering valuable data on emissions hotspots and sectors contributing most to global warming. This tracking allows governments to develop tailored emission-reduction strategies.

○ One prominent example is **Google Earth Engine**, which has been used to track carbon emissions globally through satellite data, enabling countries to identify high-emission areas and target their climate policies effectively.

2. Energy Transitions

○ GeoAI is used to model energy transitions from fossil fuels to renewable sources, helping policymakers understand the economic, social, and environmental impacts of various energy strategies.

○ For instance, in **China**, AI models are used to optimize the integration of renewable energy into the national grid, with geospatial data informing where to place wind and solar farms for maximum efficiency.

3. Mitigation Measures for Specific Sectors

○ Different sectors—such as agriculture, transportation, and manufacturing—contribute differently to climate change. GeoAI helps policymakers develop mitigation strategies tailored to each sector.

○ For example, **India** uses AI-driven tools to assess the carbon footprint of its agricultural sector and has implemented policies to promote sustainable farming practices, using GeoAI to monitor crop health, optimize irrigation, and reduce emissions from agricultural practices.

31.2 GeoAI's Contribution to Climate Negotiations

Supporting Multilateral Climate Agreements

The role of GeoAI in multilateral climate agreements is increasingly important, as it provides verifiable data on emissions, land use, and environmental change. This data supports negotiators in setting clear, measurable goals and tracking progress in real time.

1. Data-Driven Decision Making

○ GeoAI provides critical environmental data that can inform decision-making processes during climate negotiations. Whether it's tracking the global carbon budget, monitoring deforestation, or assessing the impact of rising sea levels, GeoAI enables negotiators to base their decisions on accurate, up-to-date data.

○ During the **UN Climate Change Conference (COP26)**, for example, satellite-based emissions monitoring and GeoAI tools were used to assess deforestation rates in the Amazon, influencing policy discussions on conservation.

2. Real-Time Impact Monitoring

○ One of the key advantages of GeoAI is its ability to monitor climate impacts in real-time. This capability is crucial during international negotiations, where negotiators need to adapt to rapidly changing environmental conditions.

○ For example, in **Hurricane Katrina**, GeoAI was used to track the storm's progress and assess the environmental damage in real-time, providing data that influenced the recovery strategies. This kind of data can be instrumental in shaping negotiation positions regarding disaster resilience.

3. Scenario-based Negotiations

○ GeoAI simulations allow negotiators to explore a range of possible climate futures under different policy scenarios. For example, simulations can show how carbon taxes or carbon markets might reduce emissions or how different renewable energy deployment strategies might impact future climate conditions.

○ This scenario modeling is particularly valuable in climate negotiations, where decisions need to balance economic, social, and environmental factors.

4. Transparency and Trust-Building

○ Transparency in climate negotiations is essential for building trust between nations. GeoAI provides an open, accessible source of environmental data that negotiators can trust, helping to reduce conflicts and promote collaboration.

○ For example, during the **Paris Agreement negotiations**, real-time data from satellites and AI-driven climate models were used to demonstrate the global emissions trajectories, ensuring that all parties understood the urgency of collective action.

Facilitating International Climate Cooperation

GeoAI fosters international cooperation by providing equitable access to data, allowing both developed and developing countries to track their progress and align their climate actions.

1. Collaborative Data Sharing

○ GeoAI facilitates the sharing of climate data across borders. By creating shared platforms where countries can access climate models, emissions data, and vulnerability assessments, GeoAI ensures that no nation is left behind in global climate efforts.

○ One example is the **Global Forest Watch** platform, which uses GeoAI tools to monitor deforestation in real time. This platform allows both developed and developing countries to collaborate on forest protection and carbon sequestration initiatives.

2. Joint Climate Action Programs

○ GeoAI can support the design and implementation of joint climate action programs by providing detailed data on regional climate conditions. This enables countries to address transboundary issues such as shared water resources, biodiversity conservation, and forest management.

○ The **Belt and Road Initiative** in Asia has employed GeoAI tools to optimize the development of green infrastructure along trade routes, ensuring that infrastructure projects are resilient to climate impacts and promote sustainable development.

31.3 GeoAI in National Climate Policy Implementation

Informing National Emission Reduction Targets

GeoAI tools help governments set realistic and science-based emissions reduction targets. By analyzing historical data and projecting future trends, these tools provide insights that are critical for setting effective national climate policies.

1. Carbon Intensity Modeling

○ GeoAI can model the carbon intensity of different sectors—such as transportation, energy production, and agriculture—and help governments identify the most effective areas for intervention.

○ For instance, in **California**, AI-driven models help track and reduce emissions from transportation, a major contributor to the state's carbon footprint.

2. Monitoring National Progress

○ Real-time data collection through satellites, sensors, and ground-based observations allows countries to track their progress toward meeting national climate targets. GeoAI can provide updates on emissions reduction, renewable energy implementation, and deforestation rates, allowing for timely adjustments to national policies.

31.4 GeoAI's Impact on Specific Climate Policy Areas

GeoAI is revolutionizing several core areas of climate policy, from land use planning to emissions monitoring. By incorporating AI models and geospatial data, governments and international bodies can craft more precise and effective climate policies.

Land Use and Urban Planning

Urbanization is one of the primary drivers of climate change, contributing significantly to greenhouse gas emissions, deforestation, and loss of biodiversity. GeoAI tools provide invaluable insights into land use, offering real-time data that allows cities to reduce their environmental footprints while promoting resilience to climate impacts.

1. **Smart City Planning and Infrastructure Development**

   ○ Cities are at the frontline of climate change impacts, facing challenges such as urban heat islands, flooding, and pollution. GeoAI can aid in creating smarter urban designs that integrate green spaces, sustainable transportation, and efficient waste management systems.

   ○ For instance, **Barcelona** uses GeoAI to optimize urban green spaces, such as parks and green roofs, reducing urban heat island effects and improving residents' health and well-being. This integrated planning is crucial for climate adaptation, promoting not only environmental sustainability but also economic and social well-being.

2. **Zoning and Resilience Planning**

○ GeoAI supports zoning decisions by analyzing geographical and environmental conditions to determine the most vulnerable areas for specific climate threats, such as floods or landslides. This data helps governments allocate resources efficiently to build resilient infrastructure and protect vulnerable communities.

○ **The Netherlands** leverages GeoAI to manage flood risks. By using high-resolution flood models, the country is able to better plan infrastructure to mitigate flood impacts, such as elevating buildings and designing more effective water management systems.

Agriculture and Land Conservation Policies

Agriculture is a critical sector in addressing climate change. GeoAI is transforming agricultural practices by providing data to optimize food production while reducing environmental degradation.

1. Precision Agriculture

○ GeoAI facilitates precision agriculture by using data from satellites, drones, and sensors to monitor soil conditions, crop health, and water use. This data allows farmers to optimize irrigation, fertilization, and pest control, reducing input costs and environmental impacts.

○ In **India**, AI-driven platforms like **CropIn** use geospatial data to enhance farm productivity and predict weather impacts, helping farmers adjust their practices based on climate predictions and reduce crop losses.

2. Carbon Sequestration in Agriculture

○ GeoAI can also be used to monitor soil health and optimize agricultural practices for carbon sequestration. By mapping soil carbon storage, AI models can guide farmers on the best practices to enhance soil health and capture more carbon from the atmosphere.

○ In **Australia**, the government is incorporating GeoAI tools to track soil health and carbon sequestration as part of its **Emissions Reduction Fund**, ensuring that the agriculture sector contributes to national climate goals.

3. Monitoring and Protecting Forests

○ Deforestation is a major driver of climate change, and GeoAI is crucial in tracking forest cover loss, illegal logging, and land-use changes. Satellite imagery and AI algorithms enable governments to detect deforestation in near real-time and implement corrective actions.

○ **Brazil's Amazon Monitoring Program (PRODES)** uses GeoAI to track deforestation in the Amazon rainforest. By integrating high-resolution satellite data with machine learning models, Brazil has been able to better understand deforestation patterns and reduce illegal logging activities.

Energy Transition and Carbon Markets

GeoAI's role in monitoring energy transitions and carbon markets is critical for achieving global climate goals.

1. Renewable Energy Deployment

○ The transition from fossil fuels to renewable energy sources requires careful planning to optimize the location and performance of solar, wind, and hydropower systems. GeoAI can predict the most effective locations for renewable energy projects based on geospatial data, climate conditions, and energy demand.

○ In **Chile**, GeoAI has been used to identify the best locations for solar energy projects, based on solar radiation data, elevation models, and land use patterns. This strategic planning has helped the country increase its share of renewable energy in its energy mix.

2. Carbon Trading and Market Monitoring

○ GeoAI plays an important role in monitoring emissions reductions in carbon trading systems, ensuring that countries and companies are meeting their targets. By using remote sensing and AI-powered models, GeoAI tools track carbon stock changes, ensuring the transparency and accuracy of carbon credits.

○ **The European Union Emissions Trading Scheme (EU ETS)** relies on GeoAI to monitor emissions from various industries and verify the effectiveness of emission reduction strategies. The data provided by GeoAI also helps inform adjustments to national and regional climate policies.

31.5 Facilitating International Climate Cooperation through GeoAI

In climate negotiations, particularly within global frameworks like the **UNFCCC** and **Paris Agreement**, cooperation between countries is crucial for effective climate action. GeoAI plays a key role in fostering cooperation, transparency, and trust among nations.

Data Sharing and Transparency in International Negotiations

GeoAI enables countries to share environmental data transparently, promoting accountability and mutual trust.

1. Global Climate Observing Systems (GCOS)

○ The **Global Climate Observing System (GCOS)**, supported by GeoAI, enables countries to track and share climate data, from temperature anomalies to sea-level rise, across borders. GeoAI's real-time monitoring capability allows negotiators to base their discussions on current data, fostering trust between parties.

2. **Monitoring Global Forests and Biodiversity**

○ The **United Nations REDD+ Program**, aimed at reducing emissions from deforestation and forest degradation, uses GeoAI tools to monitor forest cover, emissions from land-use change, and the effectiveness of forest conservation efforts.

○ Real-time satellite monitoring, powered by GeoAI, allows for transparent reporting, helping countries meet their climate obligations under the **Paris Agreement**.

GeoAI in Multinational Climate Action

GeoAI plays an important role in facilitating joint climate action among nations, particularly on transboundary issues such as water resources, biodiversity conservation, and emissions reductions.

1. **Shared Water Resources and Cross-Border Climate Adaptation**

○ Water resources are often shared by multiple countries, and effective management is vital for avoiding conflict and promoting cooperation. GeoAI can track transboundary water sources, allowing countries to collaborate on climate adaptation strategies, such as the management of river basins and water use in drought-prone regions.

○ The **Nile Basin Initiative**, for example, uses GeoAI tools to track water levels, climate variations, and potential flood risks along the Nile River, ensuring that the riparian countries—Egypt,

Sudan, Ethiopia, and others—coordinate water management and climate adaptation strategies.

2. **Joint Marine Conservation and Fisheries Management**

○ The sustainable management of global marine resources is another area where GeoAI is supporting international cooperation. GeoAI-powered models track ocean temperatures, fish stocks, and coral health, helping countries design marine protected areas (MPAs) and sustainable fisheries management systems.

○ The **Coral Triangle Initiative**, a multilateral marine conservation project in Southeast Asia, utilizes GeoAI to monitor coral reef health, marine biodiversity, and the impacts of climate change on marine ecosystems. By sharing geospatial data, participating countries work together to ensure the sustainability of their marine resources.

31.6 Conclusion and Future Directions

GeoAI has proven itself to be a powerful tool in the context of climate policy and global negotiations. By integrating advanced geospatial data with artificial intelligence, GeoAI enables better decision-making, more accurate climate models, and more effective cooperation among nations. From emissions monitoring to climate adaptation, the integration of GeoAI into climate policies and international negotiations is essential for meeting global climate goals.

Looking forward, the use of GeoAI in climate policy will continue to grow, driven by advancements in satellite technology, machine learning, and data-sharing platforms. However, as the technology becomes more integrated into climate policy, it will be crucial to address ethical considerations, such as data privacy, bias in AI models, and equitable access to these technologies.

In the future, GeoAI could play an even greater role in fostering climate resilience and sustainable development. By improving the accuracy and accessibility of environmental data, it has the potential to help countries—both developed and developing—create effective, science-backed climate strategies that prioritize the health of the planet and its inhabitants.

Chapter 32: GeoAI for Sustainable Energy Transition and Management

32.1 Introduction to GeoAI and the Sustainable Energy Transition

The transition to sustainable energy systems is one of the most pressing challenges of the 21st century. With the global population steadily rising and energy consumption intensifying, traditional energy sources like coal, oil, and natural gas are no longer viable for the long-term health of the planet. The global demand for energy is increasing, yet the environmental consequences of fossil fuel use—rising CO_2 emissions, air pollution, and environmental degradation—underscore the need for a shift to renewable energy sources like wind, solar, and hydropower.

GeoAI, a fusion of geospatial analysis and artificial intelligence, plays a pivotal role in this transition by optimizing renewable energy resource management, improving energy grid systems, and enhancing energy efficiency. Through advanced data analytics, GeoAI helps overcome challenges associated with the deployment of renewable energy resources, ensuring that they can be harnessed efficiently and effectively while also managing the inherent variability and intermittency of resources like wind and solar.

Overview of the Energy Transition

The transition involves multiple phases, from sourcing renewable energy to integrating it into existing grids. Solar, wind, and hydropower are the primary sources, each presenting its own set of challenges, such as intermittent production, dependence on geographical conditions, and high infrastructure demands.

GeoAI's Role in Sustainable Energy

GeoAI supports this transition by improving the identification of suitable sites for energy production, forecasting energy demand, optimizing grid performance, and facilitating better decision-making through predictive models. For instance, GeoAI can pinpoint areas with optimal solar radiation for solar farm placement or identify wind corridors for wind turbine installation.

32.2 GeoAI in Renewable Energy Resource Management

Solar Energy

Solar energy, despite its potential, faces challenges related to inconsistent sunlight due to cloud cover, the angle of sunlight, and the location of solar power plants. GeoAI helps overcome these challenges by enabling precise solar resource mapping.

- **GeoAI for Solar Resource Mapping**: Using satellite imagery and remote sensing data, AI models analyze factors such as latitude, elevation, cloud cover, and weather patterns to determine regions with the highest potential for solar energy generation.

- **AI for Solar Power Prediction**: AI systems can process vast amounts of data, forecasting power generation for specific solar panels or systems based on geographic location, local weather conditions, and system design.

- **Case Study**: In India, the National Institute of Solar Energy (NISE) uses GeoAI tools to evaluate solar resources across the country. Through satellite imagery and GIS-based models, it identifies locations with optimal solar radiation, helping the government roll out large-scale solar power plants.

Wind Energy

Wind energy is another crucial aspect of the sustainable energy transition. The intermittency and variability of wind speeds present challenges that GeoAI can mitigate.

- **Wind Resource Assessment**: GeoAI uses geospatial data, including weather patterns, topography, and terrain, to create highly accurate wind maps. These maps guide the placement of wind farms to ensure maximum efficiency.

- **Wind Turbine Placement Optimization**: AI algorithms analyze these maps to recommend the best locations for turbines, minimizing energy loss and maximizing output.

- **Case Study**: In Germany, GeoAI tools are used to optimize wind turbine placement along the North Sea coast. Satellite imagery and historical weather data are combined to create a dynamic wind resource map that informs turbine placement for maximum energy generation.

Hydropower and Other Renewable Resources

- **Hydropower**: The ability to predict and monitor river flows, rainfall patterns, and terrain through GeoAI models is key in assessing potential hydropower sites. By analyzing topography and water velocity, AI models predict the feasibility and sustainability of hydropower installations.

- **Geothermal, Biomass, and Tidal Energy**: GeoAI is also used to assess geothermal energy potential by mapping geological conditions and predicting geothermal heat flow. Similarly, tidal energy resources can be assessed using coastal and marine spatial data, optimizing the placement of energy-generating turbines in the ocean.

32.3 Energy Grid Optimization with GeoAI

GeoAI has a transformative effect on energy grid management by enabling real-time monitoring, improving the integration of renewable sources, and enhancing grid reliability.

Energy Distribution and Grid Balancing

- **AI-Powered Grid Management**: GeoAI optimizes the energy distribution system, balancing the supply from intermittent renewable energy sources with the demand in real time. By using predictive analytics, AI helps anticipate periods of high demand or low supply and adjusts energy distribution to prevent grid instability.

- **Case Study**: In California, AI-powered grid management tools have been integrated into the energy network to reduce energy loss and ensure the smooth integration of renewable energy sources like solar and wind. These tools predict demand spikes during heatwaves and adjust the energy supply accordingly.

Smart Grids and AI Integration

- **Smart Grids**: These grids leverage GeoAI for automation, allowing systems to adapt to changing energy inputs from renewable sources. With integrated sensors and predictive analytics, smart grids can efficiently manage energy flows and detect faults early.

- **GeoAI in Distributed Energy Systems**: GeoAI helps optimize the performance of decentralized renewable energy systems like solar panels and electric vehicle (EV) charging stations, ensuring they work together seamlessly within the grid.

- **Case Study**: In New York City, the utility company Con Edison utilizes GeoAI to enhance the city's smart grid. The system processes real-time data to allocate energy where it's most needed, reducing congestion and ensuring optimal energy delivery during peak times.

Renewable Energy Storage Management

Energy storage is critical for balancing supply and demand, especially for intermittent renewable sources. GeoAI can optimize battery storage systems by predicting periods of high energy generation and adjusting storage capacity accordingly.

- **AI for Battery Management**: AI models help optimize the charging and discharging cycles of energy storage systems, reducing wear and tear on batteries and extending their operational life.

- **Case Study**: Tesla's Powerwall, used in homes to store solar energy, employs machine learning models that predict the household's energy needs and the availability of solar power, ensuring optimal battery usage and cost savings for the homeowner.

32.4 Site Selection for Renewable Energy Infrastructure

Selecting the right sites for renewable energy infrastructure is one of the most critical steps in ensuring that energy systems are effective, efficient, and minimally invasive.

GeoAI in Site Evaluation

- **Geographical and Environmental Considerations**: Site selection for renewable energy infrastructure must account for various factors such as solar irradiance, wind patterns, terrain, land use, and environmental impacts. GeoAI tools integrate these factors into comprehensive models that identify the most suitable sites for energy production.

- **Remote Sensing and Machine Learning**: Satellite imagery, drones, and sensors are combined with machine learning algorithms to identify optimal sites for wind farms, solar parks, and hydroelectric projects.

- **Case Study**: In Spain, the use of GeoAI for wind farm siting has led to the installation of turbines in areas with consistent wind patterns, optimizing energy production while minimizing environmental disruption.

Land Use Planning

GeoAI also plays a role in integrating renewable energy infrastructure into existing land-use plans. Using GIS data and AI algorithms, planners can ensure that energy projects are compatible with other land uses, such as agriculture, conservation, or urban development.

32.5 Enhancing Efficiency in Energy Production and Consumption with GeoAI

GeoAI's application goes beyond the infrastructure phase—it continues to optimize energy systems in real time, improving both production and consumption efficiency.

Real-Time Monitoring of Energy Systems

GeoAI helps in monitoring the health and performance of renewable energy systems such as solar panels and wind turbines. Through sensors and machine learning, AI algorithms detect inefficiencies or faults, triggering predictive maintenance to reduce downtime.

- **Case Study**: In a wind farm in Denmark, GeoAI tools monitor turbine health, identifying parts that are likely to fail. This proactive approach reduces maintenance costs and increases overall efficiency.

Energy Consumption Optimization

GeoAI can also predict energy consumption patterns in cities, businesses, and homes. By integrating data from smart meters, weather forecasts, and energy production systems, AI can recommend optimal consumption patterns.

- **AI-Powered Demand Response**: GeoAI can inform demand response programs, where consumers are incentivized to reduce energy use during peak times. These programs can help avoid blackouts, reduce the need for fossil fuel backup generation, and lower energy costs.

- **Case Study**: In Tokyo, AI-driven energy management systems have been employed in residential buildings to optimize energy use. These systems use weather predictions, real-time usage data, and solar power availability to adjust energy consumption dynamically.

32.6 GeoAI for Energy Policy and Strategic Planning

GeoAI can provide policymakers with critical insights into how renewable energy resources can be utilized most effectively to meet national and global energy goals.

Policy Support and Decision-Making

GeoAI tools help design energy policies by analyzing geographical data and predicting the outcomes of different energy strategies. Whether for increasing renewable energy capacity or optimizing grid integration, AI models provide the evidence needed to inform policy decisions.

- **Scenario Modeling for Policymakers**: AI can simulate the impacts of various policy scenarios—such as subsidies for renewable energy or taxes on carbon emissions—providing decision-makers with data to support their choices.

International Cooperation in Energy

GeoAI also facilitates international energy cooperation by providing transparent, data-driven insights into global renewable energy potential. By integrating geospatial data from different countries, GeoAI helps assess cross-border energy flow possibilities, especially for regions reliant on shared natural resources like river systems or solar radiation.

32.7 Challenges and Future Directions in GeoAI for Energy Management

Despite its potential, several challenges must be overcome for GeoAI to fully realize its potential in the energy sector.

Data Accessibility and Standardization

Integrating large-scale datasets from satellites, sensors, and IoT devices can be a logistical challenge. Establishing standardized formats and ensuring data accessibility will be key in enabling widespread use of GeoAI in energy systems.

Ethical and Regulatory Issues

As with any AI application, issues of privacy, security, and fairness must be addressed. The use of personal energy consumption data and the deployment of AI systems in energy markets must be transparent and equitable.

32.8 Conclusion: The Role of GeoAI in Accelerating the Energy Transition

GeoAI offers immense potential in transforming the global energy landscape. By optimizing the management of renewable energy resources, improving grid performance, and enabling more efficient energy use, GeoAI will be crucial in achieving a sustainable, low-carbon future.

Future Directions

As AI technology evolves, its integration with renewable energy systems will become even more sophisticated. Enhanced models, real-time data processing, and the inclusion of emerging technologies like blockchain and IoT will further optimize energy production, distribution, and consumption.

GeoAI's role in the energy transition is not just about technology—it's about empowering nations and communities to make smarter, more informed decisions that will shape a sustainable future.

Chapter 33: The Future of GeoAI in Earth Observation: Innovations and Challenges

Introduction: GeoAI's Evolving Role in Earth Observation

GeoAI, a fusion of artificial intelligence (AI) and geospatial technologies, represents one of the most transformative advancements in the way we monitor and understand Earth's systems. It combines AI-driven data processing with geospatial intelligence, enabling the analysis of satellite imagery, environmental data, and other Earth observation (EO) inputs. This chapter explores the future of GeoAI in Earth observation, discussing innovations, emerging trends, and the challenges that could shape its trajectory. From next-generation satellite systems to autonomous drones, GeoAI promises to provide unprecedented insights into the dynamics of our planet, offering tools that can monitor climate change, urbanization, and natural disasters with greater precision than ever before.

With the increasing complexity of global environmental challenges—such as climate change, biodiversity loss, and pollution—GeoAI offers the potential to revolutionize Earth observation. It will enable decision-makers to monitor, predict, and manage the planet's health more efficiently and accurately. However, its widespread adoption faces several obstacles, ranging from technical limitations and data privacy concerns to the need for international collaboration.

This chapter will explore the innovations in GeoAI for Earth observation, emerging trends in its applications, and the key challenges that need to be addressed for GeoAI to reach its full potential.

33.1 Innovations in GeoAI for Earth Observation

GeoAI's integration with Earth observation technologies, such as satellites, autonomous drones, and Internet of Things (IoT) sensors, is driving new possibilities in environmental monitoring. Below, we examine some of the most significant innovations that are reshaping Earth observation capabilities.

Next-Generation Satellite Systems

The development of next-generation satellite systems has drastically improved the resolution, frequency, and global coverage of Earth observation data. These advancements enable more detailed and real-time monitoring of environmental variables, providing a clearer picture of the state of the planet.

- **High-Resolution and Multi-Spectral Imaging**: One of the key advancements in satellite systems is the increase in both spatial and spectral resolution. Satellites like the European Space Agency's Copernicus Sentinel series and NASA's Landsat satellites provide multi-spectral imagery that can track environmental changes across various wavelengths, from visible light to infrared. By leveraging these capabilities, GeoAI can extract more precise data on soil moisture, vegetation health, deforestation, and urban development.

- **Case Study: Copernicus Sentinel-2 and AI-Powered Agriculture**: In agriculture, AI models combined with Sentinel-2's multi-spectral imagery are being used to monitor crop health, predict yields, and detect early signs of pests or diseases. By processing satellite data with machine learning algorithms, GeoAI can help farmers optimize irrigation, reduce pesticide use, and increase crop productivity, contributing to more sustainable farming practices.

- **Temporal Monitoring**: Another major advantage of modern satellites is the frequency at which they can collect data. GeoAI can take advantage of the high revisit rates of satellites to detect subtle changes in environmental conditions, such as shifts in land use, vegetation growth, or urban sprawl. By analyzing these changes over time, AI-powered models can offer predictions about future trends, informing proactive management strategies.

Autonomous Drones for Earth Observation

Drones, or unmanned aerial vehicles (UAVs), have become a vital component of Earth observation, providing flexibility and resolution that satellites alone cannot match.

- **Advantages of Drones in Earth Observation**: Drones offer high-resolution, real-time data collection and can be deployed in areas that may be inaccessible to traditional satellites. Whether used for monitoring forests, conducting wildlife surveys, or surveying post-disaster environments, drones are invaluable tools for localized and detailed environmental assessments.

- **AI-Driven Data Processing**: As drones collect vast amounts of geospatial data, AI systems are increasingly tasked with processing this information. Machine learning algorithms can analyze drone imagery for specific environmental features, such as land degradation, water bodies, or biodiversity indicators. For example, AI can help assess the health of coral reefs or detect illegal fishing activities by identifying anomalous patterns in drone imagery.

- **Case Study: Monitoring Deforestation with Drones in the Amazon**: In the Amazon rainforest, autonomous drones are used in conjunction with AI algorithms to monitor illegal deforestation. The drones capture high-resolution imagery of forest areas, which is then processed by AI models to detect changes in vegetation cover. The ability to detect illegal logging in near real-time allows for swift intervention by local authorities, reducing the overall impact of deforestation.

Integration with Internet of Things (IoT) and Real-Time Data

The integration of GeoAI with IoT technologies has significantly enhanced Earth observation by enabling continuous, real-time data collection from a variety of environmental sensors.

- **Real-Time Environmental Monitoring**: IoT sensors, which can be installed in urban areas, forests, rivers, and oceans, provide a steady stream of data on a range of environmental parameters, including air quality, temperature, soil moisture, and water levels. AI models can process this data in real-time, enabling immediate responses to environmental hazards such as floods, heatwaves, or pollution events.

- **Smart Cities and Smart Agriculture**: In urban settings, IoT sensors, combined with AI-driven geospatial analysis, help city planners manage resources more effectively. For instance, AI can optimize waste collection, improve traffic flow, and enhance air quality monitoring. In agriculture, IoT devices track soil moisture levels, temperature, and crop conditions, while AI models help farmers make decisions about irrigation, fertilization, and pest control.

- **Case Study: Flood Prediction in the Netherlands**: The Dutch government has implemented an IoT-based flood monitoring system that collects real-time data on river levels, rainfall, and soil conditions. This data is processed by AI models to predict flood events and guide flood management efforts. The system has helped the Netherlands improve its flood preparedness, reducing the risk of costly and deadly disasters.

33.2 Emerging Trends in GeoAI for Earth Observation

As GeoAI continues to evolve, several key trends are shaping the future of Earth observation. These trends include the integration of big data analytics, geospatial deep learning, and the development of integrated monitoring systems.

Artificial Intelligence and Big Data Analytics

The sheer volume and complexity of geospatial data generated by satellites, drones, and sensors require advanced AI and big data analytics to derive meaningful insights. With the continuous growth of Earth observation data, the integration of AI and big data will be pivotal in addressing global environmental challenges.

- **GeoAI and Big Data Integration**: Big data refers to large datasets that are too complex to be processed by traditional data analysis methods. In Earth observation, big data includes satellite imagery, environmental sensor data, social media inputs, and weather data. AI is crucial for analyzing these datasets and identifying patterns that can inform decisions on land use, resource management, and environmental conservation.

- **AI for Climate Modeling and Environmental Predictions**: One of the most promising applications of GeoAI in big data analytics is in climate modeling. AI can process enormous volumes of data from different sources, such as satellite imagery, historical climate data, and atmospheric models, to predict climate change trends and inform mitigation strategies. For example, AI models can predict future sea-level rise, extreme weather events, or shifting agricultural zones based on current climate patterns.

Geospatial Deep Learning

Deep learning, a subset of machine learning, is particularly effective at processing large volumes of spatial data and detecting complex patterns in Earth observation data.

- **Object Detection and Classification**: Deep learning algorithms, such as convolutional neural networks (CNNs), excel at identifying specific features in images, such as forests, water bodies, roads, or buildings. These algorithms are widely used in satellite and drone image classification, enabling automated mapping of land cover types and changes in the environment.

- **Change Detection**: One of the most important applications of geospatial deep learning is in change detection. AI systems can compare satellite images taken at different times to identify environmental changes, such as deforestation, urbanization, or the spread of agricultural lands. This helps in monitoring the progress of conservation efforts, assessing the impact of human activities on ecosystems, and detecting the effects of climate change.

GeoAI in Integrated Environmental Monitoring Systems

As the Earth observation community moves toward more integrated monitoring systems, GeoAI is playing a key role in providing real-time, holistic assessments of the environment.

- **Ecosystem and Biodiversity Monitoring**: The integration of GeoAI into ecosystem and biodiversity monitoring allows for a more comprehensive understanding of environmental health. By combining satellite data with field observations and ecological models, GeoAI can assess habitat fragmentation, species migration, and ecosystem dynamics.

- **Marine and Coastal Monitoring**: AI-powered tools are being used to track changes in marine ecosystems, including coral reefs, fisheries, and coastal erosion. These systems combine satellite imagery, sensor data, and oceanographic models to provide real-time insights into the health of marine environments, helping policymakers take timely action to preserve marine biodiversity.

33.3 Challenges in GeoAI Adoption for Earth Observation

Despite the exciting potential of GeoAI, several challenges must be overcome to fully harness its capabilities in Earth observation.

Data Quality and Availability

One of the most significant challenges in GeoAI adoption is the availability and quality of geospatial data.

- **Inconsistent and Incomplete Data**: While satellite data is increasingly available, it is often inconsistent in terms of resolution, frequency, and spatial coverage. For instance, some regions of the world may not be adequately covered by satellite imagery, while other areas may have sparse sensor data. Inconsistent data quality can lead to inaccurate results in AI models, limiting their effectiveness.

- **Limited Access to Data**: While many satellite data sources are becoming more accessible through initiatives like Copernicus, some critical data is still held by private companies or governments, restricting its use for broader environmental monitoring. Ensuring equitable access to geospatial data is crucial for enabling global environmental efforts.

Data Privacy and Security Concerns

As GeoAI technologies collect vast amounts of data, concerns about data privacy and security become increasingly important.

- **Privacy Concerns**: GeoAI often relies on large-scale data collection, including personal data such as movement patterns, environmental exposure, and even facial recognition. While this data is essential for environmental monitoring, its collection raises privacy concerns. Regulatory frameworks must be established to

marginalized communities, such as those in rural or impoverished areas. Ensuring that AI models are trained on diverse and representative data is essential for avoiding these biases.

● **Ensuring Fair Access to GeoAI Solutions**: As GeoAI technologies become more widespread, ensuring that marginalized communities are not excluded from their benefits is essential. These communities, often disproportionately affected by environmental hazards, must have equitable access to GeoAI-driven insights. This requires inclusive policy development, transparency in decision-making processes, and targeted interventions to ensure that GeoAI solutions are used to improve conditions for all.

Transparency in AI Models

Transparency in how AI models make decisions is essential for building trust and ensuring accountability. In the context of GeoAI for Earth observation, transparent AI systems can help policymakers and citizens understand the basis of predictions and actions.

● **Interpretable AI**: Many AI models, particularly deep learning models, operate as "black boxes," meaning that their decision-making processes are not easily understandable by humans. This lack of transparency can be problematic, especially in high-stakes environmental decisions where accountability is critical. Efforts to create interpretable AI models are crucial for ensuring that stakeholders understand how and why certain decisions are made, leading to more informed, just, and transparent governance.

33.6 Overcoming the Challenges of GeoAI Adoption for Earth Observation

To realize the full potential of GeoAI, several challenges must be addressed:

Improving Data Quality and Availability

Data consistency, accuracy, and accessibility are paramount for effective GeoAI applications. As the quantity and complexity of data increase, developing robust systems for managing and sharing this data will be crucial. One of the challenges in data quality is the uneven distribution of satellite and sensor coverage, particularly in remote or conflict-prone areas.

- **Addressing Gaps in Global Data Coverage**: Developing global, consistent, and up-to-date datasets requires collaboration across borders and sectors. International initiatives such as the Global Monitoring for Environment and Security (GMES) program are working toward more uniform data distribution, ensuring that GeoAI applications are based on comprehensive and accurate data.

Ethical Data Governance

As mentioned previously, GeoAI technologies raise significant ethical concerns related to privacy, security, and algorithmic fairness. Creating governance frameworks that address these concerns will be essential to mitigate the risks associated with GeoAI.

- **Global Regulations and Standards**: Governments and international organizations must collaborate to create policies and regulations that govern the ethical use of GeoAI in Earth observation. These regulations should establish standards for data privacy, algorithmic transparency, and access to environmental data, ensuring that GeoAI applications are used responsibly and equitably.

33.6 Conclusion: A Future Shaped by GeoAI

The future of GeoAI in Earth observation holds tremendous promise, with innovations in satellite technology, autonomous drones, and AI-driven data processing offering the potential to revolutionize how we monitor and protect our planet. The ability to track environmental changes in real-time, model complex scenarios, and make data-driven decisions will empower governments, businesses, and individuals to respond proactively to global challenges such as climate change, biodiversity loss, and natural disasters.

However, for GeoAI to reach its full potential, the challenges of data quality, privacy, governance, and international collaboration must be overcome. Ethical frameworks must be established to ensure that GeoAI applications are transparent, fair, and accessible to all. As the field continues to evolve, we must remain mindful of the need for collaboration across disciplines and borders to ensure that GeoAI serves the greater good and contributes to a more sustainable, resilient, and equitable world.

By addressing these challenges and leveraging the power of GeoAI, we can create a more informed, proactive approach to Earth observation that benefits all of humanity.

Chapter 34: Conclusion: The Path Forward for GeoAI and Planetary Health

Introduction

Over the past several decades, the integration of artificial intelligence (AI) with geospatial technologies—known as GeoAI—has dramatically reshaped the way we observe, analyze, and manage the Earth's environment. Through the convergence of machine learning algorithms, satellite data, remote sensing, and other geospatial technologies, GeoAI has become a game-changer in planetary health. The convergence of these technologies provides unprecedented tools for monitoring the health of our planet, mitigating the effects of environmental degradation, and striving toward a sustainable future.

The growing body of research and the real-world applications discussed throughout this book highlight the immense potential of GeoAI to solve complex environmental challenges. These challenges are diverse, ranging from climate change, deforestation, and biodiversity loss, to urbanization, pollution, and resource depletion. The ability of GeoAI to harness vast amounts of geospatial data and transform it into actionable insights is opening new frontiers for environmental monitoring, management, and policy development. But while GeoAI is a promising tool for improving planetary health, its future potential is inextricably linked to how we address the challenges of adoption, data access, ethics, and international cooperation.

This concluding chapter will reflect on the key themes explored throughout the book, summarizing the contributions of GeoAI to environmental management, discussing future prospects, and outlining the challenges that lie ahead. Most importantly, it will offer a call to action for further research, innovation, and global collaboration, urging the development of strategies that will maximize the potential of GeoAI for the betterment of planetary health.

34.1 GeoAI: Revolutionizing Earth Observation

At the heart of GeoAI's transformative power lies its ability to enhance Earth observation in ways that were previously unimaginable. Earth observation, traditionally reliant on ground-based data collection or periodic satellite imaging, has been revolutionized by the integration of AI technologies. These technologies allow us to monitor changes in the Earth's surface, atmosphere, and ecosystems in real-time and with unprecedented accuracy.

GeoAI enables rapid processing of massive volumes of geospatial data, extracting patterns, anomalies, and trends from sources such as satellite imagery, remote sensing data, and sensor networks. Machine learning and deep learning algorithms are trained to identify environmental changes, such as deforestation, desertification, changes in land cover, and shifts in biodiversity. This approach facilitates the detection of threats to planetary health in real time, enabling quicker responses to environmental crises.

One notable example of GeoAI's capabilities in Earth observation is the monitoring of deforestation in the Amazon rainforest. Using satellite images combined with machine learning algorithms, GeoAI has been used to track illegal logging activities, land use changes, and the rapid degradation of forest cover. Similarly, in urban areas, AI-powered algorithms have analyzed the effect of urban sprawl on the environment, identifying trends in the spread of impervious surfaces and assessing the impact on local ecosystems.

Beyond simply identifying environmental changes, GeoAI can also predict future trends by modeling climate dynamics, land use change, and environmental interactions. This predictive power is especially crucial for policymakers, allowing them to anticipate problems and take proactive measures.

34.2 The Promise of GeoAI in Addressing Global Environmental Challenges

As the world grapples with a host of interconnected environmental crises, GeoAI provides a unique opportunity to address many of the most pressing challenges. Climate change, biodiversity loss, and resource depletion are among the most urgent global threats, requiring coordinated efforts across borders and sectors. GeoAI offers the tools to tackle these issues more effectively by providing the data-driven insights needed to inform policy and drive action.

Climate Change Mitigation and Adaptation

GeoAI is playing an integral role in climate change mitigation and adaptation strategies by improving climate modeling, forecasting, and risk assessment. AI algorithms are now capable of analyzing massive amounts of environmental data to model climate scenarios, predict the impacts of different policy interventions, and guide climate resilience efforts.

For instance, AI-driven models can simulate the effects of various emissions reduction strategies on global temperature trends. Similarly, GeoAI is used to assess climate vulnerability at regional and local levels, identifying areas most at risk from rising sea levels, heatwaves, or extreme weather events. By offering targeted insights, GeoAI helps policymakers develop more effective climate adaptation strategies, whether through urban planning, coastal management, or disaster preparedness.

A real-world example is the use of GeoAI to assess the resilience of urban areas to climate change. In cities like New York, AI algorithms analyze satellite data to predict areas vulnerable to flooding, heat stress, or air pollution, helping local governments develop resilience plans that minimize the impacts of climate change on the population.

Biodiversity and Ecosystem Protection

In terms of biodiversity, GeoAI's capabilities are providing valuable tools for monitoring and conserving endangered species, protecting ecosystems, and addressing threats like habitat loss and fragmentation. GeoAI helps track species migrations, identify critical habitats, and assess the health of ecosystems using high-resolution satellite imagery and AI-powered analysis.

AI-powered models have been used in Africa to track animal populations, such as elephants and rhinos, and predict their movement patterns across protected areas. This data supports anti-poaching efforts and helps ensure that conservation resources are allocated effectively to protect species in peril.

Furthermore, GeoAI plays a role in the restoration of ecosystems by modeling the potential impacts of reforestation or wetland rehabilitation efforts. For example, AI models can predict how restoring a forested area might affect local biodiversity and water quality, enabling better planning and decision-making.

Sustainable Resource Management

GeoAI is also helping in the efficient management of natural resources such as water, energy, and land. By integrating geospatial data with machine learning models, GeoAI optimizes resource allocation, reduces waste, and ensures that resources are used sustainably.

In agriculture, AI-powered systems monitor soil health, crop conditions, and irrigation needs, helping farmers improve yields while minimizing water and pesticide use. In water management, GeoAI analyzes rainfall patterns, river flows, and groundwater levels to optimize water distribution and mitigate the impacts of droughts or floods.

34.3 Key Themes and Insights from the Book

This book has explored a wide array of applications where GeoAI has made significant contributions to planetary health. The key themes that have emerged throughout the chapters include:

Environmental Justice and Equity

One of the most important aspects of GeoAI is its potential to ensure environmental equity. GeoAI can identify marginalized communities that are disproportionately impacted by environmental hazards, such as air pollution or lack of access to clean water. Satellite data combined with AI algorithms helps map pollution hotspots, monitor water quality, and assess the spatial distribution of environmental risks, ensuring that no community is left behind in environmental monitoring and protection efforts.

For example, in cities with high levels of industrial activity, AI models have been used to map environmental pollutants and identify areas where people are most at risk of exposure. These insights can then inform policies aimed at reducing pollution levels in vulnerable communities.

AI in Environmental Policy and Governance

GeoAI has a transformative impact on environmental policy, offering decision-makers the real-time data and predictive insights they need to craft more informed policies. Whether through disaster preparedness, climate change mitigation, or biodiversity conservation, GeoAI enables better governance by providing data-driven solutions for complex environmental challenges.

One notable case is the use of GeoAI to monitor compliance with environmental regulations in mining and agriculture. Machine learning algorithms analyze satellite imagery to detect illegal activities, such as unapproved land clearing or deforestation, and flag them for further investigation.

The Integration of AI with IoT and Remote Sensing

The integration of GeoAI with the Internet of Things (IoT) and remote sensing technologies is crucial for data collection and analysis. IoT devices, such as environmental sensors placed in forests, oceans, or urban areas, collect real-time data on air quality, soil health, water quality, and more. GeoAI uses this data to generate actionable insights, optimizing decision-making in sectors like agriculture, forestry, and urban planning.

34.4 Future Prospects of GeoAI in Solving Environmental Challenges

The future of GeoAI is full of promise, with emerging technologies pushing the boundaries of what is possible in Earth observation and environmental management.

Technological Advancements on the Horizon

The next wave of GeoAI innovation will likely be driven by advancements in autonomous technologies, such as drones, robots, and satellites. These technologies will provide even more detailed and real-time data, further enhancing the capabilities of AI models in tracking environmental changes. Quantum computing is another area that could significantly boost the power of AI algorithms, enabling faster processing of vast amounts of data.

GeoAI for Global Climate Agreements

GeoAI has the potential to play a pivotal role in international climate negotiations. Real-time data from satellite systems, combined with AI modeling, can provide governments and organizations with accurate assessments of emissions reductions and the effectiveness of climate policies. By providing transparency, GeoAI could help facilitate more ambitious and cooperative global climate agreements.

Advancing Global Sustainability

GeoAI's role in supporting the United Nations Sustainable Development Goals (SDGs) is crucial. Whether it's tracking deforestation, assessing water scarcity, or optimizing energy consumption, GeoAI has a key role to play in helping nations achieve their sustainability targets.

34.5 Key Challenges to Overcome

Despite the promising outlook, there are several challenges to the widespread adoption of GeoAI technologies:

Data Access and Quality

One of the primary challenges is ensuring open access to high-quality, real-time data. In many regions, particularly in low-income countries, access to satellite data, sensors, and even basic computational infrastructure remains limited. Overcoming these barriers will require international collaboration, investment in infrastructure, and the democratization of data.

Algorithmic Bias and Equity

GeoAI algorithms are not immune to biases, and ensuring the fairness of AI models is crucial to their successful application in environmental monitoring. Developers must ensure that AI models are trained on diverse datasets and account for the specific needs of marginalized communities to avoid perpetuating inequities.

Ethical Governance and Regulation

As with any emerging technology, GeoAI's deployment must be governed by ethical principles that prioritize transparency, privacy, and accountability. Clear global standards and regulations will be essential for guiding the responsible use of GeoAI in environmental management.

34.6 The Call to Action: Research, Innovation, and Global Collaboration

To maximize the potential of GeoAI, it is essential to foster a culture of continuous research and innovation. Governments, academia, and the private sector must work together to push the boundaries of what GeoAI can achieve. More funding must be directed toward developing cutting-edge AI models and satellite technologies, and interdisciplinary research is needed to explore new applications of GeoAI across environmental sectors.

Moreover, collaboration across borders and sectors is essential for ensuring that the benefits of GeoAI are shared equitably. Knowledge sharing, joint research initiatives, and capacity-building programs will help bridge gaps in technology and expertise, enabling more regions to benefit from GeoAI's transformative potential.

34.7 Conclusion: A Vision for the Future of GeoAI and Planetary Health

GeoAI has the potential to transform the way we monitor, manage, and protect our planet. As we confront increasingly complex environmental challenges, the integration of AI with geospatial technologies offers powerful tools for addressing climate change, biodiversity loss, and resource depletion. However, realizing the full potential of GeoAI will require overcoming significant challenges related to data access, ethics, and international collaboration.

Looking forward, the future of GeoAI is bright. With continuous technological advancements, increased global cooperation, and a commitment to ethical practices, GeoAI can play a pivotal role in shaping a more sustainable, equitable, and resilient future for our planet.

In closing, the journey toward a healthier planet begins with informed action. As GeoAI continues to evolve, it is essential for researchers, policymakers, and citizens alike to embrace its potential and collaborate to ensure that its benefits are maximized for the good of all. The path forward is clear, but it requires a collective effort to shape a future where both humanity and the planet can thrive together.

End Note

As we conclude *GeoAI and its Role in Planetary Health,* I hope you are leaving with a deeper understanding of the transformative power of GeoAI and a renewed sense of hope for the future of our planet. This journey through the dynamic intersections of technology, science, and sustainability is a testament to what is possible when innovation is guided by purpose and collaboration.

Throughout these pages, we have explored how GeoAI is revolutionizing the way we monitor, analyze, and protect Earth's delicate systems. From conserving biodiversity to mitigating climate risks, and from enabling precision agriculture to addressing environmental justice, GeoAI has proven itself to be a versatile and invaluable tool in tackling the most pressing challenges of our time.

However, this is just the beginning. The real story lies in the potential that is yet to be unlocked. GeoAI, like any tool, is only as powerful as the intent and ingenuity of those who wield it. It requires visionaries to develop new applications, leaders to advocate for ethical use, and communities to embrace its possibilities. It also demands collective action to ensure equitable access to its benefits and to address the ethical dilemmas that arise as we push the boundaries of innovation.

The health of our planet is not just a scientific challenge; it is a moral imperative and a shared responsibility. GeoAI, with all its promise, serves as a reminder of our capacity for ingenuity and collaboration. It challenges us to rethink how we interact with the environment, how we design our cities, and how we ensure a sustainable future for generations to come.

As you close this book, I encourage you to take the insights and inspirations you've gained and apply them in your own way—whether it's by pursuing a deeper understanding of GeoAI, advocating for environmental policies, or simply making more conscious choices in your daily life. Each action, no matter how small, contributes to the larger mission of preserving and restoring our planet.

Finally, I want to thank you for embarking on this journey with me. Your curiosity and commitment to understanding the role of GeoAI in planetary health are vital to the broader effort of creating a more resilient and equitable world. Together, we can transform knowledge into action and innovation into impact.

Here's to a future where technology and humanity work in harmony to protect the only home we have—our beautiful and fragile Earth.

Warm regards,

— **Abhijeet Sarkar**

About the Author

Abhijeet Sarkar, CEO & Founder of Synaptic AI Lab, stands as a modern polymath and philosopher whose intellectual voyages chart the often-turbulent confluence of technology, consciousness, and the future of human governance. His work is not a mere exploration of disparate fields but a deeply integrated synthesis, a testament to a mind that perceives the intricate web of connections binding the digital and the spiritual, the political and the personal. To categorize his literary and intellectual contributions in a straightforward manner would be to miss the very essence of his endeavor, which is to dissolve the artificial boundaries that have long segregated these critical domains of human thought.

At the helm of Synaptic AI Lab, Sarkar is more than a technologist or an entrepreneur; he is an architect of future dialogues. The very name of his organization hints at his core philosophy: the creation of new connections, new synapses in our collective understanding, mirroring the neural networks of the brain and the burgeoning intelligence of the artificial. His exploration of artificial intelligence transcends the mere mechanics of machine learning and deep learning. Instead, he plunges into the profound philosophical questions that a future with advanced AI necessitates. His writings are a compelling tapestry where the threads of code and consciousness are inextricably woven. He compels his readers to move beyond the simplistic narrative of AI as a mere tool and to confront it as a potential partner, a creator, and even a new form of consciousness, prompting a fundamental re-evaluation of our place in the universe.

Read more at https://abhijeetsarkar.com/.